Dreams and Tears:

CHRONICLE OF A LIFE

D1082502

ERWIN K. KORANYI

Published by

 GENERAL STORE
GSPH PUBLISHING HOUSE

499 O'Brien Road, Box 415
Renfrew, Ontario, Canada K7V 4A6
Telephone (613) 432-7697 or 1-800-465-6072

ISBN 1-897113-47-1
Printed and bound in Canada

Cover design, formatting and printing by
Custom Printers of Renfrew Ltd.

© General Store Publishing House
Renfrew, Ontario, Canada

Library and Archives Canada Cataloguing in Publication

Koranyi, Erwin K.
    Dreams and tears : chronicle of a life / Erwin K. Koranyi.

Includes bibliographical references.
ISBN 1-897113-47-1

    1. Koranyi, Erwin K. 2. Holocaust, Jewish (1939-1945)--Hungary.
3. Jews--Hungary--History--20th century. 4. Jews--Hungary--Biography.
5. Psychiatrists--Canada--Biography. I. Title.

RC438.6.K673A3 2006   616.89'0092   C2006-905492-4

This book is dedicated to those whose voices were silenced a long time ago, but who will live forever in my memory.

Erwin Koranyi is an amazing man, and this is an amazing book. This is an amazing book because it chronicles the incredible story of a heroic person in a most eloquent manner. Only someone with Dr. Koranyi's profound appreciation of the complex nature of the human being could write such an honest, raw, incisive, and revealing book. It is a biography, plus. The author has a rare gift of linguistic clarity and uncanny wisdom. This book is a human adventure story, surely not a sought after adventure; a triumph of will, perseverence, and love. The author bares his soul in a most unique and respectful manner. By the end of the book, you know the man, his ups and downs, his losses and achievements, all shared with grace and humility. His intellectual conclusion will startle you, and you will come away from this novel-like true story fully appreciating that Erwin Koranyi is an amazing man. This book will challenge your thoughts, warm your hearts, and inspire your soul.

Rabbi Reuven P. Bulka

Table of Contents

Acknowledgements vi
Preface vii
Chapter 1: Born Canadian 1
Dreams and Tears I: Halcyon Days 19
Chapter 2: Father's Family 21
Dreams and Tears II: Incubus 31
Chapter 3: Happy High School Years 33
Dreams and Tears III: Gemini 48
Chapter 4: Dream Goes to Nightmare 49
Dreams and Tears IV: Houdini 66
Chapter 5: A Rainy Day 71
Dreams and Tears V: My Runaway Relatives 81
Chapter 6: The Abyss 86
Dreams and Tears VI: A Hospital Job 93
Chapter 7: The Irate Currents of the River Styx 95
Nocturnal Images: Dread 102
Chapter 8: *Rhododactylos Eios* 103
Dreams and Tears VII: Experiment and Lost Love 110
Chapter 9: A Long and Bumpy Road 113
Dreams and Tears VIII: *Chronos* 126
Chapter 10: The Change of Guards 129
Dreams and Tears IX: Demons 140
Chapter 11: On the Road Again 145
Nocturnal Images: Return and Regret 151
Chapter 12: From Caterpillar to Butterfly 152
Nocturnal Images: Random Thoughts of an Insomniac 160
Chapter 13: Voyage to the Ancestral Shores 162
Dreams and Tears X: A Sentimental Journey: Past or Future? 174
Chapter 14: *Die Wanderjahre* 176
Nocturnal Images: The Question 186
Chapter 15: Struggles and Losses 187
Dreams and Tears XI: A Seraphic Diary 195
Chapter 16: New Challenges 197
Nocturnal Images: The Answer 207
References 211

Acknowledgements

First and foremost, I wish to thank my beloved wife, Edie, whom I have so shamelessly robbed of many hours of togetherness while writing this memoir. I can never recoup the precious time gone forever.

I am grateful to my sister, Marta Sebor, who began to write her own life story and inspired me to do the same.

I credit Liza Cogan, our close friend, for her gently insistent encouragement over the years, without which I would have allowed oblivion to take over the past.

I want to thank our devoted friends Myrna Barwin, Cathy Lofgreen, and Jennifer Vered for reading my early manuscript and bravely enduring a forest of grammatical peculiarities.

My never-ceasing gratitude also goes to Heather Raff, a truly good friend, and the late Starr Solomon, who provided useful suggestions and encouragement.

I wish to thank Anne Bilsky for her editorial suggestions, some of which have been aggravated by our bitter but friendly fights over every superfluous comma and incorrect phrase.

Finally, I wish to thank my senior editor, Jane Karchmar, whose formidable linguistic skills, coupled with her empathy and exceptional sensitivity, helped to render this text enjoyable to read.

Erwin K. Koranyi

Preface

The human mind is a labyrinth. In writing a book, particularly an autobiography that is delimited by concrete facts, one never knows where one ends up. Perhaps this is why introductory words are written last. One writes an autobiography to demarcate oneself.

Looking at the sum total of my writing, I define myself as a Jew. The yellow star, once forced onto my chest, became my legacy. Jean Paul Sartre said that anti-Semitism makes a Jew a Jew. Man, so confidently treading on his ambitious road to ascend to God's image, has indeed made remarkable progress in the fields of science and technology. It is a pity that the optimistic moral prediction of visionaries fell so short of their expectations. While mature and socialized layers of the brain may predominate in peaceful times, a hidden segment of the ancient brain retains the avaricious reflexes and indiscriminate predacity that helped our ancestors survive in prehistoric times. The archaic icon of the superstitious caveman, so easily prompted by the signal of misread peril and prejudice, forever lurks behind our features. It is anchored in our anatomy. Unfortunately, it can be readily engineered into a mass movement.

Cursed, blessed, or both, my early years were embedded in the proverbial "interesting times." Such epochs invariably augment the eternal struggle between the forces of Good and Evil, the unique alloy of which we all are made. It also renders such an era the enduring target for historic scrutiny and sparks ongoing interrogation of its impact upon the soul of mankind and society. *Dreams and Tears* gains meaning only to the extent that it meets these challenges. As necessitated by the topic, historic marginalia now and then sprinkle the text. The origins of these often reach back to the middle of the nineteenth century or earlier. I try not to focus on them in detail; however, a sketchy portrayal of some historical events is essential, for I was profoundly affected by them. They represent the backdrop of my life. Similarly, a sketch of the everyday flow of the world around me during my formative years is called for.

Finally the time arrived for me to sit down and write. For years, my friends had urged me to set my chronicle down on paper lest it vanish forever in the ocean of human indifference. I always resisted, for I found it painful to relive many of my memories. It cost me an abundant flow of ink and tears. The notion that in all probability nobody would ever read these lines tucked away in the hidden recesses of my computer helped to dampen my scruples.

Even though I might not care about the potential reader, but because I am a reader myself, I must issue several caveats to those adventurous souls who may one day read this account. I am not a hero. If I were, it would be easier on the reader, for doesn't everyone like to follow the valiant stories of a brave man? Nor am I a famous personality chased by a gossip-hungry public. I am but a witness, and this commits me to tell the truth—as I see it, as I know it, as I recall it.

Am I worried about atrocious linguistic mistakes and about trespassing all the rules and traditions so faithfully followed by professional writers? Surely. For this you must forgive me if we are to proceed at all. And finally, my writing style, if I am allowed to refer to it with such a superlative term, is at best old fashioned. Now that I have done my very best to discourage you, I ask that you proceed at your own risk!

CHAPTER 1

A Born Canadian

In my heavy Hungarian accent (no use trying to escape from it), I like to perplex my Canadian friends by declaring that I am a "born Canadian." I enjoy the puzzlement this assertion generates. The expectation on the faces of these listeners as they wait to hear my explanation amuses me. Yet the statement is not entirely without foundation. I was born in 1924 in an apartment house across from the Eastern Railway Station in Budapest, Hungary. The apartment building belonged to the Canadian Pacific Railway.

Do you know those old nineteenth-century European apartment houses? They are quite unlike the sterile, modern American buildings. These apartment houses, such as the one in which we lived, were typically five to eight storeys high. They were built well before elevators or electric power were available, squared around a large inner courtyard that was paved with yellow tiles. The row of apartment doors and most of the windows opened towards this enclosure. Corridors with black iron railings ran along each floor. Such closeness, by contemporary North American standards, robbed the inhabitants of much of their privacy. Zestful family quarrels or conversations on delicate subjects could easily be overheard. Comings and goings could be observed. Everyone knew everything; friendships and hostilities between the neighbours were not secret.

Such living arrangements also offered a wide variety of olfactory experiences, desired or not, that kept changing with the time of day, representing indeed a peculiar chronometer, like the aroma of the midday meal being prepared, or the fragrance of coffee that wafted in the air in mid-afternoon. Or else the odours lingered in a permanent and reliable way, like the slightly mouldy, cool air that enveloped the large, stone, dimly lighted main staircase with the muscular image of a tortured Atlas at the entrance holding up the main balcony. Strangely, in the perception of a child, this musty odour grew almost pleasant. It had become part of the cocoon of parental protection, something that extended to embrace the entire building, and it made the familiarity of this small community safe and reassuring. Even today, it forms a magical, glowing, and warm memory.

The dusty ground floor was occupied by the busy immigration offices that were under the authority of the Canadian Pacific Railway. In the window of the office stood the model of a steamship, proudly displayed for all passersby to see from the street. I shall never forget this miniature replica that was one of the much-admired miracles of my early childhood. The model ship was about eight feet long, with tiny figurines of sailors and passengers on its top. It represented the joy and pride of the CPR's three-funneled 45,500-ton vessel, the *Empress of Britain*. Beside the ship, scenic posters featured swift trains pulled by smoke-sputtering locomotives rushing across blond wheat fields, livened by the odd poppies of the Canadian Prairies, inviting the public to participate in this faraway adventure.

Indeed, twice weekly, the inner court of our apartment building (European houses always had such interior space) was filled with a colourful crowd of peasants sitting on their cheap, woven-cane luggage while they waited for Mr. Kovacs, the manager of the Immigration and Colonization Office (as it was called in those distant days). Mr. Kovacs would appear, carrying impressive documents and, like a mother hen, with one hand raised high, he would escort the congregation in a loose formation past Baross Square, past the George Stephenson Monument, over to the Eastern Railway Station, where their long journey into an unknown future would begin.

I saw thousands of people leave for Canada from that courtyard during those depression years. I recall the folk songs that some chanted while bidding farewell to the old country: "My lover left for America, but I won't go after him . . ." Nevertheless, they did. The very first words I could decipher when I learned to read were: "Tzanadian Patzifitz Railway," as the company name would be pronounced in phonetic Hungarian. I guess this makes me a "born Canadian."

The courtyard also provided vivid commerce and much amusement. Tradesmen came and in loud, raspy voices shouted the availability of their services and wares. Some of them repaired cooking utensils or broken windows; some sharpened knives; others sold household goods. Even more popular, at least for the maids and the children, were the street singers with their barrel organs, dulcimers, or hand-driven hurdy-gurdies, singing romantic and melancholy songs and professing banal but well-meant folk wisdom. They hoped for a shower of paper-wrapped coins from above and they were seldom disappointed. This practice was forbidden, but the stern janitor, a morose, loud man with a Stalinesque mustache, booming voice, and thick red neck, was often too busy to expel them. From their experience and practical wisdom, these itinerant artisans knew this.

The maids were young peasant girls whom the meager family farms could no longer support at home, and they streamed into the cities hoping for employment as servants. They were expected to do all the work in the house for a modest income and miniscule free time. But they were young and cheerful and embellished their lives by gossiping and chatting with each other, singing off-key, and playing pranks.

Of course, along with their many chores they were expected to babysit the children of the house. That is when we children listened with fascination to frightful ghost stories, common-sense peasant philosophy, and ancestral folklore that these girls narrated with zeal to an avid, round-eyed audience. We had no television in those days.

When I was between two and five years old, we had a young German servant, Louise, of whom I was very fond, and I was sad when she left. I find it awkward to sketch for the reader a world that exists no longer and is so far removed from here by geography and the dusty course of time. But this is what autobiography is about, isn't it? And this was the world around me in my early years.

My father was young, hard working, and determined to succeed in those burdensome years following the First World War. He set up a small electrical workshop on the first storey of our building, where he produced some of his inventions. We lived on the third floor. Only in retrospect do I realize the daily worries my father must have had in trying to create a market for his electrical products and patents and to earn enough money to support us.

Father changed his family name from the original "Kohn" (as the Cohenite name was usually spelled in Middle Europe) to the Hungarian-sounding "Koranyi" so he could get a business licence from City Hall. All this happened before I was born.

My grandparents lived in the same building. I could play for hours on end in Father's workshop or else run in and out of my grandparents' apartment. They were always easy targets of my sister's and my wishes and demands. They were my mother's parents. Samuel Schwartz was born in 1854 in the small city of Kiskunhalas, and his wife, Rosa Schlesinger, was from Fegyvernek, in the Hungarian lowland. They still followed the old traditions of Judaism and kept a kosher kitchen. Grandfather took his daily prayer sessions seriously, chanting seemingly endless passages in Hebrew. It was his never-fulfilled ambition to teach me to read Hebrew.

I remember my grandmother's love for reciting poetry and her devotion for faithfully lighting the Sabbath candles every Friday night. My maternal uncle, Sandor (I also had a paternal uncle named Sandor, who lived in Czechoslovakia), was a born poet. He had an endless struggle to make a living to support his wife, Ilonka, and their daughter, Ann, not because he was lazy but because he totally lacked the skill to make money. But no family birthday or anniversary passed without an appropriate poem written by Uncle Sandor.

Looking back now, I can see Father's ambitious plans for a better future. On that vague but important plan Mother was even more insistent. She kept the small apartment immaculately clean, forever rearranging the few and precious possessions she collected with resolute forbearance. The better pieces of furniture were covered with white linen sheets, for they were not to be used. They just stood there silently, awaiting a dearly hoped-for awakening somewhere in the nebulous future when Mother's dreams would come true and all her hard work had paid off.

Mother, quick witted and with a good sense of humour, loved art and the theatre. She was a long-limbed, dark-haired woman with regular facial features and playful golden-brown eyes, not unlike her great-granddaughter Becky. All referred to Mother as "the beautiful Mrs. Koranyi." Mother had exquisite taste and a natural elegance. I still recall some of her favourite outfits: the stylish grey, shiny silk blouse she wore with the flared black skirt, grey silk stockings, and high-heeled black shoes, a long string of pearls around her neck and cascading down. Another outfit was a suit made of beige and yellow-brown woven material, and, as was the style of those days, the trendy jacket had a red fox collar. She liked to use the barely detectable scent of Guerlain's Mitsouko.

From the age of six until approximately ten, I visited many galleries and museums with my mother. I used to know them all very well. Mother's artistic preference was academic realism. She most enjoyed a relatively small, private exhibition of paintings in the Fritch Museum. Mother also frequently took us to Uncle Lackner's children's theatre. I guess all these activities were part of her larger dream. Mother's yearning for a bright future for the family, though rarely put into words, hung around us with a reliable consistency, acting like some sort of compass and resourcefully directing her gentle governance.

My sister, Marta, studied French, ballet, and piano. She performed once in a stage production at her school as the "Good Fairy of the Spring," for which she wore a lilac tulle gown with artificial violets randomly sewn onto it. But Marta was a born joker who loved to clown and frequently would cast herself in the role of the fumbling comedienne. Even as a child, she had a heart of gold. We fought a lot but we loved each other dearly. Marta, at that point, was attending the Maria Teresa Gymnasium. According to the continental customs of the times, we bowed and kissed the hands of the ladies, calling them "Auntie," and clicked our heels to the men, whom we addressed as "Uncle." Like all the girls, Marta curtsied.

I can still picture the time when Father took me to the Capitol movie theatre. I was five years old. We saw silent movies accompanied by a badly tuned upright piano, tortured by hungry music students. On this one occasion, we saw the first sound movie with Al Jolson's heart-wrenching "Sonny Boy." It was so impressive! All these new discoveries! Like the Graf Zeppelin—people ran out into the street and pointed at the miraculous object in the sky.

We were fascinated by Father's war stories. Father, like most men in his generation, had numerous military adventures in the First World War. He narrated them over and over until we knew them by heart. We soon discovered that all we had to do was say one of the key words, and it was like pushing a magic button: it unleashed Father's flow of words until Mother's visible disapproval finally stopped him.

One day, Father received a substantial order for his merchandise from a large company. I still see him, so young and handsome, so joyous and delighted, proudly showing off the letter of purchase to Mother. In those early days, father often met his close friend, Uncle Funk, a tall, magnificent man with a defiantly spreading, untamed, leonine white mane of hair and tufts of white eyebrows. He owned a large pharmacy and was a superb chemist. It was with Uncle Funk that Father used to discuss the trade "secrets" of his homespun soldering paste that eventually earned Father a lot of money. Although he had only a minimal formal education, Father had taught himself enough chemistry to earn the admiration of the charismatic Uncle Funk. When exactly all this happened, I do not know.

One of my very first memories was the happy sight of my parents returning from an outing having purchased a property. Of course I did not understand this then. What I do recall is that they came home with their faces beaming; they were carrying two small tree branches studded with ever so many ripe, shiny, red cherries lurking behind green leaves—one for my sister, one for me. It was early summer, and I was three years old. The first memory. The first miracle.

This property, in the old, mountainous and less-crowded part of the city, in Buda, later became our summer residence with so many dearly held memories. We lived there only in July and August; we spent the rest of the year in the bustling part of the dusty, busy city.

Father, of course, commuted between his workshop and the holiday residence even during the hot summer months. He drove his own car, an old Fiat that he had bought second hand. He constantly took this car apart, rebuilt it, put it together again and again with his clever hands, and drove it with great concentration. Cars were still rare in Budapest in those days. In fact, in front of our apartment building was one of those endless number of horse-drawn, two-wheeler stations with a group of coachmen whirling around them. Such surreys, or broughams, also called "fiakers," can still be seen, as tourist attractions, but in those days, they served for everyday transportation, as they were more convenient than the crowded yellow streetcars. But there were some red or blue motor-driven taxis as well.

I used to be a nervous and finicky child, underweight, with a poor appetite, and I was a wretched sleeper. In those days we had a grandfather clock emitting a flow of isochronal, rhythmic clatter and, to the inconvenience of the rest of the family, its pendulum had to be stopped for the night, as its monotonous beat kept me awake. I always had to listen to the next click, and this vigilant anticipation did not let me sleep. This was perhaps the forerunner of my preoccupation with the notion of the inescapable passage of Time. The phrase *Dum loquimur fugerit invida aetas*[1] always stuck in my mind, or as Marcel Proust lamented, the unfailing evanescence of "insolent and indifferent time." I can recall a sparkling sunlit day at the Palatinus pool when I was eight years old, as I watched the undulating aquatic lights reflecting on Mother's face, so young and so beautiful. I fervently wished to stop time so that I could forever remember her that way. And I succeeded. That picture, a mental photograph of my lovely young mother, remains permanently captured in my mind. But the merciless passage of time endured nevertheless.

The city map of a child is substantially different from that of his adult counterpart. In my mental chart of Budapest as a youngster, surely Mr. Hauer's pastry shop at Rakoczy Street was a highlighted territory. The shop was a large, well-lighted establishment with marble tables, crystal chandeliers, and stained wood walls. Mr. Hauer himself, dressed in immaculate whites, presided over everything with good nature. His white hair was covered with a snow-white cap, making him look like one of his own whipped cream-covered marzipan petit fours. But other childhood haunts also stand out on my map, like the amusement park that we called *Angol Park*, and the zoo, and the small lake with the boat rides in the city park where, to the horror of our parents, we loved to indulge ourselves by eating pretzels and sipping cheap chocolate milk on the street.

---

[1] "While we talk, envious Time escapes."

When I was a child, the world around me was not scentless and sterile like today. Beside the horse-drawn cab station were diverse, busy shops. Not only the apartment houses but also the streets were more redolent in those days. The horses, of course, emitted a strong animal smell that was not unpleasant, though pungent, in keeping with their hard work. Their bodies steamed when a steady rain fell upon their backs. The stores, too, had their own smells. Some were fragrant, like the coffee- and tea-shop of Julius Meinl at the corner, or the Stuhmer candy store farther down the street. Some were racy, like Behrenwald's cheese market nearby. Still others were aromatic, like the grocery of Morvai's provisions with the smell of freshly baked bread. The Funk pharmacy, like all the other similar establishments, spread the distinct and clean odour of ether, camphor, and herbs.

But talking about scents. Father always had some kind of hobby that he pursued for a number of years with a great deal of vigour and energy, only to direct his interest to another pastime a few years later. Soon after the property in Buda was purchased, Father became an enthusiastic rose grower. And whatever Father did, he never did it on a small scale. He planted 2,500 rosebushes in that huge garden. He knew the names of the different species

**A white-painted loggia, a trellis with climbing
baby roses, divided the garden.**

and all the tricks of growing centifolia, tea roses, Druski, French and other hybrids. He also planted many other flowers. An Italian style of white-painted loggia, replete with tumbling baby roses, divided the garden into a smaller, upper part where our summer cottage stood. The enchanting lower section with the splendour of the rose garden, fruit trees, and a round water fountain was our delight in the hot summer days. We surely had no shortage of this "queen of flowers," honoured with this name by the poetess Sappho. Our friends appreciated frequent gifts of magnificent bouquets of roses, and our apartment was filled with their noble fragrance.

Mother enjoying the garden.

How I used to love those rosebushes! For the rose is a complete life by itself, with a dramatic similarity to our own ephemeral human existence and unavoidable ultimate fate: It starts with the innocent green bud, then shoots straight and high with a glimmer of red in the tight, well-hidden, promising blossom that unfolds with magnificent glory and luxury. The fine petals then begin to curl back just as its intimate core offers its yellow pollen to the world with its deepest, most sensual scent. Finally, it bows its tired head elegantly in assent, and the slightest motion causes the delicate and vulnerable petals to fall to oblivion.

Not only were the odours of the city so different in those days, the cacophony of sounds and the multicoloured street scenery also painted a vastly different picture. The music of the church bells invaded the chorus of street noises several times a day. Chimney sweeps walked down the street, sometimes burdened with ladder and rope, and everything—including their black uniforms and their faces—was covered with soot. Children kept touching them for good luck while chanting a rhyme. Noisy streetcars, motorcars, and horse-drawn vehicles all struggled for space. Many uniformed city workers cleaned the streets of the dross left behind by the horses, scattering the hordes of sparrows feasting on it. Peasant women passed by in their elaborate handmade garb that gave a clue to the village they came from. Apprentices pushed delivery carts. Black marketers peddled smuggled saccharine and flints, items that were taxed by the state. Fresh bottled milk and crusty rolls, still warm, trailed by an appetizing cloud of aroma, were delivered to the door every morning. Cloistered nuns with unsmiling faces, never alone, always in groups of two or three, were seen with starched white headgear, their black garments covering their shoes. They appeared to be floating or rolling on wheels rather than walking, with rosaries in their folded hands.

Numerous barbershops were to be found all over town. Men would drop in every morning for a shave with the old-fashioned blade knife while they read the morning paper or consulted the chatty barber about politics or upcoming sports events. Many of these steady customers had their private, labelled shaving mugs on a shelf in the shop.

When sundown descended on the city, an army of workers appeared carrying long, slender poles, as one by one they lit the row of gaslights along the street.

In Canada, we seem to have only three seasons: we often go from winter to summer within a single week. But in Hungary, there were the four distinct periods of the year, each one lasting for three months. The winters were cold and windy. The snow swept in on us. We warmed our cold hands with cups of hot chocolate or with roasted chestnuts sold on the street corners in small pieces of paper that had been twirled into a cone. Many ladies carried fur muffs. The cheeks of the women and children turned bright red from the cold. Kids carried their skates hanging on a thong, often losing the key needed for winding the contraption onto their shoes, not an easy task while dressed in heavy winter coat and with fingers stiff from the cold. They slid along on hazardous, narrow tongues of ice patches on the street that got longer and more treacherous the more they were in use.

Our home was heated with a glazed-tile wood stove that maintained an even heat with crackling logs. Simpler dwellings often operated the stout, cast-iron stoves and metal pipes that turned an angry red from the sudden heat that died off fast.

A peek at the living room.

Soon enough, the chill of winter vanished and gave way to balmy, fluorescent spring. That is when we used to buy little nosegays of white snowdrops or violets for Mother with our saved pennies. By the time March 15, the National Day, rolled around, we went to the school parade without wearing an overcoat, and sometimes, when our parents were not around, even in our shirtsleeves. The weather got warmer, and the first bunches of ripe cherries were on sale in the stores by mid-May. When the schools closed in June, the days were really hot, one dog day following another, the parched soil marked by a net of tiny cracks like so many brittle wrinkles from the unremitting dryness.

Then, one day, dark clouds gathered, and you could smell the imminent rain in the air. Startling blasts of thunder reverberated, and the splashing summer downpour cleared the air. We loved to inhale the rising scent of the wet earth. Autumn crept in with noble, apathetic tardiness and rust-coloured decay, with shorter days and morning haze. Leafless treetops nodded in the wind.

Budapest was an outdoor city with many places for the public to go. There were many swimming establishments where families went for the weekend. One delight, of course, was the Danube. Its speeding, dark currents vainly tried to swallow the playful golden reflections of the sunshine shimmering on their uneven surface. Narrow two-seater rowboats, usually carrying a boy-and-girl team, rapidly sliced the waters. An occasional four-thwarted racing boat tried to attract suitable partners for an informal regatta. Oarsmanship was a serious matter on the Danube. Well-aged riverboats that smelled of paint, like the *Szent Istvan*, pretended to be still-powerful young vessels, as, packed with tourists, they fought their slow and steady way against the current, funnels belching and whistles screeching.

A well-kept, pretentious segment of the downtown Danube shore was the Corso, which stretched for a mile and was adorned with carved stones. This was another source of entertainment for some. Along the Corso, sitting on rows of rented chairs, the public had a good view of Society's haughty as they strolled along on self-chosen display. Their wives, showing off their stylish clothes and eccentric hats, strutted and preened so they would be written up in the next day's gossip column.

Toward the waning daylight, clattering yellow streetcars returned from the popular excursion places carrying the exhausted weekend crowd of people with their half-empty, after-picnic backpacks, alpenstocks, and bunches of lilacs that quickly shed their tiny petals. Their preteen children, still burdened with flasks, flashlights, maps, magnifying glasses, and compasses, gave up self-importance for slumber.

Some visited the omnipresent cheap garden restaurants that were always filled with the murmur and laughter of humankind. The clatter of crockery vied with the squeals of gypsy music, just as wafting scents of the flowering chamomile trees duelled with the penetrating aroma of the fried food and lager. Tall glasses full of golden liquid with a foamy white collar sat on trademark-crested beer mats on top of the red-and-white-checkered tablecloths held in place by metal clips. A finicky house cat patrolled his territory under the tables.

Oh, yes! Those languorous Sunday pleasures. Like playing soccer in the city park or feeding the animals at the zoo. Children ate thin pretzels almost the size of their heads. The affordable pleasures of the bourgeoisie.

For one week late each spring, Father displayed his electrical and chemical wares at the International Fair. This was a popular annual industrial and commercial gathering, held in and around the exhibition hall of the large central park of Budapest. We children could hardly wait for the opening of this spectacular event with its colourful crowds, loud music, and junk food reluctantly bought for us by our besieged parents. At the different exhibition booths we collected armfuls of imaginative advertising materials and colourful brochures.

All in all, it was a solid, cohesive world; cohesive like the orderly and predictable Newtonian mechanical physics itself, as physics was thought to be in those days of human innocence. I believed then that nothing could ever shake this good order, and that everything, including the clockwork of society, seemed to be built to last without any change, forever and ever. But no, it did not endure.

* * *

Many years passed, and I was twenty years old. In a narrow street, garbage was piled high. Some of the houses were in ruins. A tall, unpainted wooden plank closed off the street where dead bodies lay. This was not a huge pile of thousands of corpses; that was two streets down, near the building that we called the hospital, at one time a school. The streets, the houses, everything was crowded with masses of bewildered Jews. We all passed by the bodies. We all were hungry and looking for food—such as dead horses. We no longer cared about the small-arms fire, the burst of machine-gun chatter, the blast of artillery or exploding small bombs that the Soviet planes poured down so generously on Nazis and civilians alike during the siege of Budapest. These were the "democratic" dangers. They hit without asking any questions about one's racial origins.

My shoes were leaking and coming apart, and my coat was tied around my waist with a rope. I was there with my first wife, Lici, and she looked no better. In our day-to-day quest to survive the Nazi horrors without being killed by the would-be liberators, we were always on the move. We stayed a few days in the ghetto hospital where they knew us. In another era and in a different location, this was the well-respected Jewish General Hospital where we worked and studied. My father was taken away to dig mass graves and there, in the ghetto, he met an old man who recognized him. Yes, he was Mr. Kovacs, but he was hardly the same man we used to know. "Remember me?" he said. "Thousands and thousands of people I helped to immigrate to Canada, but I, as a Jew could not get a visa . . ." We never saw Mr. Kovacs again and never knew whether he survived the war or perished like so many others. The date was January 10, 1945. Why do I remember it so exactly? Well, we will see why later.

* * *

One day in 1996, I was visiting the Museum of Science and Technology in Ottawa. My niece, Ann, Marta's daughter, her husband, Mike, and their children, Becky and Matthew, were with me. In the museum shop, a book caught my eye: *Canadian Pacific Posters 1883–1963*, by Marc H. Choko and David Jones. Right at the beginning of the book was a photograph from the year 1915 showing the Canadian Pacific Railway's Immigration and Colonization Offices in Budapest, Baross Square 12—the house in which I was born!

I do not intend to convert the cornered reader into an unassenting disciple of history, nor do I wish to tautologize on yesteryears' well-known historic junctions. But some of these events, centred in the particular focus of persecution, had augured the eventual catastrophe that immured my youth. To that extent they need to be repeated.

The Age of Enlightenment rose imperceptibly from many sources, including the moral philosophy of John Locke. The central idea of the movement, popularized later by Jean-Jacques Rousseau and Francois Voltaire, carried the flag of tolerance, emancipation, and liberalism to most parts of Western and Central Europe. It was fervently embraced by the Jews (*Haskalah*) and ushered in a growing secularism. The latter initiated two divergent trends. One was a cultural assimilation, praised and promoted by Moses Mendelssohn in Germany in the last century. The other was the vigorous revival of a hitherto vaguely felt hope ("Next year in Jerusalem") by Theodore Herzl's Zionism (the name "Zionism" was contributed by Nathan Birnbaum). Zionism, with its full range of political affiliations, was enthusiastically followed by a growing group of young men and women.

Opposing these developments were the forces of hatred and racism. Count Joseph Arthur Gobineau, a French diplomat, published in 1853 his *Essay on the Inequality of the Human Races*, a four-volume treatise extolling the Aryan race as the sole originator of culture and all noble thoughts. It generated great interest, and by the end of the century, Gobineau societies, with a virulent anti-Jewish agenda, had spread all over Germany.

Anti-Semitism is as old as the House of Abraham itself. The modern term first appeared in Wilhelm Marr's Jew-hating pamphlet in 1879. Marr became the founder of the Anti-Semitic League, established in Dresden and Berlin. Only two years later, in 1881, a series of Russian and Ukrainian pogroms burst forth with the help of Nicholas Pavlovitch Ignatiev and Constantine Pabedonostsev. There was a revival of the blood libel charges. The decade was particularly rich in anti-Semitic activities. The infamous Dreyfus affair in 1896 incited France, and preceded by one year the publication of a forged document called *Protocols of Learned Elders of Zion*, a product of the Russian Secret Police. The Aryan race concept was emphasized by Houston Stewart Chamberlain in his 1899 bestseller, *The Foundation of the Nineteenth Century*. All these prepared the ground for the National Socialism that was to come.

Not all Jew-haters were Christians. Some were Jews. Prominent among them was Karl Marx, who said, among other derogatory remarks, "The Jews of Poland are the smeariest of races."[2] In his 1843 essay *The Jewish Question*, he wrote, "The social emancipation of Jewry is the emancipation of society from Jewry." He was not alone. Later, Ilja Ehrenburg sided with the persecutors against the Jewish writers in the Soviet Union, morally contributing to the death of many.

The most ferocious anti-Semite in the late nineteenth century was Otto Weininger, a Jew with an unsightly facial feature who was appointed professor of philosophy at Vienna University at the age of twenty-two and killed himself at the age of twenty-three by slitting his wrists "to let the Jewish blood out." Weininger detested Jews and hated women. But had he lived, he probably would have been sent to Auschwitz. One of his admirers was Ludwig Wittgenstein, who, with three Jewish grandparents, would certainly have qualified as a "full Jew" according to the Nuremburg Laws, were it not for copious donations to the Nazis. Wittgenstein was six days younger than Adolf Hitler, and all three of them lived in the same city at the same time.

There is some evidence that Hitler had been influenced by Weininger. The anti-Semitic Jew, however, is a perennial phenomenon. Today one can mention Noam Chomsky, the son of a Hebrew scholar. He is an anti-Semitic, anti-Zionist Jew who wrote the preface for Robert Faurisson's Holocaust-denying book and who even found excuses for Osama bin Laden because of the "long-standing U.S. support for Israel's brutal military occupation" of Palestine.

Zionism also had its Jewish enemies. The socialist newspaper *Arbeiter Bund* on the left and the ultra-orthodox Jew on the right did their best to distress the Zionists. The ultra-orthodox abhorred the idea of a secular Jewish state "before the Messiah arrives." They also remembered the false messiahs, like Sabbatai Zevi, centuries before. Yet for two thousand years, all Jews have prayed on Yom Kippur, the holiest day of the year, saying, "Next year in Jerusalem." Throughout history, there have been many false messiahs: in 720 CE, Serene in Syria; thirty years later, Obadiah Abu Isfahan; in 1160, David

---

[2] *Neue Reinishe Zeitung*, April 29, 1849.

Alrui in Mesopotamia; and in 1660 Sabbatai Zevi. Were they all possibly early Zionists who used the self-made title of Messiah as a means to an end?

The *Zeitgeist* permeated Hungary as well.

The position of the Hungarian Jewry was such a perplexing issue that scholars of history still cannot agree on many aspects of it. On the one hand, in 1867, under Gyula Andrassy's government, the emancipation of the Jews was recognized by the Hungarian Parliament. On the other hand, fifteen years later, during the Tisza Kalman regime, the ancient myth of the ritual blood libel at Passover was raised, an accusation first reported by Josephus Flavius. The libel, with proper agitation, gained new life when a fourteen-year-old girl, Ester Solymosi, disappeared from the small Hungarian village of Tisza-Eszlar. In the subsequent trial in 1883, the charges of ritual murder against the Jewish community leaders of the village were dropped, but in many places anti-Semitic violence broke out. This sentiment was used for political purposes by Gyozo Istoczy to form the Anti-Semitic Party, and, not to be left out, by Count Nador Zichy to establish the Catholic People's Party with an anti-Jewish agenda.

Despite this, the Jews fared well both culturally and economically. In 1910, the population of Greater Hungary was approximately twenty-one million souls, of which more than 900,000 were Jews. The population of the capital, Budapest, was 20% Jewish, and among the professionals the number was 40% or more.

The Jews themselves were sharply divided. The minority were the Orthodox Jewry, who kept to themselves, and spoke Yiddish; some were anti-Zionists on religious grounds. The majority were secular "Neolog" Jews who spoke Hungarian and in appearance and culture were undistinguishable from the non-Jewish population. They were assimilated, but nevertheless they were Jewish and proud of it. Assimilation provided them with a sense of security. Many of them thought it was chic to look down on their orthodox counterparts. Budapest, in particular, had a strong Jewish cultural influence that richly coloured the city's art, theatres, cabarets, humour, and newspapers. But this seeming equality between the assimilated Jew and the Christian Hungarian was far from reciprocal.

In alliance with Germany, the Austro-Hungarian Empire was defeated in the First World War and disintegrated, forming five chauvinistic, sovereign nations that were mutually hostile. After the Peace Conference of Trianon, Hungary lost 71.5% of its territory. The remaining population was just below eight million, and the Jewish population of the post-war country had been reduced to 473,000. At the closing days of the war, around 1918, Hungary was overtaken by the Communist Revolutionary Government of the Jewish Bela Kun. There were several Jews in prominent positions in his government, such as Otto Korvin, Bela Vago, and Erno Por. During their 133-day reign, referred to as the "red terror," many Jews and non-Jews were executed, and thousands of others, including my father, were arrested; but the anti-Semites regarded this government as a "Jewish movement."

Soon, a counter-revolution arose, led by Admiral Miklos Horthy. It nurtured extreme rightist elements and brought about what history refers to as the "white terror." Many innocent Jews were killed by them, too.

Soon after, the upheaval settled down to a moderate form of anti-Semitism, along with the usual feudalism.[3] Duels in defence of one's honour, although nominally against the letter of the law, were everyday occurrences. Even Arthur Koestler, at that time a young Zionist, in his fervour to prove that his Jewish swordmanship and bravery were as good as that of any non-Jewish student, duelled and was wounded in the Vienna woods. What characterized the spirit of the country was the humorous definition of a prominent Hungarian actor. When asked, "Who is an anti-Semite?" his maxim was, "The anti-Semite is the one who hates the Jews more than one is supposed to."

In 1920, the Teleki government introduced the *numerus clausus* ("closed number"), a legal ceiling that set a limit to the number of Jews that could be accepted in the universities. Anti-Semitic student organizations, like the Turul Society, took hold, and the slogan could be heard with an increasing frequency, voicing the "need to defend the Christian Hungarian race against the Jewish race." In 1932, Gyula Gombos, a politician of German descent, became prime minister. He was an enthusiastic, long-standing member of the Race-Protecting Party. By then, Mussolini was in power in Italy, and soon Adolf Hitler took over in Germany. Gombos made sure that Hungary followed the same ideological path as these dictators. His successor, Prime Minister Daranyi, introduced the First Jewish Law in Hungary. This law enforced a twenty percent limitation of Jews in the professions and in the field of art. The importance of this piece of legislation was not in the mere figures but in the legal precedent of race discrimination. Strangely, the economic situation, probably because of the approaching war, was still reasonably good.

---

[3] Although no longer practised formally, the *jus primae noctis*, the typical medieval law, was still in the law books in Hungary; this law gave the aristocratic landlord the right to spend the wedding night with the bride of any of his underlings.

As the war was about to begin, more and more harsh and restrictive Jewish laws were passed, and increasingly repressive governments gained power. The Second Jewish Law permitted only six percent of Jews in the professions and severely limited the economic status of the Jews. Two years later, in 1941, the Third Jewish Law introduced even more wicked measures against the Hungarian Jews. Around that time, sugar rationing was introduced. To obtain food rationing tickets, a form had to be completed with each person's religion and respective family tree exactly marked. By this means, the authorities obtained a list of the entire Jewish population. But this was just a prelude to the rapidly evolving catastrophe to come.

In the same year when Hitler's Soviet campaign began, the prime of the Jewish youth was called up for "military duty." However, this was not true military service. In fact, it was forced labour on the faraway Soviet front line under the most primitive conditions. The young Jewish men were cut off from all communication with their families, and, unarmed, they were in the absolution power of sadistic and corrupt Hungarian Army officers and staff. People doing forced labour were not given uniforms or any other kind of clothing. Many of them faced the harsh Russian winter in civilian clothes and shoes. Food was scarce and none was provided for them. They were guarded by armed Hungarian soldiers. The purpose of this forced labour was to waste these Jewish boys without any witnesses.

That they did. More and more young Jewish men were drafted, leaving behind the old people, the children, and the women. This situation rendered all potential resistance hopeless in the home country. In the horrific winter of 1942–43, approximately 44,000 young Jewish men from Hungary were killed in the snow-covered Ukrainian tundra. They were dragged there by the Hungarian military. Strangely, this was not fully grasped by the Jewish population at home, just as they were also unaware at that time of the existence of the extermination camps. This was 1942, when the Wannsee conference was held near Berlin and where Adolf Eichmann and other "technicians" decided the details of the "final solution of the Jewish question."

Dreams and Tears

Not all of these interspersed captions represent actual dreams. Some are just composites of my own memories, or stories that touched my life. Some are like old postcards or faded watercolour pictures that were found in a dusty corner of the attic. Others are thoughts that perpetually inhabit my mind. Some are nightmares that plagued me for many years, not as much with their visual images as with the emotions closely tied to them. These interludes or brief vignettes are part of my life, and some of them are portrayed separately in three Nocturnal Images. They may act as background illustrations to my narrative.

Dreams and Tears: I

Halcyon Days

Come let us go while we are in our prime.
And take the harmless folly of the time!
We shall grow old apace, and die
Before we know our liberty,
Our life is short, and our days run
As far away as does the sun . . .

From Robert Herrick, "Corinna's Going a-Maying"

On this bright summer afternoon, the sun is beating down on my back and shoulders with a steady heat that feels like tiny pinpricks on my glowing skin. To soothe the sting, I lie down on the soft, moist grass, always dewy, in our garden in Buda and listen for a while to the multitude of competing sounds of honeybees, dragonflies, and other busy summer creatures. I close my eyes and my thoughts go back to the day before, when my friend Mitzu and I discovered a large cave, the entrance obscured by a dense bush. To enter the cave appeared to be both dangerous and thrilling in a way that adults cannot understand. But this afternoon, the clock seems to stand still. My sister, Marta, and I had been playing together earlier, then hung around in the kitchen while the maid worked. Bored with one another, we went in different directions, but both of us awaited our parents' return—Father from his work, and Mother from her shopping, for she expected the grandparents for a weekend visit.

I was eight years old then, an avid reader of Karl Maj's books on the Wild West, the prairies, Indians, and the Northwest Passage. But on this lazy afternoon, I had no patience to pursue such activities, which at other times were so soothing and absorbing. What Marta and I were waiting for, and soon heard, was the tortured whining of a distant motorcar, barely managing the steep climb. Finally, we heard Father changing gears as he turned onto our street. Like hungry puppies, we both ran from different directions, running as only the young muscles and joints can propel the eager bodies of children. Past the big walnut tree, we scurried towards the gate to greet our parents. Mother unloaded the car, and we all helped carry the packages of delicacies and the oversized, ice-cold watermelon to the kitchen. There, Mother was already busy.

After a light supper, deep darkness enveloped the garden. The background melody of nature had changed. The vibrant cacophony of the sweet songbirds was gone. The cadence of the nocturnal tunes now dominated. There, the glimmer of the fireflies and the stridor of the crickets mingled with the brassy concert of the bullfrogs as they took over the night shift. The deep blue-black summer sky was lit by distant stars that appeared to be within arm's reach.

Uncle Bear, a family friend who sometimes stayed for an evening meal, talked to us of the miracles of the stellar constellations; the sextant and other ingenious seafarer's instruments of earlier times; the four principal wind directions defined by the ancient Greek sailors; and Odysseus, the heroic husband of the beautiful Penelope. Uncle Bear's stories captivated our imaginations until our eyelids fell shut and we were fast asleep.

CHAPTER 2

Father's Family

The northern part of Greater Hungary, now Slovakia, is dominated by the rugged landscape of the huge and untamed Carpathian Mountains. Its snow-covered cliff, Gerlachovke, is the highest peak, rising to 8,700 feet above sea level. The famous Tatra Range is the second highest. Lush forests of pine, spruce, and fir cover the slopes up to the tree line, halfway up the mountain. Icy, rapid, white-foaming streams and rivulets turn and twist in the midst of the mossy rocks, swirling and churning toward the lowland. On many of the windy summits, blanketed by wildflowers, romantic ruins of medieval castles stand abandoned. Their towers, visited by eagles and sometimes shrouded by clouds, silently keep their mystical past and unspoken secrets. When I was a child, these thick forests, smelling of mushrooms and wet earth, were still full of wildlife—brown bears, chamois, boar, and all sorts of birds of prey. The arable land was scarce, but sheep were plentiful and the lakes and streams were replete with fish, particularly trout.

In the highland, the majority of the population was Slovak, a Slavic ethnic group related to the Czechs. Very large Hungarian communities also lived in this locality. This region originally belonged to the Austro-Hungarian Empire. Most people spoke two or three languages. There was also a sizeable Jewish population. The more or less assimilated Jews lived in the western part of Slovakia and the ultra-religious Jews were concentrated in the eastern regions of the country, which was referred to as Rutenia or Karpathski-Ukraine. The orthodox Jews spoke mainly Yiddish, but understood all the languages spoken in the area.

Northern Hungary was once populated by the Celts and some Germanic tribes. This was far back, in the distant first century. Later, this area belonged to Moravia. As a testament to their Celtic past, the preferred musical instrument of the Slovak countryside is the bagpipe. The local Slovaks were defeated by the newly arrived Hungarians in the ninth century. They remained a poverty-stricken minority under the rule of the Magyars until the end of the First World War. This explains why most of the landowners were Hungarian noblemen. With the disintegration of the Austro-Hungarian Empire, this region joined with the Czechs, that is, with Bohemia, in 1918. The newly created union was the Czechoslovak Republic. As children raised in Hungary, we were taught to hate and despise Czechoslovakia, an enemy of the Magyars.

Close to 190 years ago, in 1808, my paternal great-grandfather, Bernat Kohn, was born in Bolesov, a small, rural community in Slovakia. He lived in Strecno, a village near the fortress, which was famous for the rich growth of poppies that painted the hills bright red at certain times of the year. According to legend, these glowing red flowers grew from the blood of fallen warriors in a long-forgotten battle. Bernat Kohn was a businessman who supplied building materials and chalk. He married Betty Lang. He died at age 87 in 1895, in Varin. He had had some kind of falling out with his son, my grandfather Simon, which is why not much is known of Bernat's life.

Simon Kohn, my grandfather, was born in 1857 in Strecno, and for a Jew, he had an unusual profession. He was a machinist. He came to live in Zilina, a small town in the picturesque Vag valley, west of the Tatra Mountains. At age twenty-seven, in the synagogue of Skale Novej-Usi, Simon married Fany Kellerman from Hrabovka, the lively twenty-two-year-old daughter of Markus Kellerman and Josephona Fishof. They had eight children, five boys and three girls, and lived in poverty. Simon spoke primarily Slovak and German, but he could also speak a broken Hungarian. My grandmother's mother tongue was German, but she could speak Slovak fluently. She spoke not a word of Hungarian, and so our rare encounters were very awkward. By the age of four, I knew all the words of endearment in German. According to Father, my grandmother's family, the Kellermans, originally came from the small Jewish community of Alsace-Lorraine. Grandfather Simon worked for the railway company as an engineer.

By the way, my father's mother tongue was German and he spoke a good enough Slovak, but his Hungarian was heavily accented, and to our riotous amusement and his annoyance, he used to make outlandish mistakes. Maybe it is a humorous punishment (or karma) that I, who laughed at him then for his accent, am now myself condemned to live with the same undesired liability in Canada!

My father was the second oldest in the family. He was not interested in education, but from earliest childhood he excelled in his ability to earn money that the large family so badly needed. He learned about machines from grandfather, and by the age of twelve, he could operate the early agricultural machines. At that young age, he became a keen competitor at harvest time, operating farm machinery and sleeping in the fields. At the end of harvest time, he returned home, proud of bringing gifts and money.

This was just one of the many ways Father earned money while he was still a mere child. He often recalled the stories of these adventures. Father was a self-made man from the very beginning. In contrast, my Uncle Sandor, the oldest in the family, was a bookworm. He married late, set up a mirror factory in Zilina, and collected antiques. Another older brother was Uncle Feri, a master printer who lived in Prividze, not far from Zilina.

The details of the long trip to the distant Zilina are hazy, but I vividly recall my first visit to Father's family when I was four years old. Before we left Budapest by train, Mother made careful preparations for the trip. We got new clothes; I was dressed in a wine-red sailor blouse with a square white collar folded over my shoulders, white pockets, and blue short pants. We were inspected several times by Mother before the departure, but I failed to pass the final scrutiny at the railway station because my pockets were bulging. When Mother discovered it and tried to straighten out my clothing, I warned her to be quiet: "I am bringing my lead soldiers, and I am going to take back the region for Hungary," I told her. To my chagrin, I had to hear that story repeated over and over again, and I liked it less and less as the years passed!

One image I recall clearly from the train ride was the marvellous emerald-green fields in which far-off cattle were grazing. They looked so tiny, it seemed to me that all I had to do was reach out and pick them up, like so many toys. Much later, I learned of Jean Piaget's theories about the peculiar stages of the perceptual development of early childhood. But way back then, it was just another wonder.

Of our many relatives, my favourites were Aunt Aranka and her husband, Hugo. They owned a big toy store in Zilina! It was located on the arcaded square. On our rare visits, I was let loose in that store and my uncle never cared how much damage I did in this veritable toy heaven. The only trouble was that Uncle Hugo loved to tease me because of my Hungarian patriotism, which had already been drummed into me by age four.

Aunt Aranka and Uncle Hugo had three children, but in those days I could communicate only with the oldest one, a lovely, genteel girl named Edith, who spoke Hungarian. Her two brothers, Laci and Zolo, spoke only Slovak, and we used to fight a lot.

There were so many cousins, scores of uncles, and a multitude of aunts in my family! Father's youngest brother, Joseph, was almost too young to be a real uncle and, therefore, he liked to assert his authority with fierce glares at us, the nasty children. He used to give us a frightening look that contrasted with his soft heart, rendering his pretended anger ineffective. Uncle Joseph was very strong. It was said that his favourite sport was boxing. He studied therapeutic massage and he was also interested in medicine. He probably had a good chance to study, because in those days, Czechoslovakia, unlike the feudalistic Hungary, was a genuine democracy with no racial discrimination. Meanwhile, Uncle Joseph earned a living by some trade, and umbrella repair work. He was a man with natural elegance, and we used to call him "Baron Kohn."

All our relatives were happy to invite us for a midday meal. In Zilina, as in Budapest and in all of Europe, the main meal was at noon, sometimes followed by a siesta. This had to do with the impractical, old-fashioned rhythm of daily life. The work started earlier than nowadays. Factories whistled in their labourers in the morning darkness of six o'clock. Schools, stores, and offices opened at eight. Breakfast usually consisted of only a simple roll, sometimes with jam or butter, and a cup of coffee. The "elevenses" were eaten at ten and included no more than a sandwich. But at around one in the afternoon came the complete meal of the day.

No dinner could be imagined without soup. We had an infinite variety of soups, the pride of the housewives. In Zilina, it was often mushroom soup, for nowhere could be found any better mushrooms than in the neighbouring forests. The meat dish, either beef or fowl, was always very well done and was served with two always overcooked, moribund vegetables. In Zilina, my favourite was the wonderful trout freshly caught in the rapid currents. Salads were served with the meal. Then came sweets and sometimes fruit.

Everything, including various sauces, stuffings, ragouts, and dressings, was all freshly prepared every day with groceries and meat bought that day. Refrigeration was still unreliable. The only canned goods I saw as a child were sardines. Alcoholic beverages were very rarely consumed at home. We never ate any game. That may have been an idiosyncrasy that stemmed from keeping a kosher kitchen.

After an unhurried lunch, the businesses reopened, and work continued until the evening hours.

As I mentioned before, we did not keep the dietary laws of Judaism rigidly, although Father's family in Zilina and my grandparents in Budapest maintained kosher dietary traditions. It was Father's view that "the Almighty, being so busy in these hurtful, brutal days, has made it His priority perhaps to look into the hearts of the people before being interested in the contents of their stomachs." He believed that the central pillar of Judaism was the *mitzvot*, good deeds, and he lived accordingly. With that, Mother was in full agreement. "When your conscience is clear, you share with others, accept the guidance of the Almighty, and really want to belong to your fellow Jews, then you are a good Jew," she used to say. Her view on the dietary law was that these mostly derived from the ancient discouragement of cruelty. "To cook a calf in his mother's milk," a revolting abomination, "must have been a practice a long time ago, if it had to be forbidden." Hence comes the law that meat and milk cannot be mixed. But "Avoid cruelty to all, and be clean. That is the spirit of the law," she used to say. Yet she kept other rituals without fail, such as lighting (*zinden*) the Sabbath candles every Friday.

The family that lived in Zilina sometimes came to Budapest. One of the saddest trips was made by my Uncle Bela and his wife, Honora. They brought their four-year-old daughter Vera, who was very sick with a malignant growth on her jaw, probably a lymphoma or sarcoma. As a last hope, they came for a consultation. Uncle Bela had had a difficult life. He had been a prisoner of war in Siberia for a couple of years. How he loved to eat! It was as if he wanted to make up for all his past deprivations. His wife, Honora, was a very quiet woman who always kept a meticulously clean home. After the despairing consultation, they returned to Zilina feeling sad and accepting fate.

On a happier occasion, my cousin Edith visited and stayed with us for a whole summer. She was by then a medical student, and did her internship in a well-known university clinic in Budapest. She was a beautiful girl with honey blonde hair. She was full of youthful spark and relished life, adored dancing, immersed herself in her studies, and dove into the busy theatre life of the town with zest. That was when I was eleven years old and already fascinated with medicine. Naturally, I always pestered Edith with naïve medical questions and asked her to point out the organs on a chicken before the family consumed the scientific specimen. Edith always happily went along with these ventures.

That same year, we made another trip to Zilina. This time, Father drove the family in his precarious automobile. It was a short trip by today's standards. The distance was about 300 miles, but in those days, with Father's sputtering car that sometimes blew tufts of evil-smelling blue fumes, and the inevitable stops for the repair of blown tires and ill-coordinated washroom breaks, it took a long time for us to arrive. We started the trip very early in the pre-dawn darkness. We waited for hours on both sides of the border before being allowed to enter Czechoslovakia after a thorough and stern inspection. Finally, we arrived late at night, by then too sleepy to stay awake for the joyful reunion.

On this trip, I learned more about my family. They were still the joking, noisy bunch of folks, a close-knit, warm, and argumentative tribe with a constant dialogue. How they competed with each other in a pretended bitter tone and faked anger! In whose house should we stay or eat? Each one enthusiastically offered his or her very best. But when politics was discussed, a measure of gloom invaded the family's mood. Over a year before, a man named Hitler had come to power in Germany. He was said to be a dangerous anti-Semite, but even before that, we'd had our own anti-Semitic government in Hungary with Gyla Gombos as prime minister. It seemed to me that nothing much had happened.

Father used to listen to Hitler's endless speeches on the radio. At ten or eleven years of age, I was not interested in politics. From what I heard, Hitler was too busy trying to stay in power. There were fights within his party and plenty of killings, including the slaughter of his crony Ernst Roehm. By Hitler's own hand, it was rumoured. Yet shortly after our visit to Zilina, Hitler disregarded the Versailles Treaty and marched his military forces into the Rhineland. Jewish refugees from Germany were telling frightening stories. But life was still good in Hungary, and we pushed aside the grim tales. We preferred to think that they were exaggerations. At any rate, those bad things had happened in Germany, and this was Czechoslovakia, a democratic country.

Not long after we returned from our trip to Budapest, in mid-September of 1935, the Nuremburg Laws were passed in Germany. These deprived the Jews of citizenship and imposed stern restrictions on them. Somewhat similar to contemporary television news, a brief black-and-white newsreel was shown in the movie houses before the main program. The prominent items in those newsreels were Hitler's speeches, the Hitler Youth, and the *Sonderabteilung* (SA) marching and singing the *Horst Wessel Lied*. The words of these marching songs were frightening: . . . *Wenn das Judenblut vom Messer spritzt, dann geht es nochmal gut* . . . (". . . When the Jewblood squirts from the knife, it is then when everything goes right . . .")

Despite all this, I was eleven years old in Hungary and more interested in the upcoming 1936 Olympics. There were all sorts of controversies. The U.S. was hesitant to participate in the Berlin Olympics because of Germany's racial laws of discrimination and the persecution of Jews. Still a child and single-mindedly possessed by sport, I felt sorry that the whole Olympics might be endangered. Hungary stood a good chance to win lots of medals in gymnastics with Istvan Pelle, in swimming with Ferenc Csik, and in sabre fencing with Atilla Petschauer.

The German representative in the Olympic Committee, Dr. Lewald, promised nondiscrimination to overcome the American objection. He invited the American representative, Avery Brundage, to Germany to inspect the equal sports facilities set up for the Jewish athletes. Brundage went, was received royally, looked, and found that the situation was "entirely satisfactory." No, there was no racial discrimination in Germany, proclaimed Brundage.

The president of the Olympic Committee, General Shrill, was most impressed with Dr. Lewald's argument: "Just how many Jews are accepted as members in the New York Athletic Club? None . . ." And it was true. The Olympics were on, heralding Teutonic superiority with an incredible fanfare and splendid glitter to an unsuspecting world. Hungary fared well at the Games, too.

In those days, I was a great swimmer. With my friend Paul Amigo, we used to bring home all available medals in the national high school competitions. We alternately got first or second positions. One day, we were approached by two coaches of the Olympic team, two talent scouts who were very keen to invite us for the training of a selected group of swimmers. The envious eyes of all the other students were on us. But then they asked about our religion and we told them we were Jews. A few minutes later, their interest gone, the coaches had disappeared.

Another favourite sport I pursued was gymnastics. I trained vigorously two or three times a week for many years and won numerous medals in national competitions.

On father's forty-ninth birthday, February 24, 1938, the *Anschluss* took place. Austria joined with Germany to form a single empire. Maybe the history books describe this differently today, but I can still see the beaming faces of the proud Austrian crowd greeting the German troops with hands raised in the Nazi salute. Towns and villages resounded with the vigorous shouts of *Sieg Heil*, the German anthem, the *Horst Wessel Lied*, and with the noisy delight and exhilaration of populace at large. This is what I saw in the movie newsreels. True, there were those rare Austrians who were scared or were mourning the loss of their freedom, but it seemed that the majority were exuberant. Just a few months later, at the end of the summer, the world was on the verge of destruction.

In this critical time, 1938, we got word that Grandmother in Zilina had fallen and broken her leg. Father and I went to visit her. This was our last trip to Zilina. I was thirteen years old. We found the once-happy family in a dreary mood. I immediately understood that this was not only because of Grandmother's condition. They were frightened of what might happen. Uncle Hugo hoped that the British would not let Czechoslovakia down and that they would understand that conciliation would only encourage Germany, increasing their Teutonic aspirations. But the more realistic Uncle Joseph believed that the British needed time to prepare; that they were not yet ready to encounter Hitler's military machine. That is why he was less than hopeful.

I found Grandmother in not too bad shape, although she was bedridden with her leg in a cast. I do not recall my cousins Laci or Zolo being around. Perhaps they had already left the country. Cousin Edith was still in Prague, finishing her studies. Uncle Hugo made a small cash deal with his long-standing best friend Kempney, an Aryan, who then reported him to the authorities. Uncle Hugo was jailed, but was set free after he lost his house and his business. Aunt Elza had married Alexander Trostler and had two beautiful red-haired girls, identical twins. We did not stay long and returned disheartened to Budapest.

History books say that Chamberlain met Hitler in September 1938. After his second visit to Germany, Czechoslovakia was sold out by Chamberlain and Daladier to the victorious Nazi dictator. The deal was that a big chunk of Czechoslovakia was given to Hitler, while Slovakia was separated from Bohemia and became a German ally. The remaining small part was supposed to remain an independent Czech entity, so guaranteed by the Munich agreement by Hitler, Britain, and France. Hitler urged the Hungarians to carve out a piece of Czechoslovakia for themselves, and oddly, he asked the same from his next prospective victim, Poland. That they both did, and with zest: Hungary occupied Slovakia's lowland, and Poland took the industrial area of Teschen. When the desperate Czechs asked Chamberlain in Munich what their destiny would be, Chamberlain's answer was, according to President Masaryk's daily diary, an "unconcealed yawn."

Just a few weeks later, on November 9 and 10, the infamous *Kristallnacht* took place, in which synagogues were burned throughout Germany and Austria. This included all twenty-one synagogues in Vienna. An estimated 20,000 Jews were arrested, and 7,500 Jewish shops and apartments were looted, burned, or destroyed. Jews were killed everywhere in Nazi Germany. It was later officially declared that no Nazi Party members could be prosecuted for the killing of Jews. Not only was the insurance money for destroyed Jewish property confiscated by the State, but Jews also had to pay "reparation" to the Germans.

Still, in the same year, on December 21, the newly appointed French ambassador, Robert Coulondre, asked the German secretary of state what the destiny of the remainder of the Czechoslovakian entity would be. Ernst

Weizsaecker, the secretary of state, answered him sternly that this was Germany's business, and English–French guarantees signed in Munich three months earlier were "totally worthless." Indeed, by the end of March 1939, all of Bohemia, including the "guaranteed" portion, was taken over by the Germans. So perished Czechoslovakia.

Hitler made no secret of his intention to rid Europe of the Jews. *Judenfrei Europa* was his goal. Passports to leave the country were readily issued to Jews by the German authorities in those days, but there was just nowhere to go. Not one country was willing to give refugee status to Jews. No country allowed them in. Yes, there were individual cases, perhaps a few thousand, but now the need was for a mass emigration. There were rumours that a Jewish state would be set up in Madagascar, but this was only talk. The Soviet Union allowed some German Jews to enter, mainly transients who continued their voyage to China. Some of them ended up in Soviet *gulags* anyway.

Even those who were the lucky owners of a legitimate immigration visa to the United States of America were denied entry because of the prevailing national policy. This happened to the 1,000 German Jews, to mention but a few, who left Hamburg on a German ship in May 1939 with legal immigration papers to enter the United States. These papers would have reached validity from the beginning of August 1939, after which date the Jews could have entered the U.S. legally. But this was only May. A three-month transit visa was needed, from May to August, but such a visa could not be obtained from any country of the world—not from South America, Australia, or Canada. A transit visa from Cuba was withdrawn. Some people on the German ship, the SS *St. Louis*, by then sailing off the Florida coast, began to commit suicide in their desperation.

After every attempt failed, the Jewish community in the U.S. requested that these people be interned on Ellis Island at the expense of the Jewish community. State Department Secretary Cordell Hull did everything in his power to prevent them from being saved. And he won. Most of these unfortunate German Jews had to return to the hell they had left behind. The majority perished in concentration camps. A number who were accepted by Britain survived. Hitler and the Nazis were delighted with the propaganda value of this issue. "See, the Americans don't want the Jews, either!" was the pronouncement of an elated Joseph Geobbels.

A similar sentiment was well reflected by another incident in April 1939. The Wagner–Rogers Bill, allowing 20,000 German Jewish children to enter the

United States as refugees, was debated in Washington. The bill was defeated. The parties of the Right ("Let the little potential Communists unite with their parents in the German concentration camps") voted against the Child Refugee Bill. Franklin D. Roosevelt acquiesced, afraid of the political consequences.

At the same time in Canada, Deputy Minister of Immigration Frederick Charles Blair and Prime Minister MacKenzie King, driven by their own anti-Semitic convictions, did their best to prevent Jews from entering this country. At the same time, Chamberlain signed the White Paper, severely limiting and eventually forbidding Jewish immigration to Palestine at the very hour of the most urgent need. This was also the time when King Edward VIII kept visiting Hitler, his idol.

Those were the days when the Haj Amin al-Husseini, the Jerusalem mufti, declared his friendship to Nazi Germany. The Husseini family worked with remarkable success from Baghdad to Damascus in the interest of the Nazis. Later, with much satisfaction, the mufti inspected the operation of Hitler's extermination camps.

Palestine was the last, and now vanished, hope for survival. There was nowhere else to go. The era of the once easily obtainable passport for Jews in Germany had also come to an end. By now, no Jew could leave Europe. The doors were slammed shut and their fate was sealed. This was the beginning of the moral meltdown of the Western world.

Dreams and Tears: II

Incubus

*Cease to ask what the morrow will
bring forth, and set down as gain each
day that Fortune grants! Nor in thy
youth neglect sweet love nor dances
whilst life is still in bloom and crabbed
age is far away!*

From Horace, Ode IX, Theliarchus

Cobwebs were hitting my face while I tried to penetrate the dense bush. Their sticky touch was unpleasant and vexing, as I struggled to get through the shrubbery to reach the clearing. The pine trees were so close to one another that the sky was not visible at all. It might as well be midnight. A thick, fermenting cover of soggy pine needles and cones made the ground slippery and dangerous. The air was frosty in this Vag Valley forest, north of Zilina. Exhaled air melted into a curling, white haze of vapour not unlike the mist of cigarette smoke. Eerie noises from a bird, like an ill omen, arose unexpectedly from within the depth of the thick foliage. I was alone. How did I get there? Where to turn now?

Alarmed, I was angry with myself for landing in such a dangerous predicament. There was a mossy boulder on the right side. Huge tree trunks left only a narrow gap for me to pass. I must get through that shrubbery to reach the clearing. More cobwebs and a gamey smell. A growl arose from behind me, and without looking I knew that it was a huge brown bear. I also knew that it was not a true bear but something much more malignant towering over me menacingly. It kept growling. I turned and saw exposed white teeth. I screamed . . . screamed . . . and woke up in my bed in Uncle Hugo's house in Zilina.

What a dream! And why? My heart was still pounding. My brow was moist, cold, and sticky, but nobody heard me. I did not really scream; it was more like a whimper. My thoughts wandered. What lies ahead of us? The Last Judgment?

When I thought about that dream at a much later period in my life, I remembered Albert Camus's maxim: *Don't wait for the Last Judgment. It takes place every day.*

CHAPTER 3

Happy High School Years

The carefree days of childhood vanish so swiftly! The Olympic Games of 1936 electrified me. I recall that I heard the exciting news of Hungary's victories announced by a crackling radio whilst we were on an excursion at Acquincum, and ancient Roman town in the outskirts of Buda. We often went there, and in my fantasies I tried to reconstruct the place on the shore of that gurgling stream in the midst of bird-soiled and moss-hooded boulders, wondering how it must have looked back in Roman times. I admired the now empty sarcophagi, carved out of rock. I loved those mute old stones even though they filled me with a curious, inexplicable sadness, not just because of the inevitability of death but also because of the merciless, unidirectional passage of all-consuming time. Inspired by Uncle Bear, I learned to love Greek mythology and Roman history. Agamemnon, Odysseus, Orpheus and Eurydice, Perseus and Andromeda—they all belonged to my early childhood. On this midsummer's excursion to Acquincum, yet another member of Father's family, his youngest sister Elza, still unmarried, was with us. She was a rare visitor from Zilina.

Many important events were in the making. After having lived a dozen years in the same apartment, we were moving to a much more stylish location. It seemed that Mother's plans for the future were slowly coming through. The move itself went smoothly under Mother's supervision. But for me, this move became a memorable event for an entirely different reason. A particular section of our library had always been kept under lock and key. Through the glass panel I could read the intriguing titles of the books without having access to them. The move gave me a unique opportunity. I got hold of the book of primary interest, a red canvas-covered volume by Dr. Bauer entitled *The Woman*. Locked in the bathroom, I read as much as I could with great excitement, but understood little of that popular scientific work. However, at that age, the tempting title together with the banned status of the book were sufficient to fill me with strange enchantment and dizzying novel sensations.

My jolly, cheerful, and always sentimental sister, Marta, was studying at the Forstner Institute, a prominent school. She was learning French and German and was expected to behave like a "young lady." She conformed to this role only with reluctance and at times with some awkwardness.

But she was not alone in this aversion to comply. Another keen (alas, too keen) expectation of my ambitious mother was the progress I was expected to make at school. To ensure that prospect, beginning in Grade 1, I always had a private tutor to supervise my homework. This eventually made me feel that the official curriculum was really not my business at all. Mother's hopeful demands clearly worked in a counterproductive fashion. This slacking interest suffused most subjects excepting biology and Latin.

By Grade 5, I was supposed to study some Latin, an extracurricular activity that was not yet required by the school program but resolutely advocated by Uncle Bear. I still can picture the decrepit old Latin professor, surrounded by his musty books, whom I visited in the asphalt-melting heat of the summer. He laboured to impress me with how competent he was in his subject. He also had bad breath. God only knows how I retained my love of Latin after such an experience!

I much preferred to spend time with friends, particularly with Mitzu, who was the grandson of a Hungarian general. Mitzu and I loved to walk the hidden, verdant trails in the mountains in Buda and hunt sparrows with peashooters. He was a zealous Catholic and studied at the Piarist Gymnasium, while I attended the St. Stephan Gymnasium. I learned from Mitzu some Catholic prayers and chants in Latin: ". . . *Requiem aeternam dona eis Domine, et lex perpetua luceat eis . . .*" (". . . grant them eternal rest, O Lord, and may light eternal shine upon them . . ."[4]); ". . . *fiat voluntas tua, sicut in coelo et in terra . . .*" (". . . Thy will be done on earth as it is in Heaven. . ."[5]); etc. In those years, race and religion were not issues between us or at least we did not talk about them.

I also spent hours studying anything but the school curriculum, including anatomy. And I read a lot. But again, not from the obligatory reading list. I am anxious to point out that it was not altogether my mother's fault that I limped along so miserably in my school performance. Apart from being just lazy and interested in everything else but school affairs, the realization that schooling was not leading anywhere was also a powerful hindrance in my progress, awakening in me a feeling of defiance. By then, no Jew was being accepted for university studies. My father, forever a realist, did his best to influence me to learn a useful and lucrative trade.

---

[4] From 4 Esdras (Apocrypha) 2, 34–35; sung in the Requiems of Faure, Mozart, and Verdi.
[5] From The Lord's Prayer.

I always envied those fortunate souls who gained lasting inspiration at a later phase of their maturity and were blessed to remember their high school teachers with warm appreciation. This was denied to me, as it was to everyone in my class. Not that I forgot my teachers. They stand out clearly in my mind in minute detail. Much later in my life, many of them inadvertently contributed to my education by being living illustrations of diverse psychopathologies. One, a professor of mathematics, was the prototype of a sadist. I recall several instances of beatings he meted out to different boys (he had his preferred subjects) using a swishing slender cane that could draw blood. We could read the mounting arousal on his face as his palm smoothed the pants on the buttocks of the bent-over boy before the ordeal began. His eyes burned gleefully, then became hazy from the excitement, reflecting an unmistakable ecstasy before the cane came down countless times upon the unfortunate victim. The process was thinly disguised as "discipline."

Other professors were of a different sort. Some were obsessive-compulsive individuals with rigid ways, insistent on exacting, often irrelevant, details, immaculately dressed, one of them with his hair parted with geometric exactness in the middle of his skull ("Mr. Symmetry"). He was a bachelor who rented an apartment that faced the cheapest and busiest red-light district in town. He kept a pair of binoculars near the window.

Slapping the faces of students was routine among several teachers, not motivated by sadism or discipline. It simply represented an unchecked impulse stemming probably from the daily drudgery of their lives or from the disillusionment of their occupation into which a blind destiny had swept them and kept them captured forever as hopeless prisoners of poverty and boredom.

Some indulged in quasi-homosexual embraces, "rewarding" the student. Another, an overweight man of fifty who taught literature, not only had high blood pressure but also suffered (I did not know it then) transient ischemic attacks, a temporary impairment of blood circulation to the brain that usually precedes a stroke. He was also a vicious anti-Semite. Still another was a self-admiring, grandiose man with an elaborate hairdo and a typical narcissistic personality.

Only two professors truly impressed me. One was a delightful eccentric, a science teacher named Professor Geduli. He was like a never-grown-up naughty boy, with pockets full of small sacks containing live snakes and frogs. It was rumoured that he was an international expert on the osseology of reptiles. The other, who scored a mark in my mind on a single brief occasion, was a young Latin teacher, Professor Javor. In a poetic fervour and almost in tears, he wished to share the depth and beauty of Horace's *Leucone* with us. I learned this magnificent Latin poetry by heart. At that time, I thought that I was learning it for his sake. In fact, I did it for myself. Thank you, Professor, Javor, wherever you may be!

Other than the above, most of my professors were Nazis, semi-Nazis, or at least anti-Semites.

Instead of Christmas, we celebrated Hanukkah in mid-December. This holiday commemorates the heroic fight of the Maccabean tribe against Antiochus Epiphanes, the Syrian king, in 161 B.C. The policy of Antiochus IV, as he was also called, was to impose Hellenization upon the Jews. To humiliate those who resisted and still adhered to the old religion, pigs were supposed to be sacrificed to Zeus in Jerusalem's Holy Temple. Finally, the Maccabees revolted.

Hanukkah means "the purification of the Temple" and celebrates the time when the single holy candle burned miraculously for eight days. Therefore, on this "Festival of Light," we used to burn different-coloured candles on each of the eight nights. We gathered around the flickering tongues of pale yellow light under Grandfather's orchestration. We sang simple and sweet Hebrew melodies. After dinner, the spinning-top games (*dreidls*) earned hazelnuts for the children. But the gaiety of the guileless holiday was less spectacular than the spirit of Christmas that dominated the mood of the entire population.

In mid-December, the last day of school before the winter break, the city turned herself into a huge, glittering Christmas tree with many delightful twinkling lights all over. The snow fell in plump, swirling flakes, sometimes getting caught for a second on my eyelashes. In a joyous mood, I frolicked along the street. I kept bouncing my school bag rhythmically against the walls of the houses, trotting and hopping with outstretched tongue to taste the snowflakes. The beauty and ethereal purity of the memory begs for the talent of Dickens to describe this enchanted scene. It remains in my mind as the very last relic of my childhood.

Around that time, I fell in love for the first time. I met a Christian girl, Eva, at a drama production at school. Doe-eyed, with a slightly turned-up nose and a pageboy hair style, she was very pretty, with pouting, natural red lips and arched, innocent eyebrows peeking out from under golden bangs that gracefully framed her face. She staged a short ballet creation, and by the end of her performance, I was in flames. She was one year younger than I and lived not too far from us. In retrospect, I must confess that I really did not know her well enough, but this did not prevent me from bestowing on her

37

incredible attributes. Her tendency to blush gave away her shyness, and I felt enchanted by this innocent platonic love. Oh, Artemis, goddess of the moon and virginity! Eva's slender, little-girl body barely suggested her hidden potential for the future unfolding of magnificent femininity. Like a heartsick troubadour, I often made slow and devious detours to pass her house in the hope of catching a glimpse of her. Can it be that my rapture and devotion were not just for Eva but were for the worship of love itself, a love that I liked to compare in those youthful days with Dante's yearning for Beatrice? Was I indeed in love with my own budding youth?

Soon I was due for my Bar Mitzvah. That was a much simpler affair then compared with now in North America. I studied the Holy Books, learned to chant the pre-selected chapter of the *Haphtorah* and a few blessings in Hebrew. In the afternoon, we had a family party. I was allowed to invite some friends, and I got some books and fountain pens for presents. But it was an important and exhilarating event for Grandfather, who beamed with pleasure and pride. Now I was a full-fledged Jew in the tribe, Grandfather explained, someone who could join the *minyan*, the ten men required for community prayer.

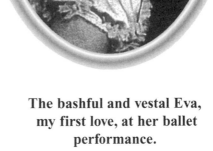

The bashful and vestal Eva, my first love, at her ballet performance.

This remained in my mind because eight months later, Grandfather died of pneumonia. He was eighty-four. The clothes of the mourners were slashed, the mirrors were covered with linen sheets, and a memorial candle was lit that lasted for seven days. The *Kaddish* was recited in dignified rituals by Uncle Sandor (my mother's brother, not Sandor from Zilina), and also by a maternal cousin Pista. The family sat on low, hard benches for the seven days of *shiva*.

Pista was my grandfather's favourite grandson. He was the one to carry my maternal grandfather's name into future generations. Pista's father established a cogwheel factory, married Elsa, and had two sons. Pista was the elder one and studied engineering. When Pista's father died of Spanish flu, Elsa married Albin, who developed the factory to even further fame. They became very, very rich and lived in a huge mansion on Mount Gellert. It was filled with antiques, valuables, and paintings. They had money invested in Switzerland and elsewhere. For Grandfather, however, it was not the material wealth that mattered but the importance of the first-born son, his *Kaddish*, and the conveyor of his family name.

There was another Bar Mitzvah present for me to unwrap. Sort of. Being informed that the religious festivity represented an initiation into manhood, a trusted household servant who used to wear a tight-fitting black skirt around her wide, womanly hips, took it upon herself to do some initiation of her own. Only the fragments of a string of tableaus, mere shards of visual images, remain from this salacious, once-ever affair: she, stepping out from a ring of crumpled black skirt, which fluttered down around her ankles; her forbidden-to-see, slutty, yet enticing lingerie, a quartet of stretched garters holding up a pair of thigh-high, somewhat laddered stockings with seams trailing up, a margin of cool, pale skin above them; her deft, cajoling and thrill-savvy fingers surprising me as they possessed my body. Her wet lips delighted and tormented me with expectations. A whiff of cheap perfume and a redolent female musk enveloped me. Full mast and rigged-to-sail, I sunk easily into her yielding, shimmering self, breathing in the faint, salty scent of her perspiration. Soon I was thrown into a seemingly never-ending chain of unbridled spasms, dissolving slowly in a visceral deliverance. I was animated by a new sensation of levity, but soon a nagging regret rose up in my soul. Thus, at that early age, and not by my deliberate choice, either (although far from being against my wishes), I discovered the mystique of sex inherent in human nature. I did not suspect then how many more brilliant, beautiful, and unspeakably monstrous and demonic layers abide in the mind. This earthly "gift" remained our secret and, although it was not a romantic encounter, in some curious way changed me.

When Father and I returned from our last visit to Zilina, we heard more and more about the atrocities to the Jewish communities carried out by the Hungarian gendarmes in those former Czechoslovak areas that Hungary had recently occupied. Fortunately, we thought, not realizing what enthusiastic Nazi supporters most of the Slovaks were in those days, Zilina remained in the hands of the Slovaks and would be relatively safe. This killing and deportation of Orthodox Jews perpetrated by the Hungarian gendarmes was a localized affair. The news about it barely reached Budapest. But after the war, it became evident that it happened with the full knowledge of Admiral Horthy, who hated the Orthodox Jews, even though he was benevolent towards the assimilated Jews. His benevolence mainly consisted of turning his back on these events while others, such as his faithful one-time officer Endre Baky, did the dirty work.

Prime Minister Gombos died and was buried with military honours. Although he worked hard at it, the "glory" of introducing the First Jewish Law in 1938 fell to his immediate successor, Prime Minister Daranyi. The next year, the Second Jewish Law came into being a few months after the February third terrorist bombing of the Dohany Synagogue by the Hungarian Nazis in Budapest.

Life in Budapest was quiet in those days. In the school, an obligatory paramilitary exercise called *Levente* was introduced. This was twice-weekly pre-military training, for two hours each time, starting at age twelve and obligatory for all boys. But for the Jewish boys in the class, like myself, there was a difference. Since Jews were eventually called up in the army for unarmed, forced physical labour only, all Jewish boys had to put on a yellow armband for the *Levente* exercises (converted Jews wore white armbands). This was when I was fourteen years old. For the first time in my life, I had to wear a visible sign of race discrimination, not unlike my ancestors in medieval times. I recall that I did so with a feeling of defiance and pride, half accusing the non-Jewish Hungarians who stared at us, hoping to awaken in them guilt for their indifferent backwardness and primitive thinking. At least, that was my expectation.

We all studied German in high school for eight years. Hungary was in a German cultural sphere. The second modern language was usually French, four years of it, but because of the Hitler–Mussolini pact and the formation of the Berlin–Rome Axis, the second modern language was changed to Italian. I really loved Italian, a beautiful language—the modern version of Latin—with fabulous literature.

Sadly, the year was not over just yet. Czechoslovakia was the remorseless price paid to Hitler by the Western Powers at the end of September 1938. And for what? For less than twelve months of peace? At 4:45 a.m. on September 1, 1939, eleven months after Czechoslovakia was sacrificed (". . . bringing you peace with honour . . ."), the German military attacked Poland—that very

Poland that five months earlier, with the encouragement of the Germans, occupied a part of the dying Czechoslovakia. Days before this unsuspected attack on Poland, Hitler made a shameless pact with Stalin; and they, like two wicked outlaws, divided the prey between the two of them. With that, World War II was on, with eager, single-minded determination of the part of the Germans, and with reluctance and trepidation by England and France.

The German Stuka dive bombers reaped horrendous civilian damage in Warsaw, as well as on the fleeing population on nearby highways. The world soon learned the meaning of the merciless *Blitzkrieg*.

My earlier Hungarian patriotism evaporated rapidly. If you are cursed with it, cancer also happens to be your own body, the product of yourself, your very own flesh, but it is a murderous growth nevertheless and you don't have to like it! As the rate of anti-Semitism rose to new heights, so grew my determined Judaism, sprouting deeper and deeper roots, and my Jewish identity became steadily stronger.

I was sixteen years old when I hoped to immigrate to the United States. With my friend Steven, I went to the American Embassy, which also housed the visa section in Budapest, and enquired about immigration. We were told that there was a waiting list, a quota. How long is it? we asked. Whether the clerk meant it seriously or was just joking, I will never know, but he answered: "Nine hundred years." At sixteen, a typical teenager hoping to live forever, I said without hesitation, "Put us down on the list anyway."

We heard nothing from our relatives in Zilina, but there were rumours that they, like all Jews, would be settled in the Eastern part of the country. Then my father's oldest brother, Sandor, arrived from Zilina with his wife and mother-in-law, three pathetic refugees. They were in horrible shape.

Shaking from anxiety, they related that the Jewish population was concentrated in a ghetto. Conditions there were terrible. Then one day, the entire community was put into unbelievably crowded cattle cars and the train left. To where? No one knew. Observing all that, Sandor was happy that Grandfather Simon had died earlier and so was spared the inhumane experience. Grandmother, who still used her crutches, was also put in the overcrowded cattle car, and the Slovak *Hlinka* guard threw her crutches after her. Surely she never reached the destination alive, wherever she was taken.

Edith, now a physician, married her dear fiancé Valer Glaser. But on the very same day they married, Edith was forced to leave. She was thrown into the cattle car, destined for that still-unknown little place, Auschwitz.

The entire family had left, dragged "probably to a forced-labour camp."

Sandor told us, with no details of how they did it, that Laci, Zolo, and another cousin, Paul, had escaped earlier. Sandor had heard that Uncle Joseph was arrested and taken to a frightful jail in Ilava, but knew no details.

Not only Uncle Sandor but many other Jewish refugees arrived from Slovakia around that time.

These unfortunate people with illegal status in Hungary had no papers. Some spoke Hungarian with a heavy accent or did not speak the language at all and had no connections in Budapest. It will forever remain the shame of the Jewish community of Budapest that in those harrowing times, they turned their backs on the few Czech and Polish Jews who succeeded in cheating death and came to Hungary. My father was beside himself, but there was nothing he could do for his family, except for his brother Sandor. Sandor was placed with his wife and mother-in-law in our house in Buda, and all their needs were looked after. They were depressed, almost in shock. The only other thing my father could do was to support as many of the illegal Slovak refugees as possible, sustaining them with money, forged papers, jobs, and clothing.

Soon my father's name was well known among these refugees. I got to know quite a few of them, including a short little man by the name of Dolly Heisler (he had half a dozen other names as well), who was a veritable Houdini, an escape artist, and whose stories must be told one day. One of the refugees, in fact Heisler's roommate, was Jan Sebor, who later became Marta's husband.

Mother, Ian, Marta, Heisler--wearing his hunter's hat--and myself.

Youth is ephemeral . . .

Around that time, a mysterious postcard arrived at our address. It was sent from a place called Birkenau. The printed lines were crossed out and signed by Father's brother Bela. He asked for money and food parcels to be sent to a numbered account via the Central Bank. We did what we could. We sent money and a food parcel. Above all, we tried to find the whereabouts of Birkenau, this puzzling location. Nobody knew it. I recall that I even asked my geography teacher how to locate that place. He had no idea.

Much later, I read William L. Shirer's book *The Rise and Fall of the Third Reich*. With a sudden jolt, I realized then what that old postcard had really meant. Immediately before people were gassed in Birkenau's extermination camps, they were urged to write such a postcard to their relatives who were still free. The cynical trickery helped to maintain calm and false hope among the relatives of these unfortunate victims, and the money was pocketed by the Germans. Every step was well planned. Yes, poor Uncle Bela, how he liked to eat! Despite our efforts, his last plea for food remained unfulfilled. And his wife, Honora, how she loved cleanliness! Cleanliness was the first luxury that was denied the unfortunate, demoralized victims. How deprived and distressed they must have been before they were killed. They were separated from their children, for in the camp, children were slaughtered immediately and without mercy. Another sister, Ilka, with her husband and youngest child Ivan, also perished in Auschwitz, as did Father's youngest sister Elza, with her beautiful daughters, the red-haired twins.

But at that time, we still did not suspect their doom. We lived in a naïve credulity. Just a few hundred miles away and totally isolated from the sight of these horrors, we continued to maintain our daily lives in gullible innocence.

Slowly my baccalaureate was approaching, a terrifying examination at that time, which ended high school and theoretically entitled entry to university. In anticipation that no university study was possible for us, Jewish parents changed their expectations. We Jews are very adaptable people; centuries of persecution have taught us to be like that. No longer was there any talk of becoming a professional—a physician or a lawyer. We were encouraged to learn some useful trade that would enable us to earn a living.

I recall the harrowing examination, finally obtaining my baccalaureate, which I considered to be a useless piece of paper. After the examination, I met Marta and my parents in the open theatre on Margaret Island. We saw Shakespeare's *A Midsummer Night's Dream* and had dinner at the plush Palatinus Hotel. My parents worried about my approaching obligatory recruitment into forced labour service. My cousin Pista, who had graduated in engineering, was called up to a labour camp even though his work at the cogwheel factory, by then an important military establishment, should have exempted him. Albin, his stepfather, still ran the cogwheel factory. The military commander in charge insisted that Albin, under his authority, continue his work. Despite that, Albin could not get Pista out of forced labour. But my parents imagined that Albin's situation was now improved and that working for him would offer me a measure of security.

Once again, I became infatuated. It came like a sudden fever. This time, the young lady of my love was Masha, who was three years older than I. But this love was different from the one three years ago towards the vestal Eva. This one was more earthy and sensual. At that stage of her life, Masha had a flamboyant and daring appearance. She looked somewhat wanton with her teenage garishness, her strawberry blonde hair forever uncombed, her challenging eyes sparkling, and her shapely body imparting a hint of suggestive femininity. It was as if she emitted a magical, come-hither pheromone, the alchemy of bewitchment. Yet it was deceptive, as all these attributes were addressed to the male gender at large, rather than being directed just towards me. And what rendered it irresistible was that all these distinctive features were not deliberately planned on her part but arose casually from her fresh womanhood. Her vivacious banter rolled gaily from her hot-pink lips. As rapidly as this emotion engulfed me, it soon dissipated.

I began to work in the cogwheel factory for a few months. It was interesting, at least in the beginning. I worked on a Reineckert lathe machine, but once I had learned the necessary calculations and how to set up the modules for different tasks, it soon became humdrum.

My mind was on medicine, my Paradise Lost. I read a lot of medical books, studying anatomy and biology whenever I could. Reading has been my analgesic from way back. It was an immersion into a different world of magic that put me in a trance. I remember the impact of some of the books, the thoughts they planted in me. The Russian classics filled me with a mellow sadness and apprehension, probably as they were meant to. Cronin's *The Citadel* was an inspiration to my tortured love for medicine. *The Gold of Caxamalca* by Jacob Wasserman saddened me for the barbaric destruction of a benevolent society. I loved Thomas Mann, Axel Munthe, and Romain Rolland. And poetry, Hungarian poetry, is, and always was, outstanding. Ady Endre, Babits, Toth Arpad, and Jozsef Atilla were not approved by the Fascist school. Some were even forbidden in those days as "reactionary" or "communist." I loved Ady Endre, the Hungarian Baudelaire, in particular. I adored George Faludi and his free translation of the ballads of Francois Villon, and like many in our circle, I can repeat quite a few of them by heart even today. Similarly, I still can recite magnificent Latin poetry, such as Quintus Horatius Flaccus, my very favourite. One book had a uniquely enduring influence on me. This was one of the works of Roger Martin du Gard: *Jean Barois*. To me, it was the gripping struggle of a scientist as his rationalism and agnosticism that arose from his logical thinking fought with his archaic, mystical, religious inner core. The Rational paired with the Spiritual. The result was the magnificent testament of Jean Barois that carved out a permanent influence on my world.

One day, I heard that some Jewish youths, all frustrated medical students like myself, had found ways to pursue some sort of medical studies. There was a course being given in the Jewish General Hospital of Budapest. I inquired and was directed to the Department of Pathology, which was housed in a small, separate building. A stunning young woman of my age, with charcoal dark hair and steel-grey eyes that emitted an aura of sharp wits, appeared in a white coat and sternly directed me to wait outside. Somewhat disheartened, I stood waiting on the snow-covered hospital grounds until she came out again and called me in.

She seemed to regret that she had been so curt and officious. A cup of hot coffee was offered. She, too, was a "pseudo-medical student," a participant in the Laboratory Assistant course, the very same course I had heard about. Her name was Alice Breuer, but everyone called her Lici. When she concentrated on a topic of interest, her slender fingers raked her raven-black hair. Lici radiated life, energy, and intelligence.

That same day, we observed an autopsy. This was the first autopsy I had ever seen. It was not the dissection of deformed cadavers resembling soaked brown cardboard and smelling of formaldehyde, the kind on which we later worked. This one was a person, alive a few hours earlier, with a band around her wrist showing her name. A young woman still with a trace of make-up and a ghost of lipstick, a small patch of gauze stuck to her arm where not long ago the intravenous fluid fought against destiny and lost. In hindsight, this description might sound corny and overstated, but I was often pervaded by waves of such exaggerated sentiments in my youth. I still feel the regretful passing of this person.

This course was unique. It was given for about forty Jewish girls and boys fervently wishing to learn medicine. The lectures were given by the heads of different departments of the Jewish General Hospital. These outstanding physicians were themselves burning with the desire to teach. For these mentors, a long-overdue university appointment was as unattainable as was our hope for university entrance. It was a good match. In exchange for the course, we worked half-days in different departments as "orderlies" or "assistants." We ate in the hospital cafeteria and listened to and soaked up professional chit-chat, a language that soon invaded our vocabulary.

In addition to this program, some of us found ways to bribe the night watchman in the Anatomy Institute so that we could do our dissections at night when the building was empty and the regular students were absent. Some might think that the midnight dissection in the abandoned Anatomy Institute was an eerie, haunting exercise, but if anything, it reminded me of the secret dissections performed in the Middle Ages by Andreas Vesalius. All went well until one day when we were confronted by a group of anti-Semitic students led by one named Dunai. We were thoroughly beaten up. But we still found ways to continue to study.

Somehow, we had to sell this full-time venture to our parents, promoting the idea that eventually these undertakings would bring us closer to the fulfillment of our dream. To support this, we found some benevolent professors like Huzella and Kisely from the Histology Department who knew that we were Jewish. They not only permitted us to attend their lectures, but they also encouraged us to write the examinations. Naturally, this was entirely unofficial and the examination results, for want of official documents, were written on letterhead. These typed letters with the marking of our colloquia served as powerful means to persuade our parents of the ultimate usefulness of our plan in those difficult days. Now these venerable records survive only as so much bittersweet memorabilia.

We could also register as "guest students," and for a small fee, we could "passively" participate in some lectures without any official recognition or credit. We indulged in these programs with vigour and determination. Lici was bright, cultured, and an enthusiastic student. She lived in Budapest and shared a room with her girlfriend. Lici came from Kormend, a small town near the Austrian border of Hungary where her parents, sister, and brother lived. She is the kind of complex person who defies all efforts to portray faithfully. She could be cutting and critical one time, warm and loving another time. Impatient by nature, she possessed remarkably minimal practical sense and unashamedly accepted, if not demanded, assistance in trivial, everyday matters.

One time in late 1943, I took Lici to meet Mitzu. After all, Mitzu and I had been close friends from the age of six. When I rang the bell, the door was not opened immediately. Finally, Mitzu's mother answered, and without inviting us to enter (the place used to be my second home for many years), she said that Mitzu was "away." Just then, I saw Mitzu through the crack of the door. It hurt.

A patient arrived at the hospital under police escort. He had been sent from the detention center and was placed into a small cubicle, sort of a large broom closet with no bathroom. The guard sat in front of the door and made sure that the prisoner's shoes and clothes were removed. He locked them in a suitcase himself, which he kept under his personal care. In my white lab coat, I had free access to the prisoner's room. He was a Jewish illegal immigrant from Slovakia, a dentist who spoke a heavily accented Hungarian. He had no papers and so was caught. He was now in despair. He needed help to escape.

The next morning, I placed a bundle of clothing, including shoes, a hat, and dark-framed glasses, in the common bathroom. Passing his room, I gave him the prearranged signal. The guard waited in front of the bathroom. What if he were caught? Surely they would have no difficulty getting out of him who had helped him. He (I never learned his name) emerged soon, confidently walking down the corridor. The guard lifted his head briefly from the morning paper, took a passing look at him, and resumed his reading while he waited for the shuffling steps of his hospital-shirted prisoner. I never saw our Jewish dentist again, although I heard that he later became one of my father's protégés.

By then, the Third Jewish Law was in force, legislation with close kinship to the Nuremburg Laws of Nazi Germany. This law, fortified with draconian punishments laid down in the Criminal Code, forbade marriage between a Jew and a non-Jew and declared sexual intercourse between a Jew and a non-Jew to be "race defilement" (*Rassenshande*). It was directed towards the idea of "purification and race hygiene." According to this law, a Christian with two Jewish-born grandparents (in the case of children born out of wedlock, one grandparent) was considered to be a Jew. People with two Jewish grandparents were *"Mischlinge* [mixture] of the first degree" and with one Jewish grandparent were *"Mischlinge* of the second degree." Plans to eventually sterilize them were under consideration.

The Nazi notion of *Lebensunwertiges Leben* of the Jew (a life not worth living) came from the Nuremburg Laws. Under the same label, mentally ill patients also were taken to the extermination camps. Interestingly, Carl Gustav Jung, by his own free choice since he was a Swiss citizen, became the president of the New German Society of Psychiatry (founded by the Hitler appointee Dr. M.H. Goring ". . . for physicians who are willing to practise psychiatry according to the philosophy of the National Socialists . . ."). Jung also became the editor of the *Zentralblatt fur Psychotherapie*, in which he wrote on the topic of the "harmful influence of Jewish psychiatry."

Only after the war did most Jews of Budapest become aware of the details of what had been happening in the concentration camps. The first reports were delivered to the Western world in August 1942 by two escapees from Auschwitz, Szmuel Zygenboym and Schwarzbart. Through Bruce Teicholz, the Hungarian Jewish community leader, Kasztner was also made aware of this disclosure. However, Sumner Wells, Cordell Hull, and others prevented the publication of these horrendous revelations. A frustrated Zygenboym, in his despair, committed suicide the following year "to draw attention to what he had to say." He died in vain.

So many other things we did not suspect. My cousin Pista, having been sent to a forced labour camp somewhere on the Soviet front, was dead by then, and we did not know. Some boys in his group became ill with typhus, which had been rampant in the area. The entire group was locked in a barrack that was then set on fire by Hungarian and German troops. Those who tried to get out of the burning barn were machine-gunned. This is how Pista died. We knew nothing about his death until after the war. Atilla Petschauer also died in this way. Remember him? He was the sabre-fencing champion of the world and the Olympic hope in 1936—but he was just another Jew.

$\mathcal{D}$reams and $\mathcal{T}$ears: *III*

Gemini

Nothing begins and nothing ends
That not payed with moans
For we born in other's pain
And perish in our own.

From Francis Thompson, *Daisy*

Aunt Eliza of Zilina, Father's youngest sister, married late. But she had twins. Two beautiful, red-haired girls with green eyes and irresistible smiles. How tragic!

Immediately past the sign *Arbeit macht frei* over the huge gate in Auschwitz is where the incoming trains unloaded their living and dead human cargo. Many were unable to endure days spent on the crowded trip in a metal boxcar with no food, water, or sleep, in extreme heat and in bone-chilling cold. There, on that very spot, sat Dr. Joseph Mengele in his immaculate uniform and shiny boots, the devil playing God at age thirty-two.

A flicker of the swagger stick held in his white-gloved hands, left or right, decided life or death according to his whim. In the background, a fine orchestra assembled from the prisoners was playing Wagner, Bach, and Mozart. People wearing glasses, the old and the sick, mothers with children, like Elza, went to their death immediately. Those unfortunate ones who were condemned to life mostly worked and starved to death, or worse. Some others were spared for a little while. For Dr. Mengele had a pristine scientific mind. He needed living specimens for his scholarly experiments, like intravenous injection of phenol or gasoline. One of Dr. Mengele's keen research interests was twins . . .

CHAPTER 4

Dream Goes to Nightmare

We studied with a single-minded tenacity. We still had time to enjoy diversions, and at nineteen, I did not need much sleep. To start the day, I usually met Lici at seven o'clock for a morning swim at the popular indoor pool on Margaret Island. Lici cut a stunning figure in her bathing suit. With her dark, shiny, shoulder-length hair tucked under a rubber swim cap, she looked sporty, the perfection of ripe girlishness, a paragon of sublime womanhood. After a quick breakfast, we were off to the Jewish General Hospital for our precious "laboratory assistant" course, then on to search for some other study programs.

As "guest students" at the university, we could attend selected lectures but without the right to take any examinations or to obtain any form of credit. We had to select the subjects with care. Only the subjects that were not too popular were advisable options lest the Jew-hating students got wise to our scheme. We chose anthropology and archaeology. We even managed to write some examinations, after we persuaded the well-meaning professors. Some of them, like Ottokar Kadic, were perfectly aware of our situation and were willing to help us.

This is the way that Lici and I got to know each other. Her attentive, bright grey eyes, her dark hair and splendid features, and her discriminating mind drew me to her like a magnet. We talked about books and symphonies. Lici loved classical music, a world of riches that until then I had left largely unexplored. It did not take too long before I fell in love with both; above all, with Lici, but also with the concerts that pleased her so much.

To be in love at nineteen was an invigorating experience that incredibly intensified my vitality and energies. I did everything possible to win her heart, but she reciprocated slowly. Eventually, we did get closer. I met Lici's sister Ibi, who visited Budapest from her little native town of Kormend. Ibi, who was engaged, was a lively, beautiful girl on a prenuptial shopping spree in the capital. Later, she was joined by her father, a kind, jovial, round man. He was a small-town Jewish merchant who thought that with benevolence and a sense of humour he could solve every world problem. He soon became aware of my sentiments towards his elder daughter. Lici's parents neither encouraged nor criticized their daughter's ambitions to study medicine by such a futile, dead-end route. Strangely, my parents took the same attitude towards my strivings. They were fully aware that it might lead us nowhere. They probably did not want our last hope to wither, even if they realized that by our own choice, we were living in a fool's paradise.

This is how our days passed. And they passed so quickly. Around the fall of 1943, I found that an assistant professor of histology, Dr. Kisely, was willing to give us a private course. Four of us "pseudo-medical" students participated. One was Adrianne Matyas, a girl from Kolozsvar who came from a family of famous physicians. Another was Vera Horowitz, Lici's closest friend, a strong and determined young woman who wore thick glasses. And of course, Lici and I shared this keen interest.

Every Sunday morning, rain or shine, though it was mostly snow and rain in those days, the four of us marched into Dr. Kisely's small and dusty office that smelled of xylol and stale tobacco. It was really just a corner, surrounded by milk-glass dividers, in the echoing corridors of the Institute of Histology. The place had been filled with retort stands, glass jars, Bunsen burners, microtomes, and the scrapings of leftover lunches. And there, patiently tutored by our friendly preceptor, we happily indulged in the apprenticeship of recognizing different tissue types mounted in fragile glass plates under the shiny copper microscope. The acquisition of this skill takes time, practice, and attentive learning, and we showed fair progress.

Yet, the wheels of history were moving resolutely. The Hungarian army was thoroughly defeated in the Soviet winter campaign at Voronezh near the Don River. Both the retreating troops and the bad news were kept away from the home country, lest this demoralizing event play havoc with the general population. The horrifying deaths of the unarmed Jewish youth doing forced labour for the Hungarians on the Russian Front in the hands of these vengeful, defeated, and retreating troops was even less suspected by us in those days. Unlike German Military Intelligence, we did not know that Hungarian Prime Minister Kallay had confidently sent the much-admired Hungarian Nobel Prize winner Albert Szent-Gyorgyi and other scientists to a meeting of professionals in Istanbul to communicate to certain people Hungary's willingness to negotiate peace with the Western Powers. Unfortunately, a fellow scientist and double agent, Gyula Meszaros, betrayed Professor Szent-Gyorgyi.

On a cool and breezy Sunday morning, March 19, 1944, the regent of Hungary, Miklos Horthy, was returning from Schloss Klessheim after a meeting with Hitler when his train was stopped near Budapest and boarded by

Dr. Edmund Veesenmayer, the German ambassador, who was accompanied by Adolf Eichmann, SS *Obersturmbannführer*, and Dieter Wisliceny from the *Sonderkommando*. Horthy was told that the Nazi occupation of Hungary (Operation Margherita 1) had begun. The German troops were assisted by two bilingual (German-Hungarian) Schwabian divisions and one division of Croat Mountain SS with Bosnian Muslims. (The Schwabians were a German minority, some of whom settled in Hungary. The Schwabians, or *Volksdeutschen*, retained their German language, their national identity, and loyalty to Germany, forever their true home country. They served in Czechoslovakia, Hungary, Serbia, and Poland in the role of the "poor, persecuted German minority," awaiting merciful liberation by Hitler.) From that day on, Hungary was no longer just an enthusiastic ally of Germany but also a country occupied by them.

In the middle of the lively histology lecture on that quiet Sunday morning, we were startled by the shrill ringing of the phone. Dr. Kisely was pale when he hung up the receiver. He told us the frightful news of the total German occupation of Hungary, and we were dismissed.

By then, the German military units were all over the city. We were in a hurry to get home. Trucks full of German troops raced about, soldiers shouting and closing streets. I passed a flock of German military men in the Erzsebet Ring. Among them, I spotted a lively young man in civilian clothes wearing a borrowed German military cap. He chatted to the soldiers in a friendly way, laughed, and turned towards me as I passed him. Our eyes met. He was Richard Strasser, a classmate of mine. He pretended not to recognize me and looked away. Remarkably, he was half-Jewish. In fact, he was the grandson of the former Jewish community leader, Shimi Krausz, a story that was always kept a secret. But Richard's sympathy was always with the Germans.

The carefully planned and well-rehearsed events by the German authorities unfolded rapidly and with an unparalleled efficiency. The Germans moved with the smoothness of well-oiled machinery. Thousands were arrested, not only Jews but also the odd sympathizers of Jews and the influential opponents of the Nazi regime. Hundreds of prominent and wealthy Jews were taken as "hostages" and locked up in the Rabbinical School in Budapest. About 10,000 Jews who were unfortunate enough to be near various railway stations or major hotels were arrested and transported to an internment camp in Kistarcsa. They were destined for special treatment. Eventually, most of them were taken to Auschwitz.

By the next day, the Ministry of Finance closed all Jewish bank accounts and safety deposit boxes. A Jewish Council (*Judenrat*) was set up by the

Germans on the day of occupation. This organization had to see that every demand made by the Germans was fulfilled without any delay, like the 2,000 mattresses requested on Sunday afternoon, the very day of occupation, to be delivered by the same evening. Some were pulled from under patients in the Jewish General Hospital.

A horrific fear seized my family and all Jewish families in both the town and the countryside. Years of denial, rationalization, and vain hopes melted away as one terrifying news item followed another. There was the appointment of Laszlo Baky, a ferocious anti-Semite, in charge of the police, and the naming of the vicious Peter Hain to the security police. The same day, the homes of 7,000 Jews were raided and emptied by the security police, who removed valuable paintings and other artworks, many stolen by Peter Hain himself. The Germans demanded 100,000 Jewish labourers. Jews could not employ non-Jews. Aryans married to Jews were free to divorce them, and the process was instantly officially recognized. Every Jew was to wear a yellow star on each garment, and the size, location, and colour (canary yellow) were specified exactly. Adolf Eichmann, SS Commander Otto Winkelman, Laszlo Baky with the Hungarian gendarmerie, and Laszlo Endre, all of them major war criminals, were already preparing the ghettoization of the Hungarian Jews.

It was around that time that American planes bombed Budapest for the first time. We huddled in the basement listening to the scream of the sirens, the muffled blasts of the bombs, the angry bark of antiaircraft fire. Immediately after the air raid, the Germans demanded that, "a hundred Jews were to be killed for each victim of every bombardment." Although this did not take place at that time, ultimately much more than this ratio of Hungarian Jews perished at the hands of the Germans and Hungarians.[6] However, at the time it was demanded, and instantly carried out, that "1,000 Jewish families leave their apartments at once, leaving everything contained in them, to be occupied by Hungarians who lost their homes in the air raid." Two days later, a second American bombing took place.

On the day of the German occupation, my mother was in a frenzy. It was agonizing to watch her. Finally, I was able to calm her down to a point. Marta, my sister, who by then was deeply in love with a Slovak refugee, Jan Sebor, also was on the verge of hysteria in her fear that harm might come to her loved

---

[6] During the eleven-month Nazi occupation, a total of 569,000 Hungarian Jews were killed; that is, 69% of Hungarian Jewry. These losses were higher than those in Romania (47.1%) and Belgium (44%) but lower than Slovakia (79.8%) and Poland (90.9%). In Poland alone, three million Jews were killed. (The Weisenthal Centre.)

one. My despair was for the comfort and security of Lici. We were very close to each other by then, but she was concerned about her family in the small rural town of Kormend. I tried to console her but the repeated screams from a nearby police station, heard clearly from Lici's apartment, meant that somebody was being beaten, which did not help mitigate her worries. Many Jews had been taken to this police station earlier. Finally, I could not dissuade her from returning to her family in Kormend. My instincts told me she would be better off, and safer, in Budapest. I watched her go on the train with a heavy heart.

The backstage machinations were well prepared and carefully calculated. Only the signal had to be given. The government decrees were followed in rapid order. Jews were forbidden to own radios. Telephone services for Jews were cut off. Jews were not allowed to travel, or to visit city parks or restaurants. Motor vehicles owned by Jews were confiscated. All Jewish business transactions were null and void retroactively to March 22. Jewish retail stores were locked and barred. Food rations exclusively for Jews were drastically reduced. We all had to line up at the nearest bank and were given a receipt for the surrender of all our personal jewellery and gold items.

(Strangely, all these gold objects and other valuables stolen from the Jews of Europe, along with the gold fillings pulled from the teeth of murdered victims in Auschwitz, ended up in Switzerland in accordance with a Strasbourg agreement of August 10, 1944, between some Swiss bankers and the SS, represented by *Obergruppenführer* General Dr. Scheid. Some of this gold, worth billions of dollars, was intended to finance the rescue operations of important Nazis via the "Odessa" movement and to support post-war Neo-Nazi ambitions. However, much of this gold has enriched some of the Swiss banks. The total value of the gold was estimated at between US$200 billion and US$500 billion dollars, with a current value in the trillions, as recently revealed by the Jewish World Congress and Edgar Bronfman, and based on documents in the U.S. National Archives. It is also peculiar that seven billion dollars in Jewish gold, deposited in Swiss banks by the Nazis, found its way to New York, Montreal, and London banks. More remarkably, after the war, the Allies paid millions of dollars of reparation using this Jewish money to "Nazi victims" like—surprise—Austria! While all these revelations were being published, an art exhibition opened in Moscow in 1996 and featured the valuable paintings that had "once belonged" to the Jews of Budapest.)

The same day that Lici left, I was notified by the *Judenrat* to report for compulsory labour the very next day. I was in a group of about thirty Jewish men, and we were taken to the outskirts of Budapest. Under the supervision of some young Nazi civilians, we were to build an air-raid shelter. This started with the heavy work of digging a very deep foundation. I welcomed the tough physical labour, although it was difficult for some of us, because I found that the distraction eased my worries about my loved ones. I took out my aggression, pain, and hurt on the tough earth and worked until the sweat was pouring from my body. Every night, we were allowed to go home so that they would not have to feed or house us.

But our misery was dwarfed when compared with the fate of the Jews outside of Budapest. The Hungarian gendarmerie, under the command of General Gabor Faragho, turned out to be the most enthusiastic collaborators of the Germans. The also excelled in their ruthless sadism against the Jews. These gendarmes were in charge of setting up the ghettos in the countryside. They were also in charge of putting the Jewish population, after cruel and humiliating body searches, into the cattle cars to Auschwitz. The relatively low numbers and the isolation of the Jewish population in these rural areas contributed to the ferocity of these savages.

Some of the high-ranking gendarme officers who were in charge of these unfortunate people and were later condemned as war criminals lived happy and full lives after the war, when they were sheltered by South America and well tolerated even by Canada—such as the gendarme Captain Imre Finta, now living in Toronto. Together with SS Captain Argermayer, he had been condemned for war crimes in post-war Hungary. (Finta was responsible for the brutal handling of the Jewish population in the ghetto of Szeged, including the internal body search of women by his gendarmes before their deportation.) Notwithstanding their barbarism, the personal documents of this war criminal group and the Archives of the Hungarian Gendarmerie were deposited by their runaway leaders, as a favour to them, and preserved with "confidentiality," in the Canadian National Archives, where I inspected these documents myself.

A special technique of intimidating the population at large, Jews and non-Jews alike, was the practice born out of Hitler's personal order in 1941 called the "*Nacht und Nabel Erlass*." This "Night and Fog Directive" was carried out by the Gestapo and the *Einsatzgruppen* (extermination squads). They picked up specific people during the small hours of the night. The helpless victims then vanished forever and no information, not even their burial places, was disclosed to their relatives. The experience was beyond description. The startled awakening in the middle of the night, the shuffle of heavy boots in the echoing corridor, the vigorous banging on the door, full-throated shouts, the last glimpse of the ashen face of a beloved one, the fading noises, car doors banging, followed by silence, loneliness, and despair. Some South American dictators imported this technique after the war.

Many Jews, caught on the streets of Budapest for one reason or other, were put in detention camps. These people were put on a train carrying Jews from the Hungarian countryside and small towns and were deported without delay to Auschwitz. Lici's friend Vera Horovitz was arrested with her father for being on the street during curfew hours. They were taken to Auschwitz and both died there. Adrianne Matyas went back to Kolozsvar to her parents and was taken from there to the concentration camp Bergen Belsen. She survived. A dear neighbour of ours in Buda, Zsuzsa, was rumoured to have been betrayed by her non-Jewish Schwabian husband for the sake of their money. Zsuzsa and her entire family were killed.

By then, Lici and most of her family had been put in the ghetto in the little town of Kormend. Her brother had been in a forced-labour camp for some time. With the help of a friend in Budapest, we stole some letterhead and an official rubber stamp from the University. I composed a "stern," official-sounding letter to Lici, "commanding" her, as a medical student, that she, in the "national interest," "must report immediately to the dean's office." In retrospect, this contrivance sounds ridiculously naïve. Nevertheless, this unlikely ploy was a complete success because of the blind and deep respect of the gendarmes for any "official" document, particularly if it was well decorated with one or more rubber stamps. Lici was allowed to come to Budapest from the ghetto of Kormend. To be sure, this was only a "temporary" permission, and she was supposed to return to the Kormend ghetto at a later time. Not many Jews were allowed to leave the ghetto officially! If not for this move, Lici probably would have followed the abysmal destiny of her family.

As a first step in preparation for setting up a ghetto for all the Jews in Budapest, at that point more than 300,000 people, we all had to move into "designated buildings." These houses, chosen for their state of dilapidation, were marked by large yellow stars on a black background over the entrance. Their former non-Jewish tenants moved into the larger and refurnished Jewish apartments. This "population exchange" took place within the first month of the German occupation. Our graceful home, the fruit of Mother's hope and perseverance for such a long time, was gone in a single day. Instead, we got a crowded, seedy hole in a pathetic building. Here, Jews were not allowed to receive visitors and were permitted to leave the house only between the hours of 11:00 a.m. and 2:00 p.m. each day, but were forbidden to commute on the main streets. The crowding was incredible in these designated Jewish buildings. Jews were not even allowed to go to city parks for a short respite.

When Lici arrived in Budapest, she was under the impression that eventually she must return to the ghetto of Kormend. She worried that her parents might be in trouble if she did not do so. She was told she could stay in Budapest "officially" if she were a resident there. Of course, there was at least one way for her to become a legitimate resident: if she were to marry in Budapest. Naturally, I made this point quite vehemently clear to her. I did not count on my mother's objection. Despite the extraordinary times and circumstances, Mother still retained fragments of her old dreams and she put up a strong resistance. After all, I was only twenty years old. But I won the argument, and within one week, with special permission, Lici and I were married. After the marriage "ceremony" (the signing of the papers) at City Hall, we went to celebrate at the only small restaurants where Jews were still allowed to go. For a honeymoon, we had an espresso coffee.

I had to continue the forced labour of building an air-raid shelter, but not for long. Another air-raid shelter was to be built in Budapest's Schwabenberg, where the headquarters of Adolf Eichmann, the leaders of the SS *Sonderkommando*, and the Gestapo were housed at the Majestic Hotel. The elite of the Hungarian gendarmes, with General Gabor Faragho, Col. Laszlo Ferenczy, and Tibor Paksy-Kiss, stayed at the nearby Lomniz Hotel. Eichmann needed some labourers, and by the order of the *Judenrat*, I was transferred there.

From that time on, I made the long and precarious trip at the crack of dawn each day to this frightful lion's cage. On my way there, I was stopped innumerable times as I passed through the city ("Hey, Jew, what are you doing here at this hour?") by the police, the gendarmes, Hungarian soldiers, and assorted Nazis; for I was, of course wearing a yellow star on my coat. These stops were particularly threatening after an air raid, but a bilingual (German–Hungarian) identification paper issued by the Germans, who owned me by then, helped me out of these prickly situations. There was also a Gestapo jail in the Schwabenberg, and the agonized shrieks of Jews who were being tortured and interrogated there could be heard all the time. I was at that point directly under German masters.

Unexpectedly, a letter and parcel arrived from Lici's mother, Cecil. She had smuggled it out of the Kormend ghetto. The parcel contained our "wedding present," a cake that Cecil had baked for us in the ghetto with the last of their precious food supply and with the warmth of her devoted heart. I never met Cecil in person. In the letter, she hesitantly confessed that Lici had always been her favourite child, and implored me to take care of her: ". . . from now on," the letter said, "Lici is your responsibility . . ." Her words remained etched in my soul. I made a solemn pledge to myself to fulfill Cecil's last wish. A few days later, Cecil was on her way to Auschwitz with her husband and her other daughter, Ibi. None of them ever returned.

Emptying the ghettos and putting the Jewish population in cattle cars destined for Auschwitz or other death camps was now taking place in hundreds of Hungarian cities except for Budapest, where the number of Jews was too

Lici wearing the obligatory yellow star for the first time.

high. The act of herding Jews into cattle cars was executed by the Hungarian gendarmes, and sometimes by the police, after a crude and humiliating body search. These cattle cars were filled to the point that people could not even sit on the floor and had to stand. One pail of drinking water and another single bucket serving as an open toilet for eighty to ninety people was placed in each car, and the doors were bolted shut. These metal cars were unbearably hot in the summer and freezing cold in the winter. Surrounded by Hungarian soldiers, the cattle cars were mainly left standing on tracks in the open fields, and then travelling for unpredictable distances. The average arrival time to Auschwitz was three or four days, sometimes more.

By then, my sister, Marta, was also doing forced labour, in the Riegler paper factory, but like me, she could return home each evening. She was in despair because her fiancé, Jan Sebor, had been caught at the Czechoslovak border with a friend of his, and they were taken to the Hungarian counter-espionage office for interrogation. Marta tried to negotiate with some people in the underground, as well as with some shady characters, to help Jan and his friend, but to no avail. Also, Marta's close friend Gabi, a lovely girl, was taken with her parents to Auschwitz from their rural home in Kadarkut. A last-minute rescue mission organized by my sister failed because Gabi's anxious mother refused to let her daughter go with the prearranged false papers that were brought to her by a stranger on a motorcycle, who was actually a daring family friend of ours. Gabi died in Auschwitz, along with her parents.

Meanwhile, Marta had to move into the factory and could no longer come home at all. She became a captive in the Riegler factory.

It was then that Lici was caught by the Hungarian police because she left the house two minutes before the permitted time for Jews. She was taken to the detention centre. Quite daringly, I was able to visit her there two or three times and to smuggle in whatever she needed; but after a short while, she was transferred to Kistarcsa, a holding camp, awaiting transport to Auschwitz. I suffered great torments, but I was quite helpless. I, too, negotiated with the same lawless creatures who, for money, were willing to help her escape, but no positive results were expected.

At that point, I heard that a young Swedish diplomat had arrived in Budapest and had just begun "to help the Jews." This sounded quite unlikely, but I understood that the help consisted of putting them under the protection of the Swedish embassy "until their immigration to Sweden." Thus, they were no longer Hungarian citizens and, as such, they became exempt from all the anti-Jewish laws, including wearing the yellow star and being subjected to forced labour.

It sounded unbelievable, but I immediately proceeded to the Swedish embassy at Mount Gellert. To my amazement, the rumour was closer to the truth than I imagined. I had to prove, though, some kind—any kind—of a "Swedish connection." Fortunately, for many years my father had had a fruitful business relationship with the Swedish wire factory of Actiebolaget Kanthal, Halstachamar, and had the papers to prove it. This was good enough. Anything would do. I also talked to this miracle man, Raoul Wallenberg, a young, intense, and energetic man, clearly driven by some deep inner force. He promised to help Lici. I got a distinguished-looking "Defense Passport" that

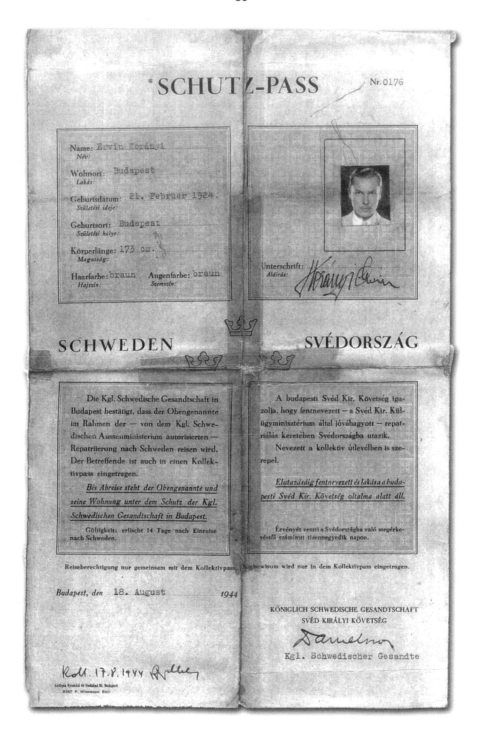

The life-saving document. Observe Wallenberg's signature in the lower left-hand corner.

Wallenberg's diary from Budapest, summer 1944. Recovered from the Lubyanka Prison and published by the Swedish newspaper Expressen on January 13, 1990. Note the name "Koranyi" on Saturday @ 16:00 and Monday @ 10:00 a.m. ("5 fanger" = "the 5 prisoner.")

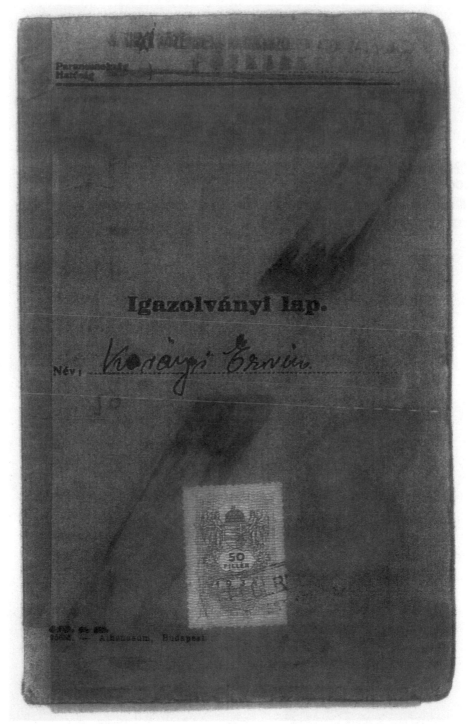

Hungarian "military booklet" modified for Jews by a hand-painted, red "Zs" ("zsido" = Jew) for the Forced Labour Services.

bore the very low serial number of "0176." At this point, Wallenberg had negotiated with the Germans and got permission to issue 5,000 such documents.

Lici had no idea of these rescue attempts. But one day, in the desolate camp where she was kept, a policeman approached her, saying, "You are a Swedish citizen, and the consul is here for you." Lici did not know what this man was talking about. Surely it must be some kind of mistake, or else he is mad, she thought. But a few days later, along with four other prisoners, she was taken to the Swedish embassy in Budapest, and there we had an incredible reunion. Not only that, but all of us, myself, my parents, and Marta, obtained the same Swedish documents from Wallenberg. We were also able to get one for Lici's brother, who, at that time, was at a forced labour camp. This was August 7, 1944. I barely dared to look at Lici, remembering the agony of Orpheus attempting to save Eurydice from Hades but failing because of a premature glance he had taken at her.

SVÉD KIR. KÖVETSÉG
BUDAPEST

A budapesti svéd kir. Követség igazolja, hogy

K O R Á N Y I E R V I N

aki 1924 évben Budapest -n született (anyja neve : Schwarcz Sári)
és személyazonosságát 01/76 sz. Védőútlevéllel igazolja, a m. kir. Honvédelmi Mi-
niszter Ur 152.730/Eln. 42/1944. számú rendelete, valamint az azt kiegészítő és az illetékes
hatóságokkal kötött megállapodás alapján a kisegítő munkaszolgálatból elbocsáttatott.
Budapest, 1944. december hó 4.

Verification by the Swedish embassy stating that, according to the quoted agreement with the Hungarian Ministry of Defence, Ervin Koranyi has been released from the Forced Labour Services.

By then, the Soviet troops were close to Warsaw and the Hungarian border as well, while the Germans constantly retreated. This caused a change in the Hungarian government. The rate of the deportations slowed down for a while, and the intensity of persecution eased. It was then that we first found out exactly what was happening at Auschwitz.

Lici and I joined an underground movement. All cell members (Dr. Szanto, Dr. Benedek, Ganz Sanyi, and others) were given a typed document signed by Walter Rosenberg, Alfred Wetzler, and Sigfried Lederer, the three men who succeeded in escaping from Auschwitz in April 1944. These eyewitnesses gave an exact account of the methods of mass killings: the gas chambers, the ovens, and the crematoria. (This document is preserved in Yad Vashem. At the time when we first read it in August 1944, copies were sent to the Vatican, to the president of the United States, and to Rezso Kasztner, a member of the Budapest *Judenrat*. But these three sources did nothing to publicize it. For that, Kasztner paid with his life after the war. His assassins in Tel Aviv were convinced that if this document had been known to all, surely mass resistance of the Jews would have taken place.) This was the first time that Lici and I learned with certainty what really happened in the extermination camps. My parents still did not know.

In a daring and exhausting trip on a train that was bombed from the air and raided by the gendarmes, we delivered the Swedish Defense Passport to Lici's brother George in the forced labour camp near the Austrian border. For one confusing moment, Lici and I got separated in the tumult. The despair I felt was beyond words. The railway station swarmed with gendarmes. Then, almost unexpectedly, we bumped into each other. I thought that our embrace would never end. We took a crazy chance by undertaking such a dangerous three-day trip, but in the end, this document saved George's life.

We rented a room in Buda and returned to the Jewish General Hospital, which had already moved to a new location, an abandoned school building on Wesselenyi Street, soon to become the ghetto hospital. We met some friends there and did what we could. We assisted Dr. Molnar Bela at surgery, and Dr. Acel Dezso organized our activities.

As "Swedes," we did not have to wear a yellow star, and were more mobile than the rest of them. We made numerous house calls and experienced the horrendous human suffering around us. Most Jews were starving, but the one-time middle class had nothing to go on now. I still recall a young, nameless woman dying of starvation. Another was a severely beaten man having Cheyne–Stokes respiration, a terminal phenomenon that I saw then for the first time. His dilated pupils failed to react to light, another sign that testified to his brainstem injury. We dealt with issues far beyond our capacity and "training" to grasp. When I complained to Lici: "What's the use of us untrained people

seeing such cases?" she answered, "We share their suffering and we are there."
Lici taught me a lesson.

We did not sleep much. In the evenings, I recall taking turns with Lici in
reading aloud Roger Martin du Gard's *Family Thibeault*, a recent Nobel Prize-
winning novel. I also recall the thought I had while we read, probably a
psychological manoeuvre: "I cannot die before I finish reading this hefty
book." A sort of contract with Karma.

The air raids became more and more severe. The British planes usually
came at night. Segments of the blue-black sky were lit up by roving beams of
reflector lights, tracer bullets, slowly sinking, huge glowing flares ("Stalin
candles"). It was difficult to distinguish one's own shaking heart from the
steady sound of the airplane engines.

First, the echoing anti-aircraft fire ruptured the background noise, then the
exploding bombs could be heard with a reverberating vibration in our spines.
Sometimes a burning plane lit up the sky, whining like a child crying. When
we saw the sheen of the long trail of the blazing and mortally wounded plane
falling like a meteor in the night sky, we thought with sorrow, "There goes
another friend."

The Americans, too, came to bomb, always during the day, almost always
on Sundays. They came with a much larger number of planes, and the air
vibrated with a deeper and deeper pitch of engine noise, even before the
bombs began to fall. Sometimes houses came apart like sand castles in the
waves of an angry sea, emitting a peculiar smell of cooking gas, dust, death,
and incinerated, acrid wood.

Groups of Jewish forced labour workers in civilian clothes and wearing
yellow armbands milled around the smouldering ruins, digging out survivors.
Among them I saw a very young Jewish physician with jet-black curly hair,
rimless glasses, and an intense look, carrying a medical bag with an air of
authority. Before such air raids, the radio station interrupted its programming
and transmitted German code language: ". . . *Achtung, Achtung. Lichtspiele.
Krokodil gross, kommen Nelken . . ."*

Even though by then Marta and my parents possessed the Swedish
Defense Passports, they remained in their apartment in the Jewish designated
house, hoping to salvage a few of our remaining possessions. But one
morning, a detail of Nazi Arrowcross soldiers entered the building, lined up all
the people in the courtyard, and accused my parents of being spies. Vicious
beatings with rifle butts followed. All of them suffered severe abuse. God only
knows what would have been their fate had a policeman not shown up just

then. This particular policeman, who knew my father well, pretended to be on official business and immediately "arrested" Marta and my parents, saving them from the Nazis.

Marta's and Father's negotiations with the rank and file of criminals also brought results. By then, Jan and his friend Heisler were in a detention camp in the small Hungarian city of Sarvar. For a fair price paid by my father, they were helped to escape and brought to Budapest. However, some of the Jewish women workers at the Riegler Factory, where Marta had had to work before she obtained her Swedish Defense Passport, were deported, and all of them died in various concentration camps. So many other young women, doing forced labour in other factories, shared their fate. Once again, Marta's survival, like the hold on daily life for all of us, hung on a delicate thread.

The Soviet military was then in Eastern Hungary, where a major armoured battle was shaping up in Debrecen. There in a fateful encounter, the German–Hungarian forces were eventually defeated.

Yet, an unspoken premonition for sinister ill fortune burned in our souls; an ominous foreboding that made us feel wretched.

Dreams and Tears: IV

Houdini

What have we done, Oh Lord, that we
are evil starred?
How have we erred and sinned to be
so scourged and scarred?
Lash us, Oh Lord, with scorpion whips,
we can but run;
But harken to our piteous lips:
what have we done?

From Robert Service, *The Under-Dog*

Now I must pursue the story of Dolly Heisler, something I promised the reader earlier. Remember him? He is the Houdini-like character, the Czechoslovakian refugee, the menace of the Nazi authorities whom I mentioned before.

Adolf Heisler or Horovitz—for Dolly had dozens of names—was a short, middle-aged fellow, a small-town Jewish merchant who was born and lived in Slovakia where he had some kind of store. Cheerful by nature, he led a tranquil, low-key life, only to lose everything when he and his fellow Jews were herded into the ghettos by the Slovaks. This awakened in him a hitherto unsuspected, dormant talent. He escaped the deportations and illegally crossed the border to Hungary. What he left behind were his civilian shackles of innocence and inhibitions.

Shortly after his escape, we were visited by another Slovak refugee, a Mr. Brown, who came to see my father, asking for help. My father's name and address had spread by word of mouth among these desperate refugees. Mr. Brown described the adventurous way he had crossed the border with another man, a Mr. Heisler. Unfortunately, reported Brown, Heisler's luck ran out, and he was shot and killed at the border.

But one week later, Mr. Heisler arrived, far from being dead, but thoroughly caked with mud, starving, limping, and without a cent. He, too, found Father immediately. Mr. Heisler had indeed been caught at the border, but did not remain in jail for long. Whatever happened to the Nazi Hlinka-guard escorting him, Mr. Heisler never volunteered to disclose.

Mr. Heisler had a bath and a good night's sleep, and was given new clothes. He was well fed and supplied with forged papers and money. At that point, in the Patria Coffeehouse in Budapest, he lit a huge cigar after the generous meal and thanked Father for his help. "From now on," he said, "I will look after myself."

And really, not much more help did he need. Mr. Heisler moved to a room that he shared with another refugee, Jan Sebor, who later became Marta's fiancé. In contrast with Heisler, Jan was tall, handsome, and a highly cultured man with a university degree from Prague. They were an odd couple. Heisler became an unofficial, self-appointed organizer of the Slovak refugees in Budapest. For instance, it was customary that whenever an illegal refugee was caught, a group of Hungarian detectives took him for a "walk" on the busiest streets of Budapest. Whoever would greet the unfortunate refugee was instantly nabbed by the detectives because who else but another illegal immigrant would greet such a creature? The police turned these unfortunate refugees into unintended "vacuum cleaners." This is when Heisler put out the word: if you are caught and taken for a "walk," hang onto your jacket button. If you see someone doing that, don't greet him. Simple.

Yet he himself was caught repeatedly despite his conspicuous semi-military way of dressing, with a green hunter's hat and carrying the well-known German anti-Semitic paper *Der Sturmer* under his arm at all times. He had a phenomenal ability to manipulate people without their being aware of it. Once he was taken to the police station. The policeman, who had knocked on his door early in the morning, told him to take all his papers with him. Of course, at that point he had none. At the police station, he was questioned by a higher officer, who was enraged because Dolly "forgot his papers at home" ("It was too early, Sir; I was too sleepy. I am a night watchman," he lied). Escorted home to fetch his papers by the same policeman who had brought him in, in no time he knew which little town the policeman had come from; and with a joyful hoot pretended that he, Dolly, was also from there. He prompted his new "friend" to tell some of his school stories. A few minutes later, Dolly repeated the same anecdotes to the forgetful, befuddled policeman, who by then was convinced that Dolly knew everyone in his small community.

They instantly became great pals. Arriving at the apartment building, Dolly asked his chum, the policeman, to wait for him at the main entrance, "while I get my papers." With that, Dolly entered the back door of a restaurant housed in the same building and instantly left by the front door. "The policeman is probably still waiting," he used to remark with a grin.

Dolly Heisler was held a prisoner at the detention center, but he escaped. Another time, he was arrested and taken to police headquarters, but he ran away. One of his master strokes was when he escaped from the Gestapo headquarters with the help of no less than an unsuspecting Adolf Eichmann, SS *Obersturmbannführer*. This was on the notorious Schwabenberg.

Dolly had a few principles based on common sense: For example, what is the difference between a prisoner and a free man? The prisoner is unshaven. Therefore, Dolly always hid some pieces of razor blades all over in his clothing. Once arrested, he constantly shaved himself—he had lots of time. On one occasion, while he was being held at Gestapo headquarters, a German soldier burst into the cell. There was Dolly, with a dozen or so other Jews. A truck had to be unloaded by the prisoners and the goods placed in a warehouse. The soldier asked for an interpreter, and Dolly volunteered. Here and there, the soldier cursed the Jews (*Verfluchtene Juden*, etc.). Dolly faithfully translated this, too, with the appropriate diction. Then Dolly decided to curse the Jews on his own account. ("Never hurts," he said later.) This indeed paid off. Now a second soldier came to replace the original one, and hearing Dolly zestfully cursing the Jews, offered him a cigarette, saying, "You can go back to the office now; I am a Schwabian and bilingual, so I can talk to them in Hungarian."

Dolly immediately realized that the newly arrived soldier must have thought that he was the official interpreter from the main office. ("Thank God for shaving.") But of course, he could not just "leave." After all, he was still inside the jail.

"I have time," he said to the soldier. This happened to be true. ("By then I had sunk so low that I did not even hesitate to tell the truth occasionally, mainly for a crooked reason." This was Dolly's maxim.)

Just then, yet another soldier joined the two of them. The most recently arrived sergeant was the driver of the Big Boss, Adolf Eichmann. Again, a comradely exchange of cigarettes all around and more soldier talk.

"I am taking the Old Man downtown," remarked the driver.

"Give me a lift," said our Dolly.

"Just ask Eichmann. He is very nice," the driver reassured Dolly.

"But I am shy. Besides which, I am new here and I have not been officially introduced to him yet. You ask him for me." This was how our Dolly blended lies with truth.

"Very well," replied the amiable driver.

Eichmann appeared.

"Heil Hitler!" shouted the driver, clicking his heels smartly. In a softer voice, he added: "The interpreter needs a lift downtown."

Eichmann nodded. Between two lines of SS soldiers guarding the place, heels clicking again and loud shouts of "Heil Hitler!" all around, Eichmann, the driver, and Dolly walked out of the Gestapo headquarters. He was a free man. For a while.

"Nobody can tell me the SS *Oberbannsturmführer* Adolf Eichmann is not a friend of the Jews," joked Dolly later, when we talked about that devil.

Dolly was arrested together with Marta's fiancé, Jan Sebor, at the Slovak border. They were taken to the infamous Hungarian anti-espionage agency. The first one to be questioned was Jan, and he got more than his share of beatings. Jan was dragged out from the interrogation room semiconscious and bleeding. Then it was Dolly's turn to be questioned.

"Don't you dare touch me!" shouted Dolly at those butchers standing around with their sleeves rolled up, ready for a new round of beatings and torture.

"And why not?" the sergeant major shouted back at him, aghast, while the butcher boys turned into statues from the surprise.

"Because I am short of stature," Dolly said. "Besides, I am not a hero. I will sign everything you want."

They all started to laugh.

"Okay, little one."

But the sergeant major did not like the fact that Dolly was constantly bowing.

"Why the hell you bow all the time?"

"I am a waiter. I am used to it," lied our Dolly.

But he got away without being beaten and was put with Jan in a holding camp called Sarvar. My father and sister helped them to escape from there.

The stories about Dolly are endless, sometimes sad and sometimes amusing. After the war, he could never return to any normal, philistine activities. First, he was black-marketing with the Russian soldiers in Vienna. He was caught and put in a Soviet military jail. Twice. He escaped, of course. Also twice.

Dolly, at ninety-two years old, was still active and the proud owner of a brothel somewhere in Germany. He passed away at ninety-six and was buried in Israel.

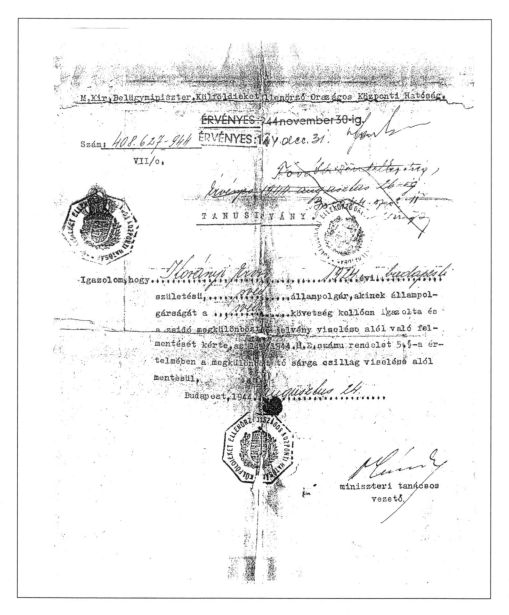

Certificate of the Hungarian Internal Ministry's "Office for Supervision of Foreigners." It states that the Swedish embassy attests to the Swedish citizenship of Ervin Koranyi, who therefore is now exempted from wearing the discriminatory yellow star obligatory for Jews.

CHAPTER 5

A Rainy Day

In the fall of 1944, one of the last years of the war, the weekend started off with sparkling sunshine and the glorious autumn colours of copper and gold. Lici and I were to have lunch with my parents, who had rented a house in Buda, and thanks to the Swedish papers, they lived there with Marta and Jan as "foreign citizens of a neutral country." We took along a little guest for the outing, a six-year-old boy from the Jewish orphanage. Lici called the little boy by the ridiculous nickname "Pipez."

He was in fact a distant relative, the son of my mother's cousin Henry. Approximately a year earlier, Henry, who was widowed, had been taken to a forced labour camp somewhere in Yugoslavia near Bor, where he was put to cruel slave labour in a mine. Before he left, Henry asked for my winter coat, a well-used, rather frayed one, because he had none. We never heard from him again. He probably perished along with the many thousands in that notorious camp, or else he died on the infamous Death March that followed the German withdrawal. His son, Tibor, nicknamed Pipez, lived in a Jewish orphanage located in the once-fashionable neighbourhood of Queen Vilma and Munkacsi streets. The orphanage had been donated by the Lindenfeld family as a charitable cause. We took Pipez out for weekends as often as we could.

Lici and I picked him up on the promising Saturday morning, October 15, 1944, and took the streetcar to my parents' place. We arrived fairly early. The family was in a good mood, and we constantly listened to the news on the radio. All of a sudden, we picked up something peculiar on the airwaves. The radio station kept announcing the name of a Hungarian general, urging him to report to headquarters immediately because the regent, Horthy, wanted to talk to him. Such a news item was most unusual. Then came further dispatches, followed by a bulletin that "Hungary is negotiating with the Soviet authorities to abandon the alliance with Germany." In between these announcements, sombre music played on the radio. We could not believe what was happening. So, was it all over? Could it be that we had really survived the war?

In our excitement, we barely noticed a subtle change of tone in the disclosures of a brand-new radio announcer who emphasized that "the negotiations with the Soviets are only preliminary," and "all soldiers are to remain in their positions." Instead of the tenebrous music, vigorous, aggressive military marches pervaded the air, filling us with a vague premonition of the Apocalypse.

And indeed we soon learned that Otto Skorzeny, SS *Sturmbannführer*, had kidnapped Regent Horthy's son. This was the same Otto Skorzeny who earlier had freed Mussolini from Allied captivity in Grand Sasso, Italy. Horthy was subsequently blackmailed by the SS to withdraw his statement of attempting to break the alliance with Germany, and they demanded that he approve Ferenz Szalasi as prime minister. Szalasi, the Hungarian Nazi *führer*, was head of the Hungarian Arrowcross (*Nyilas*) Party, a political movement supported by the *Volksdeutschen*, the Hungarian-speaking Schwabians, who were blindly extremist and anti-Semitic. The rank and file of the Arrowcross Party consisted of common killers and criminals. By comparison, the Hell's Angels of today are real angels.

We soon found out that this very political party was helped to a full and absolute dictatorial power by the occupying Germans. The previous regime, which was responsible for the deportation of hundreds of thousands of Jews to various extermination camps, and killed and tortured countless numbers of Jews, and brought about all the anti-Jewish decrees and atrocities (as the reader will recall), has been described by historians as "relatively mild and by parallel benevolent" compared with these thugs.

"All Jews up to age fifty are to report to the brick factory of Buda and to take with them three days of food."

"The Jews can only blame themselves for the fate awaiting them."

"We do not recognize half-Jews, converted Jews, Swedish Jews, Swiss Jews, or foreign citizen Jews, only Jews."

"Anyone hiding a Jew will be butchered." (The Hungarian word *felkoncoltatik* means "butchered" in loose translation.)

These declarations were on official Arrowcross government posters plastered on the walls of buildings and were publicized on the radio and by the newspapers. A central ghetto was set up in Budapest where all the remaining Jews had to move immediately and where all the "designated Jewish houses" were evacuated immediately.

We realized that my parents' rented house was no longer a safe place to stay and that we had better move out the very same evening. We contacted our former neighbour, Tivadar Homonai, an influential member of the Hungarian senate, and he, brave man that he was, invited us to his home without any hesitation. We spent the night hiding in his garage. He and his family tried to console us and spent time with us. They took an enormous chance by permitting us to stay. We also learned that on the very same night, just a few hours after we left my parents' house, the Arrowcross killers were indeed looking for us there. We had left just in the nick of time.

But the next morning, we had to be on the move once again, like sheep in a lion's cage. We separated into smaller groups, and after an agonizing streetcar trip, met a few hours later in the home of some other daring Christian family friends, the Arpadfys. Lici and I were travelling together, taking Pipez with us. Even though we had removed the yellow star from his coat, with his orphanage uniform and his head covered by a cap far too large for him and held up by his large, crooked ears, Pipez looked very Jewish. The loose cap seemed to maximize the contour of his Semitic nose. We felt that all eyes were on us.

"Pipez, take off your cap."

Unconfined, his two large ears winged into view and were emphasized by his orphanage-style cropped hair.

"Pipez, put your cap back on." He obeyed. The tiny *Yeshiva bocher* reappeared.

"Pipez, take off your cap."

We stayed with the Arpadfys overnight. After a sleepless night, we were gone. We decided to look for shelter with one of those shady characters who had helped Jan escape from the Sarvar camp. The fact that these people belonged to the world of criminals rendered them trustworthy for us. Prices were named, bargains were made, and authority was the mutual enemy. There was a lot of coming and going. They were at the peak of their form as they dealt with counterfeit identification papers.

We realized that having Pipez with us would make it difficult for us to hide. We also learned that the Jewish orphanage was under the protection of the Red Cross, and for whatever it was worth, Pipez probably had more security in the orphanage than we could offer him in our precarious, moment-to-moment state of survival. If we evaded one peril, in the next moments or hours, some other mortal danger, like the seven-headed Hydra, would threaten our existence.

Our host's wife, a lawless figure herself, undertook the task of escorting Pipez back to the orphanage. A few hours later, she came back teary-eyed. As this woman was taking him to the orphanage, Pipez turned to her: "Aunty, let me go. I want to live. I give you a *pengo*." (A *pengo* was probably worth a dime—and indeed, that was how much a Jewish life was worth in Budapest at that time.) In a short time, the six-year-old Pipez had learned the lesson well.

I was to pick up some forged papers at the outskirts of town. Lici, who came with me, waited at the nearest streetcar stop while I approached the house where I was supposed to go for those false documents. As I entered the building, I immediately sensed deep trouble looming. Could it be that my persecuted ancestors flashed some enigmatic tidings in my ear? Like the Jewish "collective unconscious"? A number of detectives or civilians started to move towards me. I ran as fast as I could, shouting to Lici to board the streetcar that had just begun to roll. When I reached it, with heart pumping and lungs bursting, I jumped onto it. The streetcar gained speed, and the people chasing us stopped in their pursuit and turned back to find another means of transportation. At the next stop, we got off the streetcar and quickly took another one, which fortunately happened to be waiting there and was going in the opposite direction. We squeezed ourselves onto the crowded streetcar. The enemy hunting us had lost our trail. We returned to the neighbourhood of our "headquarters."

My parents and Marta were already placed in an abandoned apartment. The hour of the general curfew, ordered for the entire population, was to start within a few minutes. We were still on the street, with nowhere to go. Just then, we were found by our outlaw friends and taken to a labourer's family, total strangers, in a cheap tenement house. We were deposited in their crowded one-room apartment. I must say that they received us in a friendly way and asked us no questions. As poor as these people were, they did not accept a cent and did not mention the fact that if the Nazis found us, we all, including them with their children, would be killed. I don't even know their names.

The next morning, the rain poured steadily from a gloomy sky thick with leaden clouds. As we reached the nearest wide boulevard, we saw large groups of Jews with the yellow star on their clothing marching with arms held up over their heads. They were being led by teenage boys who were shouting, firing their guns in the air, and wearing Nazi and Arrowcross insignias. Some groups were escorted by Hungarian policemen. We were soaking wet, as were the marchers. Gusts of cold wind carried the chill to our bones.

Just then, as it seemed to us that all the forces of a bitter destiny had turned against us, the sole of Lici's sandal cracked. In despair, I got some gauze bandage in a pharmacy and with cold, stiff, and clumsy fingers, nose dripping from the chill and rain, and crouching under a doorway, I tied the sandal to Lici's foot so that she could walk. We were a miserable sight in our drenched clothes. The sensation that I had lost the struggle and was only forestalling the inevitable came over me with a paralyzing effect. I realized that a single look at us would give away not only our predicament but also our identity. We thought we were done for. I took Lici to a nearby hairdressing salon, not so much to appear passable but to gain some time.

After some telephone calls, I found the address where my parents were hiding. It was a very large apartment house on the Elizabeth Ring that they used to call the "New York Palace," a well-known location. They were staying on the top floor, in an unoccupied apartment that was ready to be rented. We were warned not to take the elevator, for such traffic could have drawn the attention of the other tenants to what was going on in a supposedly empty apartment. Furthermore, my parents, Marta, and Jan were not supposed to walk around in the apartment, use the water faucet, or flush the toilet, lest someone should hear the noise. The bare parquet floor seemed to crackle and echo with an alarming resonance against the empty walls, no matter how cautiously we moved. We stayed there for only a few hours. I smelled danger wafting in the air. I urged my parents to move on, and we left. So did everyone else, one by one. I still see my mother in her dark grey wool coat with the black Persian lamb collar, soaked through by the merciless rain. She looked like a hunted deer.

Later, we learned that only minutes after my parents had finally gone, the Arrowcross soldiers came to search the place. Someone had reported suspicious movements in the un-rented apartment, surmising that Jews must be hiding there. The proximity of death was breathtaking, but by then somehow less frightening.

Lici and I decided that the best thing was simply to follow our destiny. The futility of rational planning was by then obvious to us. So we returned to our rented room in Buda to await our fate. As we proceeded, the streets were again filled with marching Jews, their arms held up over their heads. The rain was still pouring down incessantly in thick, wind-carried gouts on this blustery, grey day. The teenaged Arrowcross members had submachine guns and whips in their hands and were drunk with the headiness of power never experienced before. We saw some of them pulling elderly Jews by their beards.

We travelled on a crowded streetcar and passed yet another ravaged group of Jews. In the line, I spotted a former neighbour from the designated yellow-star building. She saw me, too. For a split second, our eyes locked. The streetcar slowed almost to a stop. I instantly grasped this poor woman's desperate and irresistible urge to be recognized and that her miserable existence be witnessed, probably for the last time in her life. But when she shouted and waved towards me, I turned around as if her lonely, heartbreaking wail were being directed at someone else behind me on the streetcar. In doing so, I lost my hat, the last hat I have ever owned. The streetcar picked up speed, and my wet hair was whipped by the cold wind. To this day, I feel guilty for not answering her call and causing more anguish to this unfortunate woman who was in distress at the threshold of her doom. But I could not help her in the least, and for us to be caught would not have diminished her torment.

Where were all these people taken? Some to the ghetto, some to the brick factory in Buda. From the brick factory, thousands of people were marched on foot to the highway and to concentration camps near Vienna, some 150 or 200 miles away. But few arrived there. The ones who could not move fast enough or stayed behind were whipped or shot on the spot. There was no rest, no opportunity to be fed, or to use the facilities. The rain was pouring down day and night. This was the way that my once so very rich Aunt Elsa, then over fifty years old, myopic with heavy glasses, and her younger son, my cousin Laci, were killed. Elsa's older son, Pista, the engineer, was killed in forced labour at the Soviet front, and her husband, Albin, was held as a "hostage" by the Gestapo.

This procession from Budapest to Vienna was one of the many infamous death marches that took place all over Nazi Europe. This one was organized entirely by the Hungarian Nazis. Corpses lay all over the highway and in the ditches. Later, we learned that Wallenberg, traveling along the same highway in his Swedish diplomatic car, saved as many people as he could.

We arrived at our rented room in Buda. Finally, we could clean up and get into dry clothes. We were aware of the continuous mortal danger, but at this point we no longer cared. If this is the end, so be it. We made coffee, boiled some chestnuts that we had found, and resumed reading *Family Thibeault*. We remained in our room during air raids, partly because it was our preference and partly because we feared being recognized as Jews in the air-raid shelter.

A few days later, we got some news. Wallenberg succeeded in coming to some kind of agreement with the new government. The thousands of Jews under the protection of the Swedish embassy could remain in certain designated "Swedish" houses for the time being. The number of these people increased rapidly as Wallenberg himself issued many thousands of documents. He knew that there were also many counterfeit documents floating about, and whenever Wallenberg himself encountered one of these bogus passports, he instantly recognized it as "genuine." At this point, the Zionist underground organized the Swiss embassy as a front for their lifesaving efforts. Some other embassies joined in the rescue operation. But those Jews who did not own such documents and who were not taken on death marches were moved into the ghetto.

Marta found out that the Swedish embassy had to be extended because of the complex administration. By then, some 80,000 Swedish Defense Passports had been issued legally or illegally. Many of these documents saved lives; many did not. Others may have saved a life one day, only to fail to do so the next time. No sane calculations were possible. Every single encounter with an authority, sometimes on numerous occasions during a single day, was *rouge et noir* at the roulette table with our lives at stake.

I know many cases where people inadvertently bought their death with their own money. It often happened that an Arrowcross soldier tore up these papers and shot the owner on the spot. But it also happened that while Wallenberg quarrelled with the German soldiers at the railway station with the Jews already sealed in the cattle cars ready for deportation to concentration camps, his assistant Per Anger, later a Swedish ambassador in Ottawa, was gathering some random names of Jews locked in the cars. Any names. Then Wallenberg read out the "list of the Swedish citizens" supplied by his assistant to the SS soldiers, who reluctantly allowed them to leave with Wallenberg. But sometimes they did not and they threatened to shoot Wallenberg unless he cleared out. And they would have done so, too. There were no guarantees, no certainties. As time went on, there was less and less respect for these papers. The Hungarian führer, Szalasi, his foreign minister, Kemeny, and Adolf Eichmann were playing a deadly poker game with Raoul Wallenberg. But Wallenberg did not have a good hand at all. He was bluffing.

From the window of my hiding place, I saw a Hungarian soldier escorting a young Jewish man with a yellow armband—one from the forced labour camp. When they reached the street corner, the young man started to run for his life. Almost like in a slow-motion moving picture, the soldier took his rifle, aimed carefully, and shot the boy dead. He did that with a detached coolness, as if he were in a shooting gallery. Destiny rang the bell and the soldier won the doll. No compassion, no regret. He sniffed at the barrel of his gun, satisfied that his aim was still good.

Marta was then "employed" by the Swedish embassy, and we were all able to move to a protected building, one of the satellite embassies at No.1 Jokai Street. At that time, the Jews still left in Budapest lived in three kinds of buildings: the ghetto; the "defended" houses filled with Jews having Swedish or Swiss Defense Passports; and, supposedly the "safest," the satellite embassies like the one at No.1 Jokai. This address is now commemorated with a marble plaque for the horror it later witnessed. By comparison, at that time, No.1 Jokai Street appeared to have the highest security, almost the security level of the official Swedish embassy itself, or so it was believed. Of course, many Jews still lived all over the city as Aryans with fake documents or were disguised with deceptive uniforms, like soldiers, Red Cross workers, or even Arrowcross officials.

A friend of ours, now a prominent physician in Pittsburgh, Dr. Katherine Detre (née Drechsler), was walking around the city dressed as a streetcar ticket collector, complete with a leather bag full of tickets and other paraphernalia. The trouble was that she always had to walk on the streets, with little chance to sleep. After the war, we used to tease her that even today she still looks sleepy. Another friend, Ervin Geiger, wearing a fake Red Cross uniform, was found out and shot dead on the spot, as was another young man, a Jew wearing an Arrowcross uniform. And so were many others.

Generally, it was easier for women to exist in this way, partly because they were not as conspicuous as men, who had to be in the Army and could be betrayed by circumcision. In Hungary, only the Jews were circumcised. By then, so many counterfeit papers were floating around that the Arrowcross officials did not accept documents of any kind from males. Two or three Arrowcross hooligans, armed to the teeth, lingered on selected street corners, simply demanding that the passing men pull down their zippers and show them their penises on the spot. If they were circumcised, they were shot dead right there and then on the street with no further questions asked, no matter what kind of papers they had or what explanation they offered. One of our jobs in the ghetto hospital was to teach men how to stick their "foreskin" with mastic to the front of their penises to appear uncircumcised.

Life in the Jokai Street "embassy" was about survival. A group of Hungarian gendarmes was housed there to guard this "extraterritorial building." The officials, like Marta, did paperwork, mainly typing the defence passports. The rest of us just lingered. Boredom alternated with great angst and sinister premonitions, hunger with despair, yearning with weariness. We had slightly more food than the people in the ghetto, where the daily ration was estimated to be 690 to 790 calories per day, with 150 grams of bread daily, 40 grams of flour weekly, 10 grams of oil and 30 grams of legumes. Also, 100 grams of meat per week could be had "when available," which was never the case.

From somewhere, the once so-loved Masha showed up in the Jokai Street embassy with her mother. She came only to place her mother in a location that was thought to be safe and secure. Masha was married by then and stayed with her husband somewhere else.

The Soviet troops were closing in on Budapest. Standing on the rooftop at daybreak, we could hear the distant rumbling of heavy guns sounding louder every day. This first faint noise grew steadily more brassy and resonant as the front line pushed closer each day. Occasionally, the flash of some remote artillery fire painted a yellow flare along the night skyline, briefly outlining the rooftops. Yet the liberating troops appeared to be so unreachably remote! Will they ever arrive? Will they be in time to save us? We did not dare Karma by asking questions like that.

The American and British planes stopped their raids on Budapest. Not long after, it was the turn of the Soviet planes to come. They were much smaller. Their bombs also were smaller, but about half a dozen of them were chained together and poured down at the same time as some kind of small-calibre machine cannon fire. At least some of them seemed to be around at all times. They flew just over the rooftop level. No air-raid sirens sounded, partly because there was no point in it. The Soviet troops were so close. The electricity often failed, and then one day it was completely gone. We were freezing all the time. The cold penetrated the walls and our bones. Since water was no longer available, snow had to be melted for cooking.

Eight of us slept in the one-room apartment. This was a great luxury compared with the ghetto, where the average was fourteen people to a room. A young boy, Tom, and another man, Robert Markovits, the owner of a hat factory, were staying with us in the same room. Later, Robert's brother, Dr. Markovits, joined us as the ninth. By then, the noise of the guns had grown stronger. On Christmas day of 1944, the Soviets closed the ring around Budapest. As is the time-honoured military custom, the Soviets sent some emissaries with white flags over to the German–Hungarian lines, "wishing to prevent unnecessary bloodshed." The answer: the emissaries, to the last man, were shot dead by the Nazis.

The besieged city now imprisoned its population. The artillery fire stopped. An eerie silence ensued.

Only later did we realize that the Soviet military had regrouped. The elite troops were replaced with a division consisting of less-than-reputable citizen soldiers, "volunteers" from a huge Soviet jail. They were given a free hand. With that, there began bitter house-to-house and room-to-room fights. This lasted for two months. Often it happened that hand-to-hand combat was fought bitterly in the very same building for a couple of days, with different floors held by troops from opposite sides.

One would think that under such circumstances, the Nazis might have other things to worry about than the extermination of the remainder of the Jewish population. But no, far from it! Since they could not transport Jews from the encircled city to the concentration camps anymore, they took the Jews in small groups to the shores of the Danube, where they shot them in the head and threw their bodies into the water.

One day, December 26, 1944, to be exact, Pipez and the 110 other children at the Jewish orphanage were taken, undressed, to the Danube for execution. With horror, the children faced the submachine guns and saw the piles of bloody, nude corpses. Then, a miracle! For no reason, they were turned back at the last minute and taken to the ghetto. The Arrowcross evildoer "got a new order." He became confused, insisting that only seventy-eight of the children could be left alive "against a receipt," according to the order, and the rest of them were to be killed. Finally, he left all of them in the ghetto.

Dreams and Tears: V

My Runaway Relatives

And though you come out of each gruelling bout,
all broken and beaten and scarred
Just have one more try—it's dead easy to die,
it's the keeping-on-living that's hard.

From Robert Service, *The Quitter*

I do not know the fate that befell some of our relatives in Zilina in full minutiae. Nor am I familiar with the details of the lives of those through the war years who escaped from Zilina. But I will narrate what I heard, can recall, and could verify. This is the story of my Uncle Joseph and my cousins who ran away from Zilina just before the war broke out.

Uncle Joseph, Father's brother, always cherished life and embraced it with a bubbling dynamism. He was the youngest in the family and often urged his older brothers and sisters to pursue an inexhaustible variety of exotic endeavours and creative ideas invented by his fertile mind. Even when he would come up with simple suggestions, like going to the theatre or organizing a hike, he was faced with the reluctance and inertia of his unwilling older siblings. Joseph's frustrated exclamations of "You don't know how to live!" still echo in my memory. But this was before the war, in the "golden era" of the only democracy in Middle and Eastern Europe.

The Czechs, having been sacrificed for the elusive peace, paid dearly, and the Jewish communities living in their midst perished. Only a few of those who remained survived, and many who escaped from the immediate Nazi danger later succumbed while fighting with the British Armed Forces, the Czechoslovakian Legion, the Soviet Forces, or as partisans.

I do not know all the details of Joseph's escape, but I know that at one point he was arrested by the Nazi Hlinka guard and kept in a notorious maximum-security jail in Ilava. Apparently he was involved in some sort of resistance movement. How he escaped from the dreaded Ilava is a mystery. The next we heard, he was in southern France, working to rehabilitate wounded French soldiers. His favourite therapeutic tool was a self-invented technique of massage practised in Pistyan, a famous healing bath in Czechoslovakia, sport massage, plus his own cryptic formula. He developed it with practice.

After much hardship and many Ulyssean adventures, Joseph arrived with the Czechoslovakian Legion at a tranquil harbour, the small English town of Whitechurch that lay surrounded by calm and verdant farmlands. There, through the caprice of a fortuitous Karma, he met and married Mary Walley, an aunt to be proud of. Mary, whose idealism, love of mankind, firm belief in both the Old Testament and the New, and her deeply embedded Britishness that never faded, remained Joseph's sunshine for the rest of his life. In this warm union, Joseph finally found his equanimity.

Remarkably, Joseph was the sole member of our family who retained the name of Kohn. (My father became Koranyi in Hungary. Uncle Sandor took the name "Kucera" in Slovakia. Another brother, Franz, needed Slovakian-sounding names and papers and placed a single but insolently daring dot upon the hump of the letter "h" in his family name and through this alchemy he was transmogrified to the Slovak "Kolin.")

By marrying Joseph, Miss Walley turned into the wonderful Mrs. Mary Kohn. Joseph's fame as a medical masseur and healer kept growing. Simultaneously, he was recognized as the dean of the Kohn clan. It is a painful loss that Joseph died in his mid-fifties, well before he had had the opportunity to filter out and put to paper his decades of professional experiences.

Mary, widowed now for many years and past her mid-seventies, fiercely defies her years. With a quick wit and character all her own, she still finds an endless number of worthy causes that make her mount her tired, aging bicycle, ready to volunteer, to organize, and to give her heart and soul to help others.

Joseph and Mary had six children, my British cousins: two girls, the sophisticated Francisca and the good-hearted Jeannette, and four boys, the enterprising Simon, the ambitious Paul, the inventive Peter, and the family-archivist Andrew. All of them are Christians, and all of them are Kohns, in fact the only remaining Kohns in the family. Mary brought them up to hold a deep respect and love for their Jewish roots. All are married and have many children. With regard to offspring, my British relatives followed the opposite philosophy to mine. Thus, a new generation has sprouted and refreshed the exhausted family name.

Cousin Zsuzsa escaped from Zilina with the help of an underground Zionist organization. She was just fifteen years old, a reluctant little refugee, when she found shelter in Palestine. She had been all alone, cut off from her parents, friends, and relatives. The news that she gathered about her parents and younger brother, Ivan, only eight years old, was terrifying, particularly in her desperate state of isolation with no shoulder to lean on. Her older brother, Paul, was in England, serving in the Czechoslovakian Legion. All other relatives died in Auschwitz. Zsuzsa always had a difficult life, studded with personal tragedies. She married and soon became a widow, but consoled herself with her new family and with her two devoted children.

Zsuzsa's older brother, Paul, and two other cousins, Laci and Zolo, escaped together from Czechoslovakia. They had hoped to cross the border into pre-war Poland. They planned to join the Czechoslovakian Legion there, but they were underage. Nevertheless, they journeyed to Krakow. With no money and no connections, they were stuck there. They soon decided that the solution was to enlist in the French Foreign Legion. Age was immaterial; in situations like that, everyone was expected to tell a lie or two. In no time, they found themselves first in Lille, France, then in the Sahara, in Oran, Sidi bel Abes, Colomb Bechar, and in basic training for the French Foreign Legion, which is itself something to survive!

Soon after, the war broke out. When the Germans later attacked Belgium, the three legionnaires were sent to the European front. In Paris, they met briefly with Uncle Joseph, who was then in the Czechoslovakian Legion. The boys were sent to the northern front, which at that time was about forty kilometres from Paris, near Mountreau. They participated in the worst battles against the Germans and witnessed the disintegration of the Allied Forces. Paul and Laci were eventually evacuated to England, where they continued to fight the Germans with the Czechoslovakian Legion and the British Air Force. Zolo became separated from them in the upheaval.

I still do not know many details of Paul's survival, except that he retired from the Czechoslovakian Legion at the end of the war with a high rank and was richly decorated.

Laci also joined the Czechoslovakian Legion in England. He had always been brilliant with his hands. He could do anything. His natural talents were put to good use when he specialized in the repair and maintenance of airplanes. In that capacity, he served in the (British) Royal Air Force. Towards the end of the war, Laci married Joyce Breeze, a British girl, also in the army. They settled near St. Andrews Airfield, where Laci's unit was posted, and soon had a son, Peter.

When the last of the fighting was over, Laci was posted to Prague, a natural choice, as he knew the language. This military posting enabled him to try to look for his parents, Hugo and Aranka, and his sister Edith. He also tried to find other family members from Zilina. They had all been taken to Auschwitz and none of them came back. The final moments of their broken lives and tragic deaths remained unknown. One can only imagine Laci's mental state when he found out about these bitter losses.

Laci called his wife in England. She was only too happy to come to Prague with their son and console her beloved one. And Laci, in his agony, fervently waited for her. But on that gloomy autumn day, instead of meeting his wife and son, he was called to see his commanding officer. There, Laci learned the unbelievable: his wife and son had been murdered in a holdup in England shortly before they intended to leave to meet him in Prague.

It is hard to imagine the deep wounds a human can survive. But Laci survived, somehow. He taught himself watch repair and married again. Peggy was an English girl whose gentle, healing faith and prayers eased Laci's grief and helped the two of them build a happy family and a new life.

Zolo got separated from the others and was wounded at the French front, near Mountreau. He was treated in a military hospital near Limoges. Still a member of the French Foreign Legion, he was evacuated to North Africa, where his job was driving a truck through the Sahara Desert. Eventually, Zolo was put in a detention camp by the Vichy government, the friendly vassals of the Nazis. He managed to escape and reached England via Portugal. There, Zolo joined the Czechoslovakian Legion. Soon after, the Royal Air Force "borrowed" him. He was taken to Canada and trained as a navigator and pilot in Montreal and Winnipeg. Back in England, he flew about sixty missions over Germany. When the war ended, Zolo, like his brother Laci, found nobody alive from his family. All those who had remained in Zilina were dead. But exactly how and when they died, nobody knew. Zolo did find his girlfriend, Vlasta. They quietly got married.

In 1947, two years after the war, Zolo was restless. On November 29 of that year, the famous United Nations vote divided Palestine into Israel and a Palestinian Arab state. The sporadic fights had grown to a full-scale war after the independence of the State of Israel was declared on May 14, 1948. British rule in Palestine ended in the same month, but Sir John Glubb of Britain had seen to it that Transjordan's military was well trained and well armed. The British also left a generous amount of military equipment in Transjordan, while the Hagana, the emerging Jewish military, was disarmed. At the same time, the Israeli forces could summon only 30,000 largely untrained men and women to face the enemy and possessed only rudimentary weapons. When

Israel's independence was declared, five Arab armies joined together and attacked Israel. These included Egypt, Transjordan, Syria, Lebanon, and Iraq. The size of the Israel territory was less than the expanse of Lake Ontario.

Israel had no air force. Zolo was in Israel by then. He and Vlasta arrived in Haifa by ship in the morning, and that same night he was in Zagreb, Yugoslavia. With a rather rickety plane, he was sent to pick up personnel and equipment. On the return flight, the plane was so laden down that it could barely gain sufficient altitude! Throughout his life, Zolo remained in the Israeli Air Force. Zolo had a small house in Zahala, near Tel Aviv. He and Vlasta had two children, a son, Dany, and a daughter, Anat.

Darkness falls rapidly in Tel Aviv in the wintertime. Zolo was driving his car. The headlights lit up the bubbling torrent of rain hitting the highway. It was already like night, and everything was cold and wet, when Zolo saw the pitiable figure of a woman on the side of the road. Normally, he did not stop when driving alone. Who needs trouble? But this time, he felt sorry for the creature, who was soaked through. He stopped the car and gave her a lift. They began to talk. The woman asked where he was born. Zilina. What was his name? Zolo Bock. With that, the woman began to wail and cry.

"What's the matter?" a startled Zolo inquired.

"I was there. I saw it all. I know what happened to your sister Edith and to your mother!"

And so Zolo learned the sad story.

CHAPTER 6

The Abyss

It was difficult to imagine how the situation of the Jews in Budapest could possibly deteriorate further. But once again, merciless reality outdid our imaginations. The meagre food supply was rapidly running out. The cruelties of the Arrowcross hellions reached colossal proportions. These criminals formed death brigades that patrolled the streets for the purpose of killing Jews or suspected Jews. They captured, then tortured, Jews in the numerous Arrowcross headquarters, or took them in groups to the shores of the Danube, where they killed them and threw their bodies into the water.

One famous murderer was Pater Andrew Kun. ("In the name of Jesus Christ, fire!" was his "priestly" command to the Arrowcross squad.) Another murderer was Father Vilmos Lucska, who worked on a plan for the complete and total massacre of the ghetto's 70,000 Jews. This operation was to take place on January 15, 1945 with the help of the Arrowcross leader of defense, Dr. Erno Vajna, the Hungarian police, and the German SS *Feldherrenhalle* Division's general, August Schmidthuber. It was prevented by Raoul Wallenberg and Paul Szalai, Wallenberg's police connection. They threatened General Schmidthuber that after the war he would face the court as an ordinary mass murderer if he embarked on this horrendous plan.

Hundreds of Jews were now committing suicide, and many more were attempting it. The ghetto hospital was overcrowded beyond measure, not only with these attempted suicides but also with people who were shot, some having been fished out of the Danube. Corpses were piling up everywhere. The Defended Houses, "defended" by the Swedish, Swiss, and other embassies, were far from safe. Even the satellite embassies were attacked and robbed.

In late December, the head of our building on Jokai Street, Lajos Turi, was taken away by the Arrowcross and murdered. As well, large numbers of both Jews and non-Jews were killed and wounded by Soviet artillery fire and air raids. Everyone slept in the basements that served as air-raid shelters. I had a strong reluctance to remain in these basements. The reason for this idiosyncrasy was that with its single entrance, the basement gave me a hopelessly trapped, claustrophobic feeling. True, it was much more dangerous to stay in one of the top-floor apartments during air raids, but it had the advantage that one could smoke there. Smoking was more important to us in those days than food, which was sorely scarce. Smoking, back then, was the jubilation of life, an ovation to our survival from one moment to the next. It took away the hunger, the fear, the depression, the exhaustion.

I also developed the habit that whenever I went to sleep, I folded my pillow into a ball under my neck and faced the door. This way, both my ears were free and uncovered, and I imagined that this vigilant position enabled me to respond faster to danger. I never thought that such a habit could fossilize to become a lifetime practice. But it did set deep, permanent roots, and this conditioned reflex is still with me today.

We suddenly woke up to the reverberation of shouting and gunshots after midnight on Friday, January 7, 1945. The Arrowcross gang threatened to throw a hand grenade at our closed front door at No. 1 Jokai Street. A terrified Jewish "guard" opened the door, and a large number of Nazis immediately poured in through the gaping hole. Within minutes, with no resistance at all, they disarmed the indifferent gendarmes who, contrary to their orders, refused to defend this extraterritorial building against the Nazis. Did these gendarmes suddenly lose their courage, or had they found their genuine loyalty? Since most people were in the basement, the Nazis blocked the door and ordered everyone into the courtyard "within three minutes." They shot a few people on the spot who could not move fast enough, including a man in a wheelchair, Gyula Kallos. Then they began a systematic search of the building, from floor to floor, room by room, to find any other people who might be hiding there.

Unbeknownst to me, my sister and mother were able to sneak away in the darkness and hide in a cabinet in the embassy office. They prayed in the suffocating darkness. I was in our fourth-floor apartment with Lici, desperately looking for some hiding place. The only spot I could find was a skylight, fifty inches by fifty inches, onto which the bathroom window opened. We climbed out there and by pressing our backs to one wall and our feet to the opposite wall, we supported ourselves somehow, with one arm hanging onto the window ledge. A flimsy and now overstrained metal crossbar served as a precarious foothold over the vertical drop. Underneath us yawned a pitch-dark, four-storey deep cliff.

We heard yelling and occasional revolver shots. Our hands were numb from the strain and the January cold as we clung to the edge of the windowsill with white knuckles. Our hands froze, but sweat was running down our backs and our mouths were parched. We could hear each other's heartbeats in that undertow of anxiety. Who was the one just killed? Mother? Marta? A friend? The palpitation became the marker of time. The rhythmic beating of our pulse before we are born is the first music we hear, and it is the last decrescendo beat that we experience when we depart.

Hours passed. The perpetuity of the lead-wrought moments finally appeared to slow to a standstill. I needed to wipe my nose but I could not. We forbade ourselves to think of the sheer precipice below us; we forbade ourselves to think at all. "Good that I used to be a gymnast" went through my mind. But I had to give more and more support to Lici, whose strength was failing as her wilting muscles turned numb. Small pieces of cement began to crumble from the edge of the metal foothold, plummeting into the unlit pitfall, the sound telling us the depth of the shaft. How much longer could it hold up? The noise of the shuffling feet of some 300 people faded away now, and a deep silence took over the building. They were gone.

Two and a half hours passed. We began to crawl out very cautiously. We found Father, who had been hiding in a folding bed. Then we found Mother and Marta as they came out of their hiding place. Jan was gone. He had been found and taken away. In the basement, we saw a woman who was dying. She had been left behind but for some reason had not been killed. There were a few other women around her who were not Jews—or so they claimed. They also had not been taken by the Nazis. Our roommates were gone. The empty house was eerie and dangerous. All in all, ourselves included, about twenty of us had succeeded in hiding in the building. The rest, a total of 266, had been taken away.

Marta was in despair because of Jan's fate, but she left with my parents and went to another Swedish satellite embassy, on Ulloi Street. Lici and I found shelter for the remainder of the night in an empty apartment in the neighbourhood.

The next morning, January 8, 1945, we made a very adventurous crossing of the city to the distant Ulloi Street. It was a much larger satellite embassy, a place where Wallenberg himself stayed at times. There were three or four separate air-raid shelters there. My parents and Marta stayed in one of them. In another air-raid shelter, Lici and I found refuge and one straw mattress for the two of us. We had not eaten for quite some time by then, but we soon fell asleep, our exhaustion being greater than our hunger. It was, however, not a very long sleep.

At seven p.m., loud shouts awakened us. Arrowcross soldiers flooded the safe place, and stood in the room, dressed in their black uniforms, green shirts,

Arrowcross armbands, and self-awarded decorations. They made all the people, about 150 of us in that shelter line up. Searches, "hand over all valuables," kicks, faces being slapped, hits with gun butts. A harsh order, and we had to march with our hands held up over our heads. The winter night was cold. We were shaking. Was it the cold or the terror? It was not a very long march. Soon we found ourselves at the doorstep of the Maria Teresa barracks. We were herded down to a basement on narrow stairs to a small room. Not even half of the people fitted in, with the rest still in the street. A young, red-haired Arrowcross soldier not more than fourteen years old was sleeping on the floor, with a submachine gun over his chest, exhausted by the demanding task of killing.

The crowd was pushing into the room and there was a danger that we might step on this Nazi hoodlum. He half woke up. "Take them to the Danube," he murmured and went back to sleep. Some other Arrowcross thugs, all drunk, lay around on the floor. They made us turn around and go out onto the street again.

But again, not far. An apartment house at 41 Ferenz Ring had become the local Arrowcross headquarters. Up on the first floor, we reached a very large apartment. We all stood there, pushed against the wall. In our group, I saw Lajos Stockler, a member of the *Judenrat*. There was a "dressing room" nearby. Our coats and jackets were taken away, and we stood in our shirtsleeves. We knew that eventually we would have to shed the rest of our clothing, all but our underwear. Soon, but not yet. Questions were being asked by one of the Arrowcross soldiers, who was seated behind a small table. A search for more valuables, and more abuse. So, that was it. Finally, the end. I was very, very tired. I looked at Lici. She, too, was a hundred years old, just weary. Exhaustion deepened the dark furrows on her face, her thin, pointed nose sticking out. Terror had painted tired, grey lines under her eyes. A narrow, barely blue blood vessel arched up under her pale skin on the side of her neck, and where her jawbone protruded, a fine but visibly rapid, fluttering pulse betrayed her frightful expectation at parting so abruptly from her young life.

In the breast pocket of my jacket was half a cigarette. All I could think of was that half cigarette. But the jacket had already been taken away. It was there in that pile, somewhere in the dressing room. My early hero, Jean Barois, flashed through my mind. What noble thoughts his mind had created, what superb testimony he produced in the moment when he believed the end was near! Maybe these are my very last thoughts in my life, my epitaph, the final spasms of my tortured nerve cells. My time was running out, and all I could think of was the butt of a cigarette! Too tired for philosophy. What if we jumped in the water before they shot? I didn't know. I would see. Probably it was not worth doing so. Better to get it over with.

Now a new commotion. What? Were the police also collaborating with the Arrowcross? No. Officers. The police holding their guns at the Arrowcross cutthroats. They were talking to the Arrowcross commander. What was happening? One of the high-ranking police officers was Paul Szalai, with whom Raoul Wallenberg used to deal. Another police officer in his leather coat was Karoly Szabo. We were told to put our jackets back on and line up. And march. Back to where we came from.

We were back at the Ulloi Street embassy. Marta was crying and kissing us. So were my parents. Their shelter was left behind by the Arrowcross soldiers. We got a piece of bread but did not understand what was happening. Somebody struck a match and the stump of the cigarette was lit. I inhaled the tangy smoke deeply. Lici turned to me: "I am pregnant." I held her close to me.

* * *

After the raid, the dying Jewish woman in the shelter at No. 1 Jokai Street, Mrs. Szanto, became the toy of the Arrowcross bandits, who returned to the building several times in the next few days. The woman was terminal and could not breathe. She was dying of TB and those devils knew it. One of the women who claimed to be a Christian was looking after her. (Remember Katherine Detre, the sleepy Jewish "streetcar ticket collector"? This was her mother, and the dying woman was her aunt.) The daughter of the dying woman was the sixteen-year-old Zsuzsika, who had been taken away by the Arrowcross on January 7. One of the savages pulled a piece of luggage from under the bed and proceeded to open it.

"No, no," the dying woman objected. "Those clothes belong to my Zsuzsika."

Crude laughter.

"Zsuzsika does not need them anymore." The Nazi is replicating an obscene swing with his hips. "We all fucked Zsuzsika like that, before we killed her."

* * *

"Lasciate ogni speranza voi chi entrate!"

The 266 people captured at No. 1 Jokai Street were herded in several groups through the darkened city to No. 14 Varoshaz Street, one of the

Arrowcross headquarters. A wild bunch of Nazis were waiting for them. Kicks, beatings, face-slapping for all—men, women, children, and the aged. "Surrender your valuables, you pigs!" People were taken to different rooms for "interrogation" by these gangsters. Jan was thoroughly beaten up because he had "long hair and that proves he is a Communist Jew."

Jan was in the same room with Robert Markovits. Markovits had special treatment. They spotted him as a "rich Jew" because he used to have a hat factory. They wanted to know where he had hidden his money and jewellery. He was systematically tortured. One of the Arrowcross leaders, a woman named Csopi (alias Lujza Hay), was an incredibly cruel sadist.

A few Jews, about twenty, were taken to the ghetto. For some unexplained reason, they were lucky beyond belief. The next day, the Arrowcross wanted to have "four strong men for chopping wood." They also assembled a group of forty or fifty people "for the ghetto" and tied them together, hand to hand, with cord and wire. They were not headed for the ghetto, however, but were taken to the shore of the Danube and shot in the head. The "four strong men" (Dr. Paul George, Erno Czitron, Karl Altman, and one other) were ordered to throw the bodies of these unfortunates into the water. The strong men were taken back to the Arrowcross headquarters but were kept separate from the rest. Nevertheless, they found ways to communicate with the remaining prisoners.

Robert Markovits was beaten and tortured again. He had some barbiturate hidden in his clothing and attempted suicide with it. But he did not have enough poison and was beaten again.

The next day, a new transport was selected and went to the Danube with the killers and the four strong men. This time, none of them returned. Again, four strong men were selected (Jan Sebor, Bela Fried, Jeno Stern, and Hollander). Transport after transport went to the Danube. One of the prisoners, Mihaly Fodor, attempted to jump from the fourth floor, but he was "saved." Two others jumped to their deaths. Finally, Mihaly Fodor succeeded in jumping again and this time killed himself.

Rugged Csopi, the sadistic murderess, was jealous of the beautiful sixteen-year-old Zsuzsika. When Jan returned to the Arrowcross headquarters, he found that Markovits had been tortured again. Some others had been killed in the "interrogation room." Zsuzsika was raped repeatedly by several Nazis. Csopi was furious and grew even more jealous of Zsuzsika. Robert Markovits's brother, George, a physician, had already been killed. Robert was bruised and cut all over. Then the door sprang open and Robert's chief inquisitor motioned to him to follow for a new session of "interrogation." Markovits stood up, suddenly turned to the fourth-floor window, sprinted like a ballet dancer, and jumped through the glass. He flew in midair and seemed to be floating for the blink of an eye. Nobody will ever know his thoughts. Perhaps he enjoyed his freedom for that split second. Time no longer mattered to Robert Markovits. That split second was his own eternity.

Csopi had had enough of that "little bitch Zsuzsika." Now she was going to show her. Csopi took her Tommy gun, made Zsuzsika undress, and forced the naked girl onto the frozen January street. Hatred ejaculated through her eyeballs as she pulled the trigger. Zsuzsika fell, lifeless, her young blood spreading all over the cobblestones.

One of the leaders of the Arrowcross was Lajos Tal. By now, he was satiated with blood. Older and more cautious, he knew that the Russians were near. The small-arms fire had already been heard for days. They were just around the corner. Tal would have liked to run away, but his son George was one of the most unforgiving Arrowcross soldiers. Word reached the Arrowcross headquarters late at night that they had to evacuate the headquarters to Buda. Lajos Tal gave Jan a heavy suitcase loaded with loot and made him carry it. Two other "strong men" were also weighed down by suitcases filled with stolen goods. They were all heading towards the Lanc Bridge. Clearly, Lajos Tal wanted to stay behind and disappear, but his son George sensed it and forced his father to go along at gunpoint. But it was pitch dark. The "strong men" dropped their loads and vanished into the mist.

* * *

Grant peace of mind for those in the midst of our community whose hearts are wounded. . . . May the knowledge console them that death is the wish of some, relief for many, and the end for all.[7]

* * *

A simple marble plaque commemorating the "266 Swedish Embassy Staff" still stands at the entrance of No. 1 Jokai Street in Budapest. In accordance with Communist house rules, the "Jewish status is not to be mentioned." It is covered by the shroud of amnesia. *Alev Hashalom*!

---

[7] *Yiskor* memorial service.

Dreams and Tears: VI

A Hospital Job

Though they go mad they shall be sane,
Though they sink through the sea they shall rise again;
Though lovers be lost love shall not;
And death shall have no dominion.

From Dylan Thomas, *And Death Shall Have No Dominion*

Cousin Edith finished her medical studies in Prague and received her medical degree in early 1942. She had yearned with her heart and soul to become a physician and through weary years she spared no sacrifice to achieve her goal. But the graduation that would normally have been a jubilant experience for friends and family passed as a mere perfunctory event. Edith could not wait to get back to Zilina to be near her worried parents. By then, the situation of the Jews in Slovakia was desperate, and immediate catastrophe loomed. Edith's brothers, Laci and Zolo, had already fled. Who knew where they might be. Uncle Hugo's family house had been confiscated and his business appropriated. They, like all the Jews in Zilina, had been entirely dispossessed by the State. The neighbours and "friends" had also taken their share of the loot.

Soon a ghetto was set up in the nearby football field where I used to play as a child, just behind my grandparents' home. There, Edith found much urgent, though unpaid, work as a physician. She worked hard, trying to help where she could.

In the sordid milieu of the ghetto, Edith married her old flame. On the very day of her wedding to Valer Glaser, the ghetto was transferred to an unheard-of former Austro-Hungarian cavalry barrack in Poland, not far from Zilina. The place was called Auschwitz, a location that had been recommended only two years earlier by *Oberführer* Richard Glucks to Himmler as a suitable site for a concentration camp. It was easy to reach by train, yet isolated from the rest of the world. An excellent place for an inferno.

The railway tracks ran into the camp through a large gate. *"Arbeit macht frei"* ("Work makes you free") lied the sign over the archway. By 1942, when my family from Zilina was deported by the Slovaks to this new facility, Auschwitz was working at full capacity on the production line of murder. Soon the factory of horrors overflowed, and satellite camps such as Birkenau had to be built around them.

We will never know how Uncle Hugo was killed. But the tragedy of Edith and her mother, Aranka, was told to Zolo in Israel by a woman from Zilina who survived the *Shoah.*

Edith and her mother passed the first and immediate "selection" in Auschwitz, the crucial, life-or-death gamble at the hands of Dr. Mengele. As a physician, Edith was ordered to serve in the concentration camp hospital. She succeeded in placing her mother in the same hospital where Aranka could work as a nurse's aide.

But on December 5th, 1942, the Administrators of Death found a shortage of people to be gassed. Aranka was ordered to fill the gap, and she was tossed into the group of people to be annihilated. Edith fought for her mother desperately, saying that Aranka was needed in the hospital. No use. Edith, knowing well the fate of the group, asked to be allowed to go with her mother to be gassed. They consented. Edith spotted a woman acquaintance nearby. She shouted to her from the doomed group" "Tell my husband I love him."

This was her epitaph.

**Uncle Hugo, Aunt Aranka, and beloved cousin, Edith
—all perished in Auschwitz.**

CHAPTER 7

The Irate Currents of the River Styx

The spellbinding rescue from the flowing graveyard of the Danube, where so many thousands had perished in anguish, became an animating experience for us. Back at Ulloi Street, we finally seemed to shed the agony of dread that had ruled our minds for too long. Fear is a prison. Now an intrepid, fatalistic disposition dominated our mood. We decided to return to the Wesselenyi Street Ghetto Hospital. This venture involved crossing a major part of the city once again, always a dangerous undertaking.

We were amazed to see our beautiful city in its current miserable condition. Torn electric wires lay across the streets, buildings had collapsed, and burnt vehicles, abandoned in a frenzy, looked like the fossilized remains of a long-extinct species. Small piles of corpses of those killed in the bombardments, half-carved-up dead horses, and looted stores were visible everywhere. Smoke curled slowly from flimsy, improvised chimneys, exposing the hurried attempts of a cryptic, invisible population now living like groundhogs and trying to keep warm and cook.

The overall desolation painted a picture of the Apocalypse. Danger was everywhere. Military police pursued army-age men; Arrowcross search parties hunted for Jews; while soldiers, civilians with Red Cross armbands, gendarmes, and policemen whirled around. The closer we got to the ghetto, the more Arrowcross and SS soldiers there were to be seen.

The Wesselenyi Ghetto Hospital was actually just outside the ghetto wall. We quickly entered the gate. In the midst of a multitude of people in the crowded corridors, it was good to see some familiar faces.

We found Dr. Acel, a physician and pathologist, and asked her about her husband, Dr. Dezso Acel. Her eyes filled with tears. Her husband was dead. No, it was not the Nazis that had killed him; he had died of fulminant sepsis. She told us what had happened at the hospital in the past few months. Not long before, Dr. Dezso Acel, still vigorous, dedicated, and, as always, helpful, decided to have a cover built for the basement windows. The basement housed the operating rooms, and the whistling shrapnel fragments flew in unhindered. He explained to the hospital carpenter how to take two pieces of wood and fill the space between with sand to cover each window. To show him what he wanted, he took the carpenter outside the building. The Arrowcross gangsters stopped them. They took the carpenter but ordered Dr. Acel back into the hospital. Dr. Acel objected, offering to go in place of the carpenter but they reassured him by saying, "We will bring him back . . . we promise you, on our Arrowcross word of honour." And indeed they did bring him back, about an hour later, on a pully, the dead carpenter's hands bound behind his back with wire and shot through the back of his neck. They called out to Dr. Acel, who was forced to acknowledge that the Nazis "kept their word." Big laughter followed. It was a damned good joke, wasn't it!

Bela Molnar, the famous surgeon, was operating. He was always operating, night and day. At an earlier date, Dr. Molnar had received a rare Exemption Certificate from Regent Horthy, a unique document that granted him the privilege of living like a non-Jew and not having to wear a yellow star. This important piece of paper was delivered to him in the ghetto hospital soon after the hospital moved to this location. Dr. Molnar had not asked for such a privilege. When he got it, he showed it to his co-workers and tore it up: "As long as you are wearing the yellow star, so will I," he said. Many other physicians did an outstanding job, including Dr. Laszlo Benedek, whom I did not like. But that is another story.

The hospital was extremely overcrowded. Patients were lying on the bare floor in the corridors. All the panes of glass in the windows had shattered long ago, letting the icy January draft blow through the winding halls, the floors of which here and there were crunchy underfoot from splinters of glass. The wounded were pouring in. A young girl, not more than sixteen, was brought in with an abdominal wound. She had been shot by an Arrowcross thug and her bladder was torn open by the bullet. Dr. Molnar operated on her although he knew this patient's chances were practically zero. Many patients died of infections. But one could not just stand by doing nothing when somebody was bleeding. It is unnatural for a physician. One must do something! We had no medications, no alcohol, no clean instruments, and no electricity to sterilize them. I once assisted at an operation when that fine surgeon ran out of hemostats. He spotted one on the floor and in desperation used it as it was. He was dealing with arterial bleeding. I understood.

In spite of all this, the Wesselenyi Street Hospital was still a lucky place. There were other, smaller, Jewish hospitals scattered around the city; there was one on the Akacfa Street, and one on Tatra Street. The latter had only twenty beds but fifteen to twenty surgeons and 500 patients. On December 31, 1944, a group of Arrowcross murderers broke in, shot some patients, and wanted to take the rest to the Danube for execution. They were saved at the last minute.

But the next day, in a neighbouring house, forty people were shot and thrown into the Danube. On January 15, 1945, drunken Hungarian gendarmes and Arrowcross bandits claimed that "the Jews had opened fire on them from the hospital" and started to kill people indiscriminately. But just then, Soviet troops arrived in this part of the city, and the "heroes" ran away.

The small Red Cross hospital inside the ghetto was attacked and annihilated by the Hungarian Nazis. Another small Jewish field hospital, in Bethlen Square, was attacked by both the Hungarian Nazis and the Schwabian SS, and twenty-eight people were murdered. On January 11, the Maros Street infirmary in Buda was attacked, and ninety-two patients, doctors, and nurses were murdered. Only a single nurse survived. On January 14, the Orthodox Jewish hospice in Varosmajor Street in Buda was attacked, and 150 patients, doctors, and staff were killed. Eight days later, the small hospital of the Orthodox Holy Society at No. 2 Alma Road was destroyed, and ninety staff and patients were murdered.

In the ghetto itself, conditions were terrifying. The cold and damp had penetrated everywhere. There was no food and no water. But these were only minor problems. The stiff dead bodies, partly covered by snow, were stacked up like so many timbers, often the last-minute horror frozen onto their motionless faces and cold, open mouths. Fine ice crystals gathered on their eyelashes, rendering them statue-like, as if they had never been alive. At least they had been spared the lengthy nocturnal last walk in their underwear to the shore of the Danube.

The Blue Danube. I will never again enjoy Johann Strauss's *Gemutlichkeit* and Viennese romanticism. The water, far from being blue, was ice cold and a rather dirty brown. The dark currents carried frozen blocks of ice with indifference, some still stained with blood. It also ferried floating bodies, hands tied behind their backs with cord or wire. Nobody will ever know the exact number, but it is estimated that around 17,000 people were murdered in this way by the Hungarian Nazis on the shores of the Danube.

In Greek legends, the River Styx divided the world of the living from the land of the dead. This is why they placed a coin, an *obulus*, on the tongues of the departed, so that they could pay the price of crossing the cruel River Styx on Charon's ferry to the forever-dark Hades. Those who did not have the fare remained the burdened souls that lingered forever between the living and the dead. But who can say *Kaddish* six million times!

Any separation from a beloved one, no matter how brief and transient, is incredibly painful. The idea of surviving these horrors alone and being forced to endure the loss of someone close was unimaginable. Certainly not worth the price. "If one has to go, we should all perish together," kept humming in my mind.

Unwisely, someone told me that she had seen the "shadow of death on my face." I kept thinking about it. I, too, could see such subtle marks on the faces of some people—an omen, a sign of destiny—but I would never tell them lest they lose confidence. Thus the remark becomes a self-fulfilling prophecy.

Survival was such a fragile plight. We felt restless and unhappy. Maybe we should go to yet another satellite embassy, perhaps the one on Revai Street? And next morning, we were on our way, carrying our medical bags. This meant crossing the streets, facing the unknown, always a gamble with the ultimate price to pay if such was your Karma. The building we sought was on one of the cross streets behind the opera house. We knew the area well. Near the opera house we suddenly ran into one of the Arrowcross death squads. We found ourselves practically face to face with them before we knew it. It was too late to turn around, as such a move certainly would have drawn their attention. Proceeding towards them was equally dangerous, if for no other reason than because either boredom or officiousness could prompt them to hold us up for the customary "inspection." We knew that we were doomed unless we tried a bold move. Certainly, that would have been the end of two (or three?) of us. What now?

I turned to Lici behind me and spoke loudly to her to be certain that the Nazis heard me well. "Come, come, dear colleague! This is an emergency! As it is, we are late!"

With that, I turned to the most obnoxious-looking Arrowcross bandit whom I spotted as likely being the leader of the gang. "Is Revai Street that way, Brother?" I asked him, after having given him a Nazi salute. My body language conveyed our urgent task to attend to a life or death emergency.

"Straight ahead, Brother," answered the unsuspecting murderer, feeling proud that he had been picked out and recognized as the most important one in the group. I felt some skipping, violent heartbeats throbbing in my chest and eardrums, and my dry tongue was sticking to the roof of my mouth. But we had won the encounter, the danger had passed, and the Nazi motioned to us to go, feeling that we were the same as them. Of course, all the elaborate reasoning behind my sudden behaviour came to me only in retrospect. At the time it happened, it was merely an instinctive response for survival.

We reached the building that we sought and soon settled in. The others hiding there had a stream of questions to ask: what had happened in the Jokai

Street embassy? How did it happen? Who survived? What were the conditions in Ulloi Street? Did they still have food?

They were friendly, but there was hardly any food left in the building. We got a mouthful of meat that somebody had carved from a dead horse a few days ago. The only place available for us was in the basement. There, a single memorial candle was burning. It was quite appropriate, I thought, although I could not decide whether the memorial candle burned for those who were already dead or for those whose destiny would be fulfilled in the next few days. In fact, it burned for the sake of giving some fluttering light, throwing its oscillating, funereal yellow glow onto the gaunt, unwashed, weary faces. Skins as sallow as crumpled parchment flared in the half-twinkle, which transformed the crowded place into an eerie catacomb. There was a low-grade, sleepy fire smouldering under white ashes in an open iron oven with flimsy pipes leading to the unprofessionally chiselled-through wall. We huddled together and spent the night there.

Early in the morning, we got something to drink, one cupful for both of us. Someone asserted the daring notion that it was coffee. A sudden burst of unexpected, brassy motor noise buzzed right over our heads, the sound quenched by an almost simultaneous explosion that was followed by a sinister rolling knock and murmur. The small oven blew a flash of fire and smoke all over the basement. Earthquake? Bomb? Everyone ran towards the door to see if we were still able to leave the basement. Part of the staircase came rumbling down, and an acrid fog obscured our vision.

A man started to scream. "My wife, oh my wife!" he shouted. "She just went to the top floor!"

I ran towards the staircase. Great chunks of it were missing, but a narrow remnant of the stairs near the wall was preserved. Hopefully, it would hold. Only part of the banister was still standing, the rest was hanging in mid-air, fringed by heavy lumps of concrete swinging on scraps of the bent steel rods. With caution, it seemed possible to pass and get up that way. People watched me as I climbed. Shattered pieces of stones rolled down and fell over the broken edges of the staircase, plummeting into the depths.

On the top floor, a young woman screamed and screamed. A narrow stream of blood was running down her face. The whites of her eyes were visible around her irises and her black pupils were as large as pennies. She seemed to be unhurt, although the chain bombs had cut a big hole in her apartment wall. I got hold of her and pulled her towards the broken stairs. She resisted vigorously. "China cups, my china cups, don't you understand?" she shouted.

Obviously she was in shock or in a hysterical, altered state of mind. I hope that my present-day colleagues in the Emergency Room will not condemn me too harshly, but I solved this psychiatric crisis according to the "recommendation" of Cronin's *Citadel*. I slapped her face. It worked. It brought her back to reality. She calmed down, then became even somewhat stuporous. I welcomed this because I realized that I would have to carry her down those partly demolished stairs on my shoulders.

She had a three-inch gash in her scalp that had soaked her hair with blood. Lici and I washed her wound and cut her hair around the sharp laceration as best we could. We found some Novocaine in our bag and put in a few stitches. This made everyone feel better, particularly myself. My confidence returned.

The grateful husband then pulled out a veritable treasure from his luggage. A small container of jam! My first honorarium! I hesitated for only a few seconds. With Lici's enthusiastic approval, I exchanged it for cigarettes. Ohhh. That cigarette was good! (What did we know way back then about the as yet unsuspected carcinogenic and vascular poison it contained! At any rate, we could only worry about the next hour, not the long-term effects of a "harmless" habit!)

It was then that I completely shed all my fears. I undertook the task of delivering a written message to a certain address in the city and carrying a "parcel" back. The next day, I set out to accomplish this dangerous task. The destruction of the city was incredible. At one point, I needed a rest and entered a shelter hospital that was of course not for Jews but was for the general population. Almost all the victims had been injured in the bombing. It was a horrendous sight. Tables after tables of patients—recovering, moaning and screaming, dying. I need no further lectures on Cheyne-Stokes respiration; I have seen enough.

Finally, I reached my destination and was given three loaves of heavy, cement-like brown-black bread. I had to hide it somehow, if life was dear to me. It was extremely perilous to run around with three loaves of bread under your arm in those days.

The return trip from my excursion took a long time and was studded with unexpected adventures. At one point, I saw a German *Wehrmacht* unit not far from me on Kaiser Wilhelm Boulevard. They looked around cautiously. Then, at a hand signal, they started to cross the boulevard, running fast. A burst of machine-gun fire came from somewhere, and all of them—five or six—fell dead on the pavement. Sometimes death is instantaneous. It is curious that it was the first time I was thinking of them as human beings! A minute ago they were living people, now they were limp corpses who would never reach the homes of their loved ones.

I arrived home at last. I was amazed—almost the entire day was gone. But I had also earned a fortune. One of the three loaves of bread was ours! We also moved from the basement and stayed in the newly created ruins of a wall. We ate bread and smoked, shading the flaring ember of the burning cigarette with the hollow of our palms lest the red glow give away our secluded position. We tried to sleep, but it was cold. From the ruin of the wall, I looked out onto Revai Street. A German tiger tank stood nearby. I slept fitfully.

Nocturnal Images

Dread

The soul shall find itself alone
'Mid dark thoughts of gray tomb-stone—
Not one, of all the crowd, to pray
Into thine hours of secrecy

From Edgar Allan Poe, *Spirits of the Dead*

The firm, brassy steps on the cold marble floor echoed like the even beats of a fated metronome. The harsh crashing sound of the thick leather boot as it hit the stone floor with each step burst the silence like the volleys of pistol shots, matching my skipping heartbeats. The hall is empty, dark, and menacing.

Now another sound: a wheezing, grating rattle of respiration breaks the silence, a growl, as the fierce dog, frothing at the mouth with bared white teeth, strains against his chain in his frenzy to kill, pulling his master after him. The soldier and the dog are getting closer now, and I hold my breath. One can always fool a soldier, but there is no escape from the dog.

On each side of the long hall there are rows of doors. When I try them, they cannot be opened. They are carved out of stone. They are not really doors—they just look like doors. At the same time, they appear to be grey headstones.

The powerful dog's wheezing is now heavy as he pulls on the leash, saliva dripping and making a puddle. Two vicious beasts, on each end of the vinculum. Palpitation, cold, clammy sweat, dry mouth gasping for air. I am awake now.

The sky, like a stage setting, is halfway between black and a luminescent blue. It tints the buildings with a matching grey pallor and heralds the morning. The light consoles me. Another night has gone.

CHAPTER 8

Rhododactilos Eios

The red, fiery glow along the eastern horizon was shading off into an indigo blue sky. It heralded the arrival of daybreak. The crumbling walls, illuminated by the rose light, adopted the same blush. The stars were still faintly visible. At last, the evil night was past. The German tiger tank, which late last night was stationed a stone's throw away, was now gone. The orange flickers of artillery fire I had watched from behind the ruins of a wall continued to flare up at the edge of the horizon. But there appeared to be less small-arms fire.

In the half-light, I saw two figures walking down the street. I could not believe my eyes. A tall Hungarian officer was marching with raised arms in front of a child. A child? No, it was a tough Tartar soldier of small size in a Soviet military uniform, a quilted olive-green jacket and a fur-lined cap decorated with the red emblem of the hammer and sickle, earflaps hanging. He pointed a peculiar-looking submachine gun with some sort of round drum attached to it and was shouting incessantly in a foreign language, presumably cursing with the tidal fluency of an expert.

Was that it? Was I free? Or was I delirious? Hurray! I wanted to call Lici immediately and show her the miracle. But before I could turn around, a twin brother of the Tartar, or so he appeared, with an identical gun, stood beside me. He pushed the gun into my ribs and shouted, "*Davay, chasee!*"

I had no idea what he wanted, but he made sure that the linguistic difficulties were promptly solved as he looked for watches on my wrists. He himself had four of them, one above the other, fastened to his lower arm. He was in pursuit of a fifth one. So that is what he was saying in soldier-Russian: "Give watch!" By then I did not have a watch, and the Tartar soldier consequently lost interest in me. And why not? Civilian. No watch, no ring. No gun. Seems to be a proletarian. He went on his way to do some more liberating.

I ran to find Lici. We felt the urge to move away quickly from what we thought were the German lines, because it quite often happened that a certain territory repeatedly changed hands. The last thing we wanted was to be "liberated" from under the Russians by the Germans!

It took less than two minutes to get ready. Cautiously we moved towards the opera house. By then, the street was swarming with Soviet soldiers. We looked at our liberators with admiration. They seemed indifferent as they milled about. I spotted a soldier, grinning and quite drunk, with a basketful of liqueur bottles on his arm. He stopped in front of me, patted my shoulder, and gave me a bottle. "*Bratj, charashow*," he said. Then he was gone. I, the *bratj charashow*—good friend—stood there with my mouth open in the January cold and whistling wind, unshaven with a bristly beard, a rope holding the remnants of my winter coat closed at the waist, shoeless in the snow, without any worldly possessions, holding a bottle of expensive French champagne in my hand. Behind the opera house. I could not grasp what was happening, but surely this must have been the most stylish way to be freed!

Less than a minute later, an angry Soviet soldier with a revolver in his hand cursed me (*Tji, Vengerski bandjit*) and grabbed the champagne out of my hand. It was a surrealistic experience. But the liberation was a miraculous joy, a flurry of delight. What did I feel? I cannot quite put it into appropriate words, but the one thought I definitely recall was this: Endless numbers of people had died, but whoever was alive in that moment would live forever. We were liberated from death itself. How on earth could I describe the sensation I felt? I certainly had no words that could even begin to express that feeling! It was as if my life had begun again after a vicious, bad dream. It was strange to be reborn with the mind of an adult. For a moment, I did not know what was the dream and what was reality. Later in my life, I always associated the moment of liberation with the melody of the *New World Symphony*—the drums imitating the bombardment and the main motif expressing the hope.

What now? Instinctively we began to walk towards No. 1 Jokai Street, where the family had last been together. By telepathy or by common sense, every one of us, at that point scattered all over the city, seemed to think the same way. And that is where the marvel, the cherished reunion, took place. My parents were well, and so was Marta. To our amazement and delight, Jan also had survived but he was stunned, clearly still in shock. "Jan is alive, but unfortunately he has lost his mind," was Father's instant diagnosis. Lici's brother also surfaced from somewhere in the ghetto, emaciated, which made his huge nose incongruously bigger still, but he was alive. Our immediate family was one of the very rare ones in which both parents and children survived. Lici was not so lucky.

Surely the innumerable tragedies were now bitter, torturing memories. Yes, I felt guilty about being happy, but I could not help it. The impact of depression was still to come . . . I had to think of Robert Markovits and recall the thirteen-year-old boy one floor above us on Jokai Street who once, when asking for guidance, confessed his guilt about his awakening sexuality. He, too, was killed. And Zsuzsika!

A grieving Masha turned up on Jokai Street, her blonde hair more uncombed than ever. Her eyes were red from crying, her cheeks streaked with tears. She had looked for her mother earlier. Now she came to find out how the tragedy had happened. Despite her pitiable condition, in a dress with the strap slipping down her arm and a loose shawl not quite covering her shoulder, Masha still retained a glimmer of her past, magnetic loveliness.

"How did you survive?" she asked me.

"I was hiding."

"Why could you not—" She never finished the sentence.

In the basement, we found some canned food, some pasta, and jam, all left behind by the gendarmes who were supposed, but failed, to defend that Swedish embassy and who, after changing to civilian clothes, had cleared out in a hurry. We appropriated these few treasures and began boiling the pasta and pouring the jam over it. Everyone was ravenously hungry but we could not eat much, except George, Lici's brother, who then became miserably ill and ended up with less in his system than he had had before the meal.

We decided to go back to the "designated house" to find out if any of our property was left. The city was a sight to behold. As I crossed the place that used to be called Mussolini Square, I saw a small pile of corpses with yellow stars on their jackets. There was a broken shop window, and in it lay the body of a huge dead *Wehrmacht* soldier, still gripping his submachine gun—a macabre, bloody sight. The gory display in the shop window seemed to be masquerading as a public pronouncement gazetted by some pacifist group advertising the absurdity of war.

All along the boulevards, houses had collapsed onto the street, blocking all traffic. All wires were down. Abandoned German military vehicles were everywhere. Soviet soldiers collected the bodies of their fallen comrades. Civilians looked for food or looted stores. Soviet tanks rolled by, spreading acrid smoke. More soldiers passed, on foot, in trucks, even in horse-drawn carriages. Hungarian soldiers with their arms held over their heads stood beside a pile of rifles, surrounded by Soviet soldiers. More dead bodies of German soldiers were arranged in a straight, almost military manner. Soviet trucks stopped at every corner, and soldiers shovelled down a small pile of dried peas or beans for the starving population. People ran over and filled their pockets, like so many sparrows.

We looked at our former apartment in the "designated house." The yellow star from over the entrance was gone by now. Surely, there must be something left from our original property? I found Mother's precious, carved china cabinet, but she acknowledged the discovery with only a passing interest. She no longer cared about the kind of future she had once planned for. My heart ached for her. The windows were broken in the cold apartment and the place was dirty. Some streetwalkers had lived there after we abandoned the place.

It was January 18, 1945. The fights were over in Pest, but Buda still held out and the Nazis still murdered Jews on Buda's side of the Danube until well into February.

We tried to locate our friends and relatives who had survived. Albin, the owner of the cogwheel factory, came back from the jail where he had been kept as a hostage. He did not know anything about his family. I found a bakery and succeeded in buying four rolls. On the way home, I saw many stores that had been broken into and looted, including a bookstore, with all the fine volumes lying in the mud in front of the store.

Nobody was interested in books, except the Russian soldiers. Bibles. They said that the pages of these Bibles were excellent for rolling cigarettes. *Papirossi*, they called these dubious cigarettes. By then, the Soviet soldiers needed manpower for two purposes. One was physical work, such as clearing rubble to open the roads for traffic. The other was that they needed a certain number of prisoners of war because they had killed too many German soldiers whose numbers had to be replaced to match the Red Cross figures. It did not matter who these captives were. Only the number counted. So the civilian "fashion" abruptly changed. Men walked with an arm in a sling or limped using a cane as if they were invalids. Women wore kerchiefs on their heads and made themselves look ugly and old because of the large number of rapes by the Soviet soldiers. After one week, everyone spoke a kind of soldier-Russian. You needed only 150 to 200 words to communicate fluently. Small groups of "greenhats," the NKVD soldiers, lingered on street corners, and a typical conversation went like this:

"Tyee, Vengerski Bandjit! Igji sudah! Davay documents." ("Hungarian bandit! Come here! Give papers!")

"Document nye charashow. Malinki robotji." ("Document no good. Go, work a little.")

The *malinki robitji* (little work) was either just that or turned out to be some years in a Siberian *gulag*. One never knew for sure. So everyone had an excuse prepared in case one was caught. *"Tovarish, Ja bratj."* (Comrade, I am friend.") "*Ja wratch.*" ("I am a doctor.") The Swedish Defense Passport sometimes helped ("*Ja Swedsky*"). A less fortunate excuse was to refer to one's persecuted race: "*Ja Jewrey*" ("I am a Jew"). Sometimes it earned a pat on the shoulder or even a piece of bread; other times there would be angry outbursts of "*Tjee Zsid!*" ("You Kike!"). Sometimes it was even worse—a friend of mine was shot in the arm by a Ukrainian soldier.

On one occasion, I was snatched by the greenhats and no excuse helped. But instead of work, I was taken to the inner courtyard of a bombed-out building where there was already quite a large crowd of Hungarian men. I instantly knew what it meant. This was a Siberian transport! A sentry walked up and down at the front wall, which was in ruins, with large boulders and bricks thrown about. Suddenly, I observed a man who had also been caught. He walked up to the sentry, pulled out a bottle of something—presumably liquor—from his coat. The sentry took the bottle and motioned to the man: "*Pashli*" ("Go").

The sentry hid the bottle among the bricks and went back to his post. Of course, by then I had been thoroughly trained in such worldly affairs. So naturally I stole the bottle, walked up to the soldier and gave him the same bottle. He took it. "*Pashli*," he said, and I ran.

There was a second, even more serious encounter, when I could not run away from a Siberian transport. They took me to a railway station with a group of other unfortunate people. I saw a Russian officer passing by with kinky red hair who looked like "one of us" (*unser einz*). I tugged his coat and murmured in Yiddish, "*Redst Du Yiddish?*"

"*Seit Ihr a Jid?*" ("Are you a Jew?") he asked.

"*Emes*" ("naturally").

I was lucky. He took me to the gate. "*Pashli.*"

Soon after, I was again caught for *malinki robotji*. It was indeed a "little work." The soldier had me carry a suitcase for a couple of miles. I do not know what was in the suitcase—probably lead. It must have been lead.

Davay, meaning "give," was the second most common expression in soldier-Russian. Since this was usually accompanied by a nudge of their peculiar-looking submachine gun with a big round drum near the trigger, the enduring humour of Budapest immediately baptized this gun as *Davay Guitar*. The most common Soviet phrase was a curse word, which served all purposes and readily replaced all other phrases, not unlike the convenient word "thing," essential to overcoming every possible language difficulty. But quoting this phrase, which in a literal translation conveyed a strongly implied hint to perform a distinctly incestuous act, would certainly be impolite to say the least.

Soviet troops were marching all over, and the city resounded with their military songs, like the *Katusa* or *Djevuske* or partisan songs. The very sad news was that Wallenberg, according to rumours, had been killed by the Germans at the last minute. This assumption was corrected the next day with the news that it was the Soviets who had arrested him. Why? We could not understand it. Wallenberg seemed to have had a plan to keep the survivors together. But surely this cannot have been the reason! At any rate, he was a diplomat and would be free in a couple of days. This was our first reaction to the incredible news of Wallenberg's disappearance.

Jan became ill with flu or something. Somehow a Soviet soldier, a Jew, became friendly with Jan. The soldier decided to look after Jan and brought him food. But Jan could not eat much. After months of starvation, he was satisfied with only a few bites. But the soldier was not. He became angry, pulled his revolver, pointed it at Jan, and shouted: "*Kushai!*" (Eat!")

There was no further argument. The finicky Jan was fed and that was that. (This was the last time anybody got his way with my brother-in-law's fussy eating habits, but this successful approach, still tempting to us at times, was remarkably effective indeed. However, times have changed.) This childish, incalculable emotionalism was characteristic of many of the Russian soldiers who liberated Budapest. Sometimes they robbed you, taking not only your watch but also your clothes. They pointed a gun at you and ordered you to undress in the middle of the street in the dead of winter. Then they sold the clothing in the emerging street trade. There was also indiscriminate rape. At other times, they gave you gifts for no reason. In retrospect, I would describe many of them as "limbic," after the limbic system of the brain: in that anatomical location, raw emotions are generated and influence behaviour.

There were many Soviet women (*barishnas*) to be seen as well, usually hard-working female soldiers, whom we scrutinized with singular curiosity. Clearly, their uniforms had not been designed with fashion in mind. Their army-issue brassieres pushed their round breasts up so high that the great globes seemed to rest on a presentation cushion right under their chins.

The nearly dead city slowly began to come to life. Small tables appeared on the street, each with a chair. On the table stood a small scale and forceps. People came. They gave the merchant a gold chain that he examined carefully. Then he chipped off a small part of the gold item, weighed it, and paid for it in Hungarian currency. Since the money was devalued each day, it made no sense to sell the whole piece of gold, for the next day the money was already worthless. Black marketers began to appear and were selling dubious items reminiscent of food for Hungarian currency.

Soon I heard a rumour that the university in the city of Szeged, which had earlier fallen to the Soviet forces, was already open. Something stirred in us. Can it be? Let's go!

Memorial plaque at 1 Jokai Street, Budapest:
"Dragged away by the Hungarian Nazis and murdered
between January 7 - 17, 1945 -
for the memory of Swedish Embassy clerks and their relatives."
According to the Communist omerta it was not allowed to be said
that they were Jews and that they were killed for that reason alone.
When the plaque was mounted, Wallenberg was sitting
in a Soviet prison.

Dreams and Tears: VII

Experiment and Lost Love

"Prophet!" said I, "thing of evil!—prophet still, if bird or devil!
By the Heaven that bends above us—by that God we both adore—
Tell this souls with sorrow laden if, within the distant Aidenn,
It shall clasp a sainted maiden whom the angels name Lenore."
Quoth the Raven, "Nevermore."

From Edgar Allan Poe, *The Raven*

We instantly became friends with that middle-aged family physician, George, who had come back from Auschwitz in the early summer of 1945. He had a sharp and inquisitive mind, and beneath the veils of depression, the faint ember of a past sense of humour still lingered. But he had lost his beloved wife and young daughter and ultimately could not be consoled. The story of his survival is a remarkable study of the human mind in peril.

In June 1944, George was taken to Auschwitz from his small Hungarian town of Pecs, where he served the community as a family physician. He could not even say good-bye to his wife when he was separated from his family. They soon disappeared in the camp forever.

He was strip-searched, tattooed with a number, given a pair of striped pants and a shirt, and transferred to a small camp for slave labour. His first response was a paralyzing fear. But he settled down and invented a game for diversion and self-preservation. "I am here only as an observer," he deceived himself. "It is not really happening to me and to my family." With half his mind he even believed this naïve pretense. In a strange, Bergsonian way, he actually placed himself "outside of himself."

He did not know that this particular way of coping with extraordinary trauma is not so rare. In fact, Bruno Bettelheim writes about it in his book, *The Informed Heart*, and I myself encountered several others who dealt with catastrophe in a similar way. These included my teacher, Dr. Albert Kral, who submitted his first post-war scientific publication three days after he was liberated from Theresienstadt. (It was entitled, *On an unusual type of epidemic encephalitis in the concentration camp Theresienstadt*.)

But, George thought, an observer must observe something; he must have a project. In that phase of his incarceration as a slave labourer building roads, he was dragged from one little camp to the next, an experience he was forced to endure passively. With each change, the SS guards took away everything from everybody and doled out a shirt and a pair of pants. George became interested that even though an "equal chance" was given to everyone with each transfer, soon "capitalist" and "proletarian" social classes emerged spontaneously in the camp.

Of course, the concept of a capitalist differed vastly from our idea of riches. If you had an extra loaf of bread, a piece of soap, a knife, or a cord, you were a capitalist. But the *principle* of capitalism was the same. For two tablets of aspirin, you could buy a rearrangement of the work schedule or send someone else in your place to do the heavy physical labour. Not only that, the very same people always became the capitalists, no matter how many "equal starts" they went through. When George asked, they also turned out to have been capitalists in their pre-war existence. George found a few former capitalists among the "proletarian" population, but they were either seriously ill and physically handicapped or else they had inherited, rather than acquired, their previous wealth.

As time passed, George lost interest in his own game and carried out his daily physical labour like an automaton. This was a much more common and effective defense mechanism. He taught himself not to think and not to feel. Close to the end of the war, every morning the work brigade passed through some small Polish village in the middle of nowhere. One morning, as they proceeded down the muddy main street, a half-crazed Polish woman ran in front of them.

"Help! Help!" the woman shouted in bad German. "My daughter is dying!"

For the first time since he was in the camp, George thought of himself as a physician. He turned to the SS guard. "I am a physician," George said. "If you want, I can try to help."

The SS soldier assigned him to another guard, and George and the new guard entered the farmer's home. They found the little daughter of the peasant woman lying in her bed, choking and holding her throat, with horror and misery in her wide and teary eyes. Her face was blue and her breathing strident. Her respiratory distress was evident and so was the easy solution. She had diphtheria.

George asked for a knife, found some kind of a tube, and performed a tracheotomy on the girl. After a few painful moments, the little patient immediately felt better and breathed freely through the tube. The emergency had passed. George instructed the woman to fetch help and then returned to the road-building brigade.

When the work brigade passed through the same village again at the crack of dawn the next morning, the Polish mother was waiting for them. She asked the guard to let the doctor see her daughter again. George entered the house with an escort. The little girl was better, and was already attended by the local physician. She was waiting for admission to the distant hospital that afternoon.

George was about to turn around when the woman took hold of his hand and dragged him into the next room. A feast was displayed on the table— cream in a crystal bowl, cutlery, steaming coffee, eggs, fresh rolls, and the like. The woman made George sit down at the table. But something snapped. George, who had witnessed murder, rape, killing, whipping, and hanging, was utterly impervious to human cruelty. Nothing could penetrate his thick armour of automaton-like behaviour. But he was not equipped mentally to defend himself against kindness. This was the Achilles heel. He was suddenly defenseless. For the first time he had left home, he was supposed to sit at a table and eat. His past life came alive, welled over, and hastened a blow for which he was unprepared. His home, his wife, his daughter all entered his mind. He could not eat but burst out crying. And crying. And crying.

And crying was dangerous. Depression was dangerous. In the camp, people died of depression. They just could not survive. He went back to his brigade and his comrades covered up for him when they returned to the main camp in the evening. It was George's luck that the Russian troops entered the camp a few days later. He was liberated.

But was he, indeed? Could he ever be liberated? George knew the answer to this question. Not long after George told us his story, he committed suicide. We understood him. Carl Menninger draws a difference between two kinds of suicide. One kind is characterized by the will to kill. Such a person is a frustrated murderer who kills himself, though he does not wish to die, only to kill, and the act of fury motivates him to kill himself. The other type yearns to die because he can no longer bear any more suffering; or he hopes to reunite with a loved one.

C H A P T E R   9

A Long and Bumpy Road

On a melancholy, wintry day in later January 1945, Lici and I began marching on the road leading out of Budapest to the highway. Our goal was to reach Szeged, the second-largest city in the country, about 200 miles southeast. On foot. There, according to the rumour, the university had already reopened. The city had been taken by the Soviet military some time before Pest fell. Based on such flimsy hearsay, we launched into our pilgrimage with a firm belief in the future. If life for us up to then had been a series of wonders, why not one more miracle?

We said a painful good-bye to my parents and Marta and Jan, and we were on our way. The damp, dull day wrapped around us as we journeyed along the windy highway. The pavement was unsightly, with dirty ice patches frozen on its lacerated surface. The road curved and bent towards the far edge of the nebulous horizon and beyond. We both were in a debilitated physical shape, feeble from massive weight loss; and Lici was pregnant. But driven by a rekindled energy and determination that only quixotic visions or unfathomable foolishness can create, we ploughed along the road, step after weary step. I carried all our worldly possessions in a rucksack on my back. From now on, we thought, every step would take us closer to the realization of our goal. We would make up for the lost years.

Soon it seemed to us that we had already walked countless miles, but in fact we made only slow progress in the beginning. We reached the suburb of Kispest and made a stop at the home of Father's former foreman, who was happy to hear of our survival. After a cup of coffee, we were gone.

On the open highway, we met a rotund, jolly character, a Jewish lawyer with a flushed face and gushing banter. He, too, was on his way somewhere, so we walked together. From time to time, Russian convoys passed us. Bursts of distant artillery fire were promptly followed by the furious barking of startled farm dogs, reminding us that the front line was still nearby. We walked all day, leaving behind villages and small settlements. The rumbling of the blasts slowly died away and no more angry, billowing smoke columns, signposts of gunnery ordeals, could be seen on the horizon. Here and there, the ditches along the highway were filled with burnt-out military equipment, incinerated shells of German *Kübelwagen*, live ammunition, and discarded Hungarian military uniforms that were frozen stiff and crackled like glass when stepped on. We had some money, but no food was available. We had long ago eaten the few sandwiches we had packed for the journey.

Somewhere along the way, a patrol of Soviet military police, the greenhats, picked us up. We were taken to a building that was obviously their temporary headquarters. They collected our personal data, reassuring us that they would "check it." At the very best, it would take a few months, we thought bitterly. But they were back in a couple of hours. And they indeed knew about us, perhaps because of our involvement in the underground movement. That was when the efficiency of the Soviet information system frightened me for the first time.

With aching, burning feet and sore muscles we resumed our trek. Night fell and the curfew was in force. In the nearest settlement, we got permission to spend the night on some fresh straw in a barn. And we had a feast. We divided into three equal pieces the last piece of bread that we had gotten from the Russian soldiers, and our lawyer friend had a few cubes of sugar. We each had two pieces. I wanted to give half of my share to Lici, but she would not take it.

Early in the morning, we were marching again. The first few steps caused agonizing pain in our stiff muscles. It was as if our legs were broken. They seemed to improve as we ignored our torment. We walked and walked all day in a drizzling rain, buffeted by a cold wind. By then, our progress was slower and our feet became more tender. I was worried about Lici, particularly because of her pregnancy. A wretched mood fell over us. Maybe the entire venture was futile. Maybe all this effort was in vain. Was our information reliable? Surely we must be fools! We began to feel irritated with each other.

Evening approached. We passed through a village and asked in numerous places for somewhere to stay overnight, but this was denied us, even for payment. Was it because they were afraid of us, or because they guessed that we were Jews? A Soviet soldier held us up because the curfew hour had passed. The soldier spoke some German, and we explained that we were Jewish survivors from Budapest. He took us to a home in the village, a place where they had already turned us down, and ordered the owner to make a bed for us in the living room, near the fire. He forbade us to give any money to the peasant family. We slept all night without stirring, and in the morning we did give some money to the Hungarians. In exchange, the farmer provided us with a ride on his horse cart, taking us four or five miles down the road. Then, once again we were trudging on foot.

Lici could barely take it. At one desperate point, I tried to carry her on my shoulders, but with the additional weight of the rucksack, I was not able to do it for long. And she did not co-operate at all. My raw skin rubbed against my shoes, sending a pinching pain and shooting anguish with each step. We rested and tried to walk again. And slowly, the hazy outline of a city became silhouetted on the horizon. It was Kecskemet, a small town approximately halfway to our goal. From that first foggy sighting, it took us almost the entire day to reach the town.

But it was worth it! When we explained that we were Jews from Budapest, we were directed to a building with signs in English: "American Joint Distribution Committee." We had never before heard of such an organization, but any puzzlement was rapidly dissipated by the aroma that came from inside. It was cooked food, the best kind, reminding me of Yom Kippur evenings at my grandparents' home. The rich meal was waiting to be served as the evening star slowly rose to signal the end of the fast. As in a dream, we were ushered into a room where dish after dish was served to us, starting with soup, then bread and meat. We did not even ask who would pay for it, and surely it had to exceed by far our collective means. We could not understand that they did not want any payment. Why?

A few other people, returning from different concentration camps, were around. Surprisingly, these returnees did not ask any questions and rarely spoke at all. Some of them just stared into space with motionless features, pointy noses, and yellow, shiny parchment for skin covering their hollow faces.

We found that actually we could not eat very much. This was the first complete meal we had had for many months.

That same night, a train was to depart for Szeged. We rushed to the railway station and found a place in a cattle car. But the train would not go. A rumour spread that the Russians had detached the locomotive, as they needed it for more important purposes. But we could not leave the train because of the curfew; we had to wait until morning. And then, in the darkness of the crowded wagon, the wheels of association began to turn around in my mind. Cattle train. Armed guard. Auschwitz. A heavy feeling came over me and I thought of my family who had disappeared like that. No. Not now. I tried to think of something else.

In the morning, we went back to the "American Joint" and had a rich breakfast. Again, without any payment. Who was paying for it? But then we had to rush, as the train ride was on once again. In a cold, windowless cattle car we made the rest of the trip.

* * *

Arriving in a totally strange city is always a disquieting, as well as challenging, experience. But at that time we were not yet used to the speedy assimilation demanded by an unfamiliar environment. Out of necessity and with the practice acquired during our wandering years, the act of fitting into a new milieu eventually became routine.

It was just after daybreak when we left the train in Szeged. Fine snow dusted the cobblestones and soon melted. We walked downtown and asked for directions to the university. Unlike Budapest, the city was well preserved. No signs of destruction could be seen because the city had given up without a fight. Russian soldiers walked the streets, some of them, surprisingly, in pyjamas. Then we learned that there was a huge Soviet military hospital in Szeged.

At last, the administration building of the university—or the *Questura*, as we used to call it—was in front of us. It was still too early to enter. A dimly lit, small cafeteria was already open around the corner, and we ordered some ersatz coffee with cake made of bread and molasses.

And waited. Why not? We had waited for years. Lici looked very sad. Her family was on her mind. She still hoped that somebody might have survived. Surely, Lici hoped, her sister Ibi, who was young and strong, must have survived. We all slowly learned how to drive out or put off "for now" these spasms of tormenting thoughts.

Slowly, there was more life on the streets. The surface of the pavement seemed to have been varnished to a shiny reflection by the steady, slow drizzle. Students began to replace the labourers in the café. Everyone ordered the same thing because there was nothing else to be had, and it was useless to complain about the taste of the cake or coffee. Actually, they both tasted the same, but one was more watery than the other. Finally, the time came for us to go to the *Questura*.

With years of frustration and rejections behind us, we trembled as we awaited our turn. Suddenly, the door opened and a soldier walked in. Not an everyday kind of soldier but one of Tito's partisans. He had a Soviet-style military cap with the hammer and sickle and partly civilian dress, with the remnants of a huge, frayed, yellow star painted in his coat still showing on the front and back. His automatic gun hung from his shoulder. He confidently pushed in front of us and registered himself in the medical faculty. He was George Bleier, who later became a good friend.

His confidence encouraged us. We made our enquiries, then we laid out all our documents in front of the questor, including the typed sheets stating our participation and examinations in different courses. He credited us with one semester of studies provided we were willing to rewrite the examinations. So we did get something from our previous studies after all. Half a year. He stamped the student booklet. I looked at it. The date was February 6, 1945. One of our professors was Dr. Albert Szent-Gyorgyi!

By eleven o'clock, we were out of the *Questura*. Our next task was to rent a room. In the student lounge, handwritten advertisements pinned to the wall offered accommodation for students. We chose one, but by the time we found the place it was late afternoon. We took the room. Finally, we felt at home. To the disapproval of the landlady, we took a warm bath and thoroughly enjoyed ourselves. Also to the chagrin of the same lady, we put all the available wood into the stove in our room.

We learned that the landlady lived alone in the large apartment because her son and his family had run away to the "West." When she described her son's history, it became evident that he must have been a prominent member of the Arrowcross Party. Apparently he did not wish to be "liberated" by the Soviet troops. The landlady was not at all pleased that we were Jews from Budapest.

The next day, we met George Bleier at the university. He had originally lived in Szeged but had done forced labour in the mines of Bor, Yugoslavia. This place was notorious for its harsh conditions and the eventual mass murder committed by the Hungarian and German military. Bleier had escaped to the nearby partisans and fought the Germans in the closing days of the war.

He was a great help to us. He soon found out that the medical students could get lunch for a pittance at the Gynaecology Clinic. Indeed, when we went there that same day, there was already a lineup. In front of us were George and Eva Klein, who were both medical students (and now are world-famous cancer researchers at the Karolinska Institute). Eva was chatty. George, according to his principle of utilizing time to the utmost, was reading an article. From his shoulder hung a sack full of journals, articles, and notes, which he made use of until the moment that the plateful of split peas was served. There were only two kinds of food, and the other was baked beans. These two items on the menu alternated with predictable reliability for the rest of our stay. Eating was not a pleasure but a biological necessity and a duty harnessed to achieve our ultimate goal.

In the afternoon, we explored the city and entered a more or less acceptable coffee house. Coffee houses were still in vogue in both Austria and Hungary.

These were large establishments, much larger than the usual restaurants. Most were decorated in the Victorian style, with solid marble tables. All the daily newspapers and magazines were available. Customers were expected to stay for hours, and many had reserved tables. Most coffee houses catered to a specific public. There were coffee houses where physicians gathered; others were watering holes for lawyers or journalists; still others were patronized by writers or students. The waiters were tipped well but usually did not serve much other than coffee and many glasses of ice water. It is a veritable puzzle how these establishments stayed in business over the years.

As we entered the coffee house, we saw a serious-looking young man with dark, curly hair and rimless glasses. I vaguely recognized him. He was the intense young "physician" from the forced labour troop whom I had seen once during an air raid in Budapest. He, too, now studied medicine in Szeged. His name was Thomas Detre.

Compared to us, he was well dressed, in a dark three-piece suit. He must have been wealthy, for he smoked ready-made cigarettes instead of the self-rolled variety to which we were accustomed in those needy days. We soon got to know him. His face was pale, his cheeks were hollow, and his eyes were very dark and alive, with a quick, penetrating sparkle. He was from the small city of Kecskemet, where we had been the guests of the American Joint Distribution Committee. Tom had lived in Budapest until he had had to go and do forced labour. His father had been a physician in his home town, and both his parents had been taken to Auschwitz. Like most of us, Tom still hoped they would return. They did not. Years later, and by sheer accident, I learned about the fate of Thomas's parents. But that is another story.

Tom was very bright, a fast thinker, cynical, and often sarcastic to the point of hostility, but he had a fabulous sense of humour. In the beginning, we could not decide whether his tongue or his mind was his sharpest tool. He loved to play the devil's advocate and could successfully attack or defend every point of view. His interest was psychiatry.

* * *

Sometimes an insignificant incident helps us to readjust our perspectives. Something of the sort happened to me in Szeged. To my horror, I realized one day that I had lice. It was far from being a rarity in those days, and it was no use asking where one had acquired it. But there was a deadly typhus epidemic throughout the entire middle and eastern Europe that was killing thousands of people, particularly in the army and in forced labour and concentration camps. Sometimes this illness hit people with an astonishing suddenness. It is caused by *rickettsiae* transmitted by lice. Clearly, I needed immediate delousing.

The institute set up for that purpose was housed in a city bath and accommodated both men and women. When I entered it, I also realized that the customers of different sexes were not separated in those confused and adventurous days—at least not in the hallway. I stepped into a long hall where a line of men and women was waiting to enter different cubicles for the crucial moment of shaving off genital hair. The first in line was a woman whose face was vaguely familiar. Then, in a daze, almost as a reflex, I sort of recognized her, and the words slipped from my mouth before I had a chance to stop myself: "Good day, Ladyship!" (in Hungarian, "*kegyelmes asszony*")

She was the wife of a high-ranking government official whom we used to meet years ago in the Palatinus Hotel. Everyone stared at me. I "woke up" only to realize that we were living in an entirely brand-new world.

* * *

Lici and I suffered from the rampant Ukrainian Fever, a vicious and debilitating diarrhea that drained our energies. But we passed the required examinations with flying colours. We had taken our studies very seriously and worked late hours in the Anatomy Institute.

In those days, only one-half of the institute belonged to the university; the other half served as a laboratory for the Soviet Military Hospital. Every night, Lici and I picked up two logs from a pile of wood that belonged to the Russians. One day, we were caught by one of the Russian soldiers, a colonel who was the head of the Soviet laboratory. When we thieves told him that we were medical students, perhaps an empathetic memory stirred in him, recalling some long-ago freezing Moscow winters and student poverty. He, too, picked up some logs and accompanied us home, where the cheerful fire soon spread a welcoming heat.

We spoke in German. He was from Moscow and he told us about life in that city. He loved Moscow and he loved the concerts, which he missed. He was less enthusiastic about the Communist political system. He would rather talk about books and music. He became our occasional guest.

As time passed, Lici's mood blackened. Her hope that some of her family had survived diminished with each passing day. She began to feel depressed. Often when I woke up early in the morning, she was already up with the books in front of her. When did she sleep? She did not. Her cheeks were hollow. There were dark circles under her eyes and she looked sad. She barely reacted to any gentle embrace or attempt at consolation.

I realized that something had begun to separate us, and it was not within my power to stop this trend. It was not a lack of love but our differing karmas. My parents and sister had survived; Lici's had not. Perhaps at that time I was not sensitive enough to her mourning. I felt guilty. I loved her with all my heart, but she could not help the change within herself. As the distance between us began to grow, I, too, experienced a heaviness. Other than the work, in which I was completely immersed, nothing interested me. I felt the futility of life. I became irritable, and soon I, too, awakened with Lici in the wee hours, after a restless sleep and frequent nightmares.

I always bought some extra food for Lici and continued to worry about her. I divided our food so that she should have more. One day, I bought a piece of cheese somewhere. I insisted that she have the larger portion because she was pregnant. She balked. We had a quarrel, and immature as I had become over the matter, I threw the cheese on the floor. We went to bed angry, but in the darkness we both seemed to have the same thought: What if a mouse got the cheese before we made a truce? We put on the light, washed off the cheese, and divided it equally, as she had wanted. We made up.

* * *

One anxiety-filled night, Lici began to bleed. She was in the fifth month of her pregnancy. I took her to the hospital immediately, and she was admitted. The next day, I met our Russian friend and told him that I wanted to buy something nourishing for Lici, something she liked—chocolate, maybe. This, of course, could only be obtained on the black market. I sold one of our books and added the money to our savings, so I had enough. Our friend the Soviet colonel came along, and when he caught the black marketeer cheating with the scale, the Russian pulled out his gun and put it on the weight side of the scale. *Vae victis.* Like Brennus, the Gaul, in 390 B.C. to the Romans. Warriors never change. The black marketer was forced to match the weight of the gun with chocolate, and I could not argue with that insistent, romantic Russian man. I gained more insight into his soul by Tacitus than by Solovjev's (apocryphal) "Quiet Don."

But the chocolate did not help. Lici miscarried. I tried to console her but her mood remained low. She kept her spirits up by immersing herself in her studies.

* * *

One night, I woke up suddenly. I felt I could not breathe, but in fact I was breathing at a fast, too-rapid rate and with deep inspirations. My body was covered with clammy sweat and my heart pounded. I felt the pulsation in my chest, head, and ears. I was numb. I had to jump out of bed. I was unable to make a diagnosis, but I knew that it was some kind of emergency. It was like an impending doom. The hospital was not far, so I ran there despite the curfew. I thought that I must be having an asthma attack. They gave me a camphor injection and I went home. By then, I was well.

My sister, Marta, and Jan Sebor got married in Budapest in a simple ceremony. I was very happy for them, knowing how much Marta had hoped for that day. But Jan still needed time to heal.

This was the time when the German defense collapsed and Hitler committed suicide in Berlin. But for us this historic event was somehow anticlimactic. This was also the time when some concentration camp survivors from the western part of Germany began to return. The world's Jewish communities paid the costs of listing the names of those Jews found alive in different concentration camps. Notices hung on the walls of public places like translucent hands gesturing in the wind: "Come, we have something to tell you." We studied them eagerly every day as they were updated. Each day, a new list was posted, and new hopes rose and fell. Then the lists stopped growing.

Lici could not wait for the end of the academic year in July. She wanted to go to Kormend, her native town, in case a miracle had happened and some of her loved ones had returned. Travelling was adventurous in those days. One night, we sat in a dark cattle car filled with Hungarian peasants returning from the city market. No one knew when the train would leave. Then, suddenly, another attack of palpitations, choking, gasping, and cold sweat assailed me. We had to leave the train. But the bizarre attack soon settled, and next day we were sitting in a similar train, waiting and waiting. Finally, after much frustration, we arrived in Kormend.

Here, our mood reached another low point. I had never been there before, but poor Lici had grown up in this place, knowing each stone and tree. Her will to live crumbled under the sheer weight of her memories. By then, Lici knew the tragic fate of her family. Her sister Ibi was last seen in a concentration camp near the Baltic Sea, probably Stutthof, where she died just before the liberation. Lici's father, although very sick with dysentery and by then a walking skeleton—*Musulman*, they used to call it in the lingo of the concentration camps—actually had survived and was liberated in Bergen Belsen. But the very next day, he succumbed to his desperate state. There was never any news of Lici's mother, Cecil, who probably was killed soon after her arrival at Auschwitz. Lici's best friend, Vera, also died in the first days of her captivity in Auschwitz. She was myopic and wore glasses. People who wore glasses were automatically sent to be gassed.

Of the once-flowering little Jewish community of Kormend, totalling perhaps 300 Jewish people, only Lici, her brother George, and the three Martin boys survived.

The devastation of the Jewish community in a small town like Kormend, where everyone knew one another by their first names, was even more stunning, more personal, than the huge statistical figures pertinent to Budapest. We walked the streets of Kormend, and Lici was overtaken by her memories as she often stopped and recalled yet another family or friend who had perished. A small group of gypsies recognized Lici, and they surrounded her with genuine warmth. These people also suffered under the Nazis. They were taken to concentration camps, where many of them were killed or died, although not systematically killed like the Jews.

There were three Hungarian families who hid some goods that belonged to Lici's parents. Two of these families were helpful and cheered Lici's arrival, but not the third one. The hardware store that had belonged to Lici's father, once richly stocked with merchandise, echoed with emptiness. Their beautiful home was occupied by the Soviet commandant. We slept in a nearby shack.

We both had trouble with our teeth. Our gums were swollen and bled when touched. The teeth were loose in their bedding. I lost a number of them. What was the cause? Poor nutrition?

I soon left Kormend. I left by myself to register both of us at the small university in Pecs, where the prices and living expenses were affordable. I also had to rent us a room and arranged to move.

This small city, bigger than Kormend, was an old university town. Its formerly lively Jewish population was now practically extinct. I rented a small but very friendly room, registered us at the university, and brought Lici to our new environment. But we soon discovered a Jewish student home that was actually a number of rented rooms in one building occupied by several Jewish students, and we felt more at home there. So we moved.

We all worked very hard. At the end of the second year, we were to write a series of difficult examinations, the first *rigorosum*. We also starved from time to time, although Mother found ways to send us food parcels. But our neighbour and fellow student Carl Roth, who had just returned from a concentration camp, literally had nothing to live on. Both his parents had been killed in the camp. He was too proud to accept any friendly help, so we used to pack a sandwich, put it on the floor, knock on the door, and run away.

In the humdrum rhythm of everyday life, we only had time for social activities with the other students in the building and with some of our professors, whom we greatly respected and liked. But one day, a Jewish Russian soldier, whom we called Sacha, came to our student home. Sacha needed to be among Jews, and there were not many left in the city. So Sacha, at his own insistence, became our daily guest. We conversed half in Yiddish, half in German. Sacha always arrived with some food and a bottle of *schnaps*. We ate, he drank, and we all sang Jewish songs.

"Kinder, erst bin Ich a Russ, dann bin Ich a Jid," he would say, warning us that he was a Russian first before he was a Jew. But it did not take much liquor and sweet Jewish melodies before Sacha was *schicker* (drunk) and jumped up, proclaiming with enthusiasm: *"Kinder, doch erst bin Ich a Jid, dann bin Ich a Russ!"*—first a Jew, then a Russian.

We all understood Sacha's natural craving for the company of Jews. We ourselves felt the most relaxed when we were with our own kind. This was very different from earlier times when we used to move unconcerned in the company of non-Jewish friends. The Hungarian Labour Government, although run by some Jews among others, was once again becoming more and more anti-Semitic. Even some Jews, like Dr. Laszlo Benedek, made vile anti-Zionist statements. Our hurt was far from cured, and even small events tore the wounds open again. Like the time I saw a Hungarian peasant woman in the market sitting behind her merchandise, with her shoulders covered sacrilegiously, but probably without knowing it, with a Jewish prayer shawl or *tallith*. Whatever happened to its owner?

One day we told Sacha our worry about Carl Roth, who would starve to death because of his pride. We wanted to take him to a decent restaurant and feed him.

"No problem," said Sacha. With that, he pulled out his revolver and got Carl at gunpoint. All of us marched to a nearby restaurant. Carl later became a well-recognized physician in Israel and until his dying day he remembered this incident.

Not everything was so amusing. Our respected friend, a professor, once invited us for dinner. He was the kind of man who had never been an anti-

Semite and who helped us when he could. After dinner was finished, we sat and chatted. He turned to me and said, "Tell me, Erwin. I know for a fact that when a Jewish boy reaches age thirteen, the rabbi tells him a secret. Whatever the secret is, it has never been revealed in history for 2,000 years. You and I are scientists. Purely from scientific interest, tell me, what is the secret?"

My mouth was open in astonishment. I told him that the idea was nonsense. He smiled knowingly and did not believe me. "What hope is there," I thought to myself, "if a well-meaning, cultured, and brilliant mind like that is infested with such deep-seated ignorance, with such superstitious fallacy? What hope is there for us?"

Since then, I have often wondered if it is possible that this well-informed man had somehow confused Judaism with the pre-Hellenic Minoan–Mycenian religions known as the Eleusinian or Orphic mysteries. In the Eleusinian religion, after purification and sacrifice, the hierophant "revealed a secret" to the initiated one.

This incident was even more difficult to take because this was 1946, well after the war, well after what the world had witnessed what had happened to the Jews of Europe. And once again, pogroms broke out. Again, Jews were murdered in Poland (Kielz) and in Hungary, their sin being that they had survived the concentration camps and returned home. There was no longer any excuse of "having been forced by the Germans." These pogroms took place after the war, after the Jews returned from the concentration camps. They were not on the same scale as under the Nazis. Between liberation and 1947, "only" 1,000 Jews were murdered in the post-war pogroms (1945–46), most by the Poles, some by the Hungarians.

These killings started a Zionist movement, the *Bricha*, to help Jews immigrate illegally to Palestine. The borders of the Western countries and Palestine were still closed to Jews. The Communists refused to issue exit permits and the West still denied immigration visas. Jews lingered, many of them for years, in demoralizing DP (Displaced Persons) camps, as they refused to return to their original Communist countries. In early 1945, when an anonymous senior Canadian official was asked how many Jews would be allowed into Canada, he answered, "None is too many." On the other hand, Nazis, including the murderous 14th Waffen SS, the Ukrainian Auxiliary Police, and some concentration camp guards, were permitted to enter Canada, where they lived out their lives unperturbed, some of them on generous German military pensions.

* * *

The sudden attacks of palpitations, shortness of breath, and cold sweats, along with the terrifying sensation of panic and impending catastrophe kept recurring in an irregular and unpredictable fashion. With all my other worries, it made my life so much more difficult. And there were the nightmares again and again . . .

There was no further news of Wallenberg. By then we knew that he was in a Soviet prison, although the Kremlin kept denying it. And for what? There were rumours that he was accused of "spying." Spying for whom? Certainly that was sheer nonsense. What a shameless lie! Surely the Soviets must let him go, we believed, then we will know the truth. Who knows? Perhaps he was mistreated by the Soviets without their being aware of his identity, and consequently it was too embarrassing to let him go—so they had to kill him to hide their blunder? But surely the Swedish government would do something. Wallenberg had a powerful family in Sweden.

But there were other disquieting signs. The Communists were more and more openly anti-Semitic. Communist cabinet ministers came out with the statement that "not the Jews but the Hungarian proletariat had suffered" from the Nazis. In Budapest, Uncle Albin was arrested by the Communists. Alexander Ganz, an idealistic Communist whom we knew from the underground movement, suffered the same fate.

Spring was in the air, the weather was balmy, and we studied with the windows open. All of a sudden we heard noise and shouting. Three Hungarians were walking in the middle of the road, their gravelly voices like foghorns: "Jews to Auschwitz! Kill the Jews!"

In a second I was on the street. Without thinking, I attacked the three men. With martial fury, I hit and kicked them wherever I could. They put up some resistance, but it nearly crumbled against my paroxysm of rage that gave me a physical force far surpassing my usual strength. In no time, there was a crowd around us, and a policeman turned up. The fight stopped. Then the swarm of people began to shout, and I was attacked from all sides by the assembled group. The policeman stepped aside, and I got a thorough beating.

A few weeks later, we wrote our examinations in anatomy and physiology and returned to Budapest.

Dreams and Tears: VIII

Chronos

The clock! a sinister, impassive god
Whose threatening finger says to us: "Remember"
Soon in your anguished heart, as in a target,
Quivering shafts of Grief will plant themselves

From C. Baudelaire, *The Clock*
Translated by James McGowan

I scrutinize the dissected remains of a watch and contemplate the delicate mechanism with its small rubies and back-and-forth swinging wheels, as the fine teeth of the cogwheels bravely chew away at never-ending Time. I let my thoughts run freely. Time—what an intriguing enigma! Science, of course, perpetually attempts to penetrate this riddle and has done so with remarkable success.

About 6,000 years ago, the Egyptians discovered the helical rising of Sirius and the Nile-year, the one that consists of 365 days. Scientific Time, Cosmic Time, what Spengler would probably call "Faustian Time," is eminently measurable. Time stretches between the Celestial Beginning and the Future of the Universe. The Euclidean space-time concept of Time as just another dimension had to be redesigned. Newton's "absolute time" had to be replaced with the paradigm of "imaginary time."

All these came about under the combined impact of the Second Law of Thermodynamics, the concept of entropy, Max Planck and Niels Bohr's quantum mechanics, Einstein's General Relativity Theory, Heisenberg's Uncertainty Principle, and Friedmann's portrayal of an expanding universe. The merging of these theories yielded a fascinating concept of Time whereby it may flow backwards as well as forwards, not unlike antimatter opposing matter. Just as well, since we travel so confidently from the Big Bang towards the Big Crunch. Was there such a thing as Time before the Big Bang?

Ultimately, black holes will swallow us all, and entire galaxies will turn matter into photons. But even more wicked possibilities can be imagined.

Events like a Big Crunch, heaven forbid, may set up yet another Blast, and then we are in for a sickening Second Ride, or for a dull, unsavoury second performance!

All these stunning and enormously respectable discoveries are just great, particularly for those select few who, unlike myself, are capable of understanding these theories at a deeper, mathematical level. Yet if the universe is indeed infinite, is not then Time a non-concept? Contradictory reasoning. But did not Heidegger say somewhere that a sparrow knows more about light than a blind physicist? So if science does not provide the answer, perhaps philosophy will.

Time has a unique, subjective meaning as well, if for no other reason than because our existence is finite. It is useless to measure subjective time. A morsel of a second can feel like an eternity, and many weary years may pass with unnoticed monotony. Past, Present, Future—which is the Real one? "Neither," said Spinoza, and Berkeley agreed with him. An event succeeding the present by only a fragment of a second still must be called future. Yet a blink of an eye later, it is already within the realm of the past. This phenomenon was questioned by Aristotle. Thus, a miniscule, virtual point wedged between future and past is supposed to be the "present." How small is the present? Does the present exist at all? Does it deserve a name of its own? It was easily explained by Kant: There are "*Ding an Sich*" issues that are self evident. But the value of this explanation is minimal. Herbert Spencer reasons that we ourselves are the measure of time itself, inasmuch as we are living, while Oswald Spengler thought that the act of "naming Time" as such is a mere human strategy aimed at "winning power over it." Is subjective time simply a memory? But memory is perishable, as ephemeral life itself surely fades away.

What if memory is completely wiped out by illness? What is left? What if the future erodes, as with Marcel Proust, condemned by his allergies to live out his later life locked in a glass enclosure with no more future, but forever a prisoner of the past and his own memories—for that is all he was left with. A sort of reverse Alzheimer's disease. "Yesterday is but today's memory, and tomorrow is today's dream," as Kahlil Gibran portrayed these complexities in his book *The Prophet*. But philosophy also fails to give a satisfactory answer. "Philosophy will clip an Angel's wings and unweave the rainbow," wrote Keats in *Lamia*.

Milton surmised that in the prelapsian period, in the Garden of Eden, there was no Time. Time, he says, was only born with Eve's sin. Does the answer perhaps lie in poetry? If not, the fragile beauty of the rhyme is a gentle apology and a tender consolation by itself. As such, it is more humble, as well as more human, than what science and philosophy have to offer. Poetry at least suggests useful advice: "... *Dum loquimur fugerit invida aetas, carpe diem quam minimum credula postero* ..." ("While we talk, envious Time escapes; seize the day therefore, without the least trust that any other follows ...")

CHAPTER 10

The Change of Guards

It was a warm spring day when we arrived at the capital city, more enchanting now than ever before. The wild chestnut trees that lined the avenues were rich with pink and white lampion-like flowers, like so many incandescent miniature candelabra, as they worshipped the last of the afternoon sunshine. True, the ugly scars of the cruel siege could be seen everywhere, but the vitality, the budding beginning of new life, was resolutely arising from within the cracks of the old walls, and was overwhelming.

A colourful, vibrant swarm of humanity was toiling and trading on the busy street corners. The black market, where everything was available, boomed. Everyone was for himself, and the slow ones were left behind in that mercantile post-war spirit that so selfishly demanded survival. People rallied in the terraces of small café bars, wheeling and dealing with dubious, sometimes non-existent merchandise. Nobody seemed to sleep as the hustle and bustle continued around the clock.

Workers began to rebuild shop windows and streets. Stores began to open. Restaurants sprang up. Newspapers and funny sheets (*Ludas Matyi*) were restarted. Theatres opened and produced biting political comedies and plays like *New God in Theba*. They were packing in the public. People did not stint on food or fun. They wanted to live it up to the hilt. Nightclubs opened all over town. There were concerts and opera performances. Tickets were hard to get because the Soviet soldiers grabbed them up. Their passion for music and operas surprised us. Otto Klemperer was the new conductor of the Budapest Opera Orchestra in those stimulating, enterprising days, and the well-known charisma of the maestro fitted in well with the mood of the city. Once I saw Klemperer on the dance floor of a nightclub with a blonde angel when he suddenly interrupted the jazz band and instructed them, "*Piu allegro, piu allegro.*"

And the women of Budapest! Oh, they have always been famous for their charm, grace, and inventive spirit. But in those arduous days they certainly outdid their reputation. God only knows how, but they seemed to be "fashionably" dressed with a daring womanliness and inexpensive elegance, like mischievous sorceresses, which matched their temperament so well.

Behold: the spellbinding sight of the gentle swell of female breasts with an eye-catching bounce to their own rhythm as so many marvellous young women passed the small terrace tables of the espresso bars! We encountered so many of them with their enchanting, fluid gait on their high heels, which were far from ostentatious or tawdry. Their looks and faint, lipsticky smile merely affirmed their confident feminity and stirred the voyeur—always a light sleeper—in the male spirit. The price of the **Y** chromosome. (". . . The way her silky garments undulate/ It seems she's dancing as she walks along . . ."[8]) And not only the young but the older women, too, excelled. Mature women pitched in wherever action was needed. With good practical sense, they brought quick solutions to problems where men, now scarce, often failed. If nothing else, matronly women with white aprons, smiling faces, and chatty dispositions baked and sold their homemade goods on neat, small tables on the street, helping life to root and branch.

As many women as men flooded the universities and pursued serious studies. But a contemptible gender discrimination still existed, surprisingly more so in North America than in Europe, and it was evident everywhere. Even male and female medical students married to one another and attending the very same classes were sometimes tainted by such disobliging behaviour. After a hard day's work, some husbands settled down to their studies and indifferently expected their wives to attend to the household chores all by themselves.

The university was overflowing with students. People like us, who had waited for so many frustrating years, suddenly got a chance to study. The university policy was that everyone who was academically acceptable was permitted to register, but the critical pruning took place at the merciless examinations. Thus, the size of the classes in first and second year were enormous.

We found that Thomas Detre had left Szeged and was continuing his studies in Budapest. After the day's work, we had a party almost every night or just a spontaneous gathering, usually in our favourite espresso bar or at Tom's apartment. At sundown, around the tiny terrace tables of the espresso café, our circle of friends began to grow: Andrew Say-Halasz, a psychiatrist; Pista Mahrer, an internist; Valerie Racz, a famous and beautiful chanteuse; Karinthy, the author-journalist son of the famous writer; Andrew Noti, the sculptor; Alois Angyal, a professor of psychiatry; a bright medical student, Marianne,

---

[8] Baudelaire, *Les Fleurs du Mal*, from a translation by James McGowan.

with her lesbian lover and another charming girl in love with Marianne; and several journalists. They were all regular members of our "club."

Lici and I were, of course, regular participants, but the main event was Tom. It was always enjoyable to listen to Tom's scintillating arguments, to his elegant ways of outstripping everyone, whether it was about politics, philosophy, biology, or nonsense. He was a master polemist, with an irresistible sense of humour. He also knew how to make outrageous statements to fan the flame of an animated argument. We had our differences, but we became good friends. Thomas had an unerring flair for biology and possessed a spontaneous insight into physiology and psychology. But he was too impatient to study the details of anatomy. It was my task to teach him before the examination.

* * *

This was the time when Lici decided that she wanted to be on her own. The separation was unexpected, and it was tremendously painful for me. I suffered for the longest time and did not know how to ease my agony. I also found that beyond my love for Lici, I was incapable of resolving the feeling of responsibility for her, something that tenaciously stuck to me in memory of Lici's mother, Cecil. But for a long time, the concern and affection were so intertwined that I could not disentangle the two sentiments: deep love and the responsibility I felt for her. And to complicate matters further, Lici became ill. She kept losing weight, had an elevated temperature, slept poorly, waking up frequently with night sweats, and developed a "smoker's cough" that kept getting worse.

It did not take too long to diagnose pulmonary tuberculosis. We felt numb. The treatment of TB in those days meant she had to go to a TB sanatorium, which was located in the hills of Buda. I visited her in this distant place as often as I could, bringing her my notes from the university and whatever delicacies I could procure.

Tuberculosis in those days was the primary killer of the young, and my anxiety was indeed great. Chemotherapy did not yet exist. I felt helpless and guilty. No doubt poor nutrition, her stressful experiences, mourning for her parents, the effort of striving to achieve her goal, and her unhappiness all suppressed her immune system and played a proportionate role in the development of her illness. So much for Cartesian duality.

After Lici left me, my life became impoverished. Apart from the visits to Lici in the sanatorium, I lost interest in everything else around me, even my studies. Since I could not sleep, I stayed out late every night, and for a while I sank into the habit of drinking in nightclubs. I did not at all enjoy the liquor and its effect on my brain, nor did I cherish the self-pity, casting myself into the banal role of the abandoned lover. So I stopped. But besides the depression that I could not help, the more and more frequent and unheralded panic attacks kept torturing me. I knew very well the roots of that sudden flair of anxiety. It was a paradox. On the one hand, I felt that life was futile and struggling was foolish; but at the same time, those ominous anxiety attacks, the fear of impending doom, suggested that I still cared about living.

I decided to cure myself by facing the devil. I took a few days off and went to the Schwabenberg and rented a room in the just-reopened Majestic Hotel, Adolf Eichmann's former headquarters. I thought that by doing so I would be able to break the power of evil. (A subsequently developed behaviour therapy called this method "flooding.") "It is hard to fight an enemy who has an outpost in your head," said Sally Kempton, and this is quite true. Many physicians asserted that these attacks were "just in your head," as if it could be in a worse place!

But my experiment turned out to be a disaster. I had my supper in the elegant hotel, and I read before I went to sleep in one of those rooms from which I used to hear the agonizing screams of people being interrogated by the Gestapo. I woke up in the middle of the night with a nightmare and panic attack. I had to open the window to breathe, but in doing so, I had seen the dark abyss, the yawning black shaft, and it took all my strength to tear myself away from the fascination of a tempting oblivion.

While the immediate cause of my depression was Lici's leaving me, my melancholy was complex and had many headwaters. Dark thoughts filled my mind for months. Can it be that I feared doom just because deep down I desired extinction? There is such a thing, too, as a "genetic suicide." And how is it done? As is every living soul, I, too, am standing at the very summit of a huge pyramid—a pyramid of my ancestors. Beneath the recent, upper layer of the pyramid, which is dominated by the Hebrews all the way back to Abraham (a mere 125 generations before myself), are probably the Cro-Magnon people. Still further down the pyramid, *homo erectus* follows, then Pithecanthropus, and finally, far back in the Pliocene era, were probably the hominoids.

Following the principle of single-minded Darwinian ambition—the survival of the fittest, the striving for "reproductive success"—the multitude of beings toiled, sweated, lived, cheated, fought, killed, and died for the solitary purpose of putting none other than myself where I am right now, at the lonely peak of the pyramid. All that strife and death! Think of it! Those determined ancestors muscled through thousands of unrecorded perils and close calls over millions of years, hunting and being hunted, to win the race, to achieve victory in the futile but desperate chromosomal relay, the passing on of the piece of their unique chemicals, that microscopic Pandora's box, to the next generation.

And now, when it would be my turn, I refuse to fulfill my biological calling. The pyramid would end with me. And why not? Who could know the fate of my potential offspring? Would he or she be a "Jew"? Would he or she be a "Nazi"? No third possibility seemed likely to me in those bitter times. Not with our macabre inheritance of being a carnivore. And out of the struggle came the resolution based on skepticism, disappointment, and cynicism. No, I did not want to play the pyramid game any more. I did not want to pursue this mad genetic lottery. By the will of a single link, the long chain would be broken.

But I remained with the burning need to understand what makes humans the most miserable of all species. Does the magnificence of the human soul share the same root as the outrageous devilment of the mind? The Romans seemed to suspect it: *"Homo hominis lupus est,"*[9] they used to say. But it explains nothing. One day I hope I will know the answer, for I have a deep-seated need to know!

* * *

As the months passed, Lici felt somewhat better. The therapeutic pneumothorax seemed to help her. I was present in the operating room when her pleural adhesions were separated (Jacobeus procedure). She spent only seven months in the sanatorium, a trifle of time by the standards of such institutions. She used to joke when I visited her: "There are two kinds of people in the sanatorium. There are those who are pale, haggard, worn down, and coughing, and there are those who look healthy, strong, and well rested. The first kind are the visitors, the second the patients."

There was some truth in it. Even more so because in those days I burned the candle at both ends. Thomas, although only a third-year medical student, was treated as an equal by several professors of psychiatry. He was left in charge of the largest mental hospital in Budapest (Angyalfold) when Professor Nyiro went on a vacation. This was an opportunity for Thomas to prove

---

[9] "Man is men's wolf."

himself. We all pitched in to help him and worked together. For weeks, we went without sleep. But we met the challenge.

* * *

The political situation changed rapidly. In the first national election, the Communist Party got only 8% of the vote, and the Socialists probably 25 or 30%. So we had a government with the leadership of the rest of the Liberal parties. But the Communists, with the Soviet troops behind them, forced a "unification" with the Socialists, whose leader, George Szakasics, was arrested. When the next election was held, an official sign at the polling station advertised the view that "only traitors use the boot," meaning that you could openly vote Communist. The Communists obtained a 95% majority! (Always engineered to be slightly less than the 97% figure in the U.S.S.R.) A jump from 8% to 95% in a couple of years was indeed impressive. With that, the Communist regime was in full power.

The Political Police of the Communists were housed, appropriately, in the very same building where the Nazi Arrowcross Headquarters used to be located: No. 60 Andrassy Street—the "house of horrors" under both the Nazis and the Communists. And they probably still employed the very same staff, the well-trained murderers! These, and the dour, priggish bureaucrats, ran the country from then on.

The Communists insisted on a process they called "denazification." All institutes had to be "denazified," universities included. But the Communists also had an endearing term for the "little Nazi" whom they claimed to be "just a poor, misled, proletar." Since the national colour of the Hungarian Arrowcross Nazis was green, and of the Communists was, of course, red, we used to joke that "the paprika got ripe—the green turned to red."

The Orwellian denazification occurred in front of committees. And the committee at the university, where I had to appear, was headed by a former "little Nazi." He was a person by the name of Dunai. No, you probably do not remember him. Dunai was the Nazi student who beat us up at the Anatomy Institute where we studied at night, long before the siege of Budapest, and before the German occupation. He was now the chairman of the denazification committee. When I objected, I got in trouble because Dunai was just a "little Nazi" who, in fact, in the Communist vocabulary, was the one who really suffered from the Nazis, not the Jews! The humiliation was that I had to prove to Dunai that I was not a Nazi! I was, of course, an offspring of the contemptible "middle class."

Besides the Political Police, a new branch, the Economy Police, came into existence. Their favourite technique was to organize raids on restaurants, where they went from table to table demanding that guests turn out their pockets in front of everyone else to see if they possessed any foreign currency. Then they had the waiter make out their bills and asked the guests to explain how they could afford it, where they worked, how much money they earned.

One of the problems with the Communists was that they had absolutely no sense of humour. In Budapest, this was in direct collision with the spirit of the town. A new anti-Semitism arose in Russia, invading the satellite countries. One after the other, the Soviet Jewish writers and philosophers were arrested, and many of them were killed in the Soviet *gulags.*

Informers were rewarded, which was just a natural in a political system that in the U.S.S.R. erected monuments to Pavlik Morozow, the Komsomol child who betrayed his father to the Soviet authorities. In Hungary, they tried to turn everyone into an informer and were successful in many instances. Most people in Budapest lived in apartment buildings. All of these buildings had janitors, and each acted as a spy. They had to report all the activities of the tenants to the political police, not only those of a political nature, but also sexual tidbits. The latter was always good for the purposes of blackmailing people and turning them into informers. This was a time-honoured method developed in the organization that ran originally under the name of Cheka, then GPU, then NKVD. The founder was Dzerzhinsky; then the mad Yagoda and Yezhov headed this institution. The club eventually was named KGB by the detested Laurence Beria. Naturally, the process of denazification was primarily used to dispose of all other political opponents.

There were obligatory meetings to attend, donations of money to be given, time and work to be eagerly offered, compulsory mass demonstrations—with roll calls of names just to be sure. More and more people became "Communists," at least on the surface, for career reasons. They were called "the careerists" by the Party.

The process of "conversion" to communism reminded me of Franz Kafka's *Metamorphosis* or Eugen Ionescu's metaphorically described transformations into "rhinoceroses." There was an endless amount of new social and political terminology, like the Orwellian "Newspeak," that assailed one's intelligence. Daily life was run by austere mandarins and pedantic bureaucrats. There were open meetings for party members—thank Heaven not for me—extolling "self-criticism" and "constructive criticism" on political matters.

By then, the first-year university registration was restricted to those with "pure worker or peasant background only." Sound familiar? With my Jewish middle-class background, I was suspect; even more so because I found it difficult to keep my mouth shut. My impulsive utterances and sarcastic comments got me into more and more trouble.

Dr. Laszlo Benedek, who had done a wonderful and daring job saving lives during the siege in the ghetto hospital, now became a leading Communist who declared that he would see to it that "all Zionists [would] . . . be thrown out of the Jewish General Hospital."

There was no more news about Raoul Wallenberg. Just the mention of his name was anathema. What had happened to him? Faint hope was still held for his safety, but it was peculiar that in those days, Swedish government voices demanding his release were never heard.

The war in Palestine was finally on, and we faced with horror the menacing threat of obliteration of the small Jewish community in Palestine, not only by a dozen well-armed Arab states but also by an adversely inclined Great Britain and a hate-filled Soviet Union. The original Israel, as her borders were drawn by the United Nations, was a farce. According to some sources, Israel was never really meant to live and thrive. Those who doubt this need only look at the original map and judge for themselves what the United Nations had designed: a tiny bit of land consisting of three longitudinally arranged triangles with connecting corridors, the whole not wider than a few miles. A minimum military offensive could cut this tongue of land into three parts in no time. Part of the Negev and Be'er Sheva would be in Arab hands, as would Jaffa. Jerusalem would be "international," and the port of Haifa would be shared between Arabs and Jews.

Jews, not Israelis, because a special United Nations committee convened in June 1947, consisting of Britain, Belgium, China, Syria, and Canada, did not approve naming the entity the "State of Israel." Instead, they recommended it to be called the land of the "Jewish Agency." Surely the sentiments and intentions of Israel's Arab enemies must have been well known to the United Nations, as were the calculated military chances of survival in such a region.

No, Israel was not meant to stay alive, but it was a nice, self-serving gesture to support the idea of Israel without actually expecting such a state to materialize. This empty gesture would surely mitigate the West's guilt for having done nothing to save European Jewry. Even bombing the railways leading to the ovens of Auschwitz, so often implored by Jewish leaders at the height of the German mass murders, was refused by the Allies. This was requested in the hope that such interruption of transport would slow down the efficiency of the Nazi killing machine. After the war, mistakenly, U.S. military experts argued that such bombardment would "not have been technically possible." Yet there were documented Allied air bombardments close to Auschwitz, a mere thirty miles from the gas chambers.

Today, it is common knowledge that the veto of bombing the crematoria or the rail lines leading to the extermination camps came from President Roosevelt's chief advisor, John J. McCloy. This same McCloy went out of his way after the war to help many notorious war criminals. This clear reluctance to save some of the Jews increased our belief that world opinion notwithstanding, we Jews had better take care of our own affairs. Reliance on the "good will" of others was, to say the least, perilous. Survival appeared to be more important than the gracious approbation of others. And yet, politically inconvenient as it may be, Israel did survive.

Remember Uncle Albin, the one-time industrial magnate? Remember that his wife and two sons were murdered by the Nazis? He survived the war, then was arrested by the Communists. They released him for a short while. His factory remained State property, as did his home and other possessions. Albin, always a fighter, began to build up a small workshop, a venture that was still possible in those days, but he was too successful. He was arrested again and taken to a *gulag* in Siberia, where he died. Between the Nazis and the Communists, their entire family was wiped out, and the Swiss banks got richer.

Uncle Baer died of a stroke. His gentle world had come crumbling down in his last few years. He could not grasp the horrors of the times and he just withered away. His ethereal sphere, his values, his love of classics could not stand up to the harshness of the changed circumstances. If I close my eyes, I can still see him dressed immaculately as always in his three-piece Burberry suit, brown shoes and gaiters, stiff starched shirt, and beige gloves, holding his brown crocodile attaché case and light brown walking stick with the ivory head. His ancient Greek and Latin education, his fervour to teach, did not belong in the twentieth century.

The report of one more death reached me: Mitzu, my old friend from the age of six, grandson of the famous general, raised in a Jesuit high school and in the Ludovica Military Academy. Mitzu, who had humiliated me when his friendship or courage fell short of my expectation, had died. Close to the Austrian border, as the commander of a tank, he had leaned out of the bay of his armoured vehicle and a Russian machine gun nearly cut him in half.

A Jewish classmate of mine, Andrew Kulcsar, who was frail and the best student in the school, was killed in one of the concentration camps. Another, Thomas Szanto, was murdered in a forced labour camp by Hungarian Nazis.

Paranoid, like the rest of the mad dictators, Stalin had the delusion that the "Jewish doctors were plotting to kill him." This started a mass arrest of Jewish doctors all over the U.S.S.R. and also in the satellite countries. ("If it rained in Moscow, you were obliged to open your umbrella in Budapest," we used to say, and then look around to see if the wrong person had heard it!) At the same time, the Communists found that "Budapest was too crowded" and began to order people to leave for other, police-selected villages.

Of course, all who were chosen to leave Budapest were believed to be enemies of the Communists. When forced to live as strangers in a small village, they could easily be watched and thus rendered harmless. Because of the crowding, people had to share their apartments with two or three families. Why was there such crowding in Budapest? The Communists had brought a large number of people from the countryside to the city. This was a clever manoeuvre, and very beneficial for the political police. After all, it was like this in Moscow. When two or three families share a single apartment with one kitchen and one bathroom, it is not conducive to fomenting meaningful secret political revolt.

One day, a famous couple got their notice to move from Budapest to a tiny muddy village. The husband was Dr. Tibor German, a professor of ear, nose, and throat diseases, and a Jew. His wife was Gizi Bajor, an actress, a prominent life member of the Hungarian National Theatre and an Aryan. Both were well known, much loved, and widely respected. The night before they were supposed to leave, they committed suicide. Tibor German was the uncle of Thomas Detre.

One more little victim: the shapely, stagey, straw-blonde Sari Okos, probably not the greatest actress but young and enthusiastic, who played in a performance of *New Gods in Theba*. She was ordered out of Budapest to live in an unheard-of village, where she died of appendicitis.

This was the time when Tom decided that he could no longer stay in Hungary. He was one of the last who could leave the country with a passport on a train. Tom went to Italy, where he hoped to establish himself as a refugee and finish his university studies. He left with one piece of luggage, no money, no knowledge of the language, and no connections.

The city seemed empty after Thomas left, and our circle of friends began to fall apart. One reason was a growing distrust. One never knew whom to trust. Frightening stories about political arrests circulated. Ganz Sanyi, whom we knew from the resistance movement and who had been a dedicated Communist all his life, for which he spent time in jail before the war, was now arrested by the Communists. (To his chagrin, and quoting Freud, I used to tell him that Communism, with its saints, heretics, lore, and holidays, was his religion.)

A few months later, he was released, and we met him. He remarked that the Communists were right to arrest him. Why? "Because I am an idealist. Idealists are always dangerous. They [the professional *apparatchick*] want the materialists whose interests make them Communists. Then they have a hold on them. Idealists cannot be bought, cannot be controlled. Materialists can. Besides, I know the ins and outs of resistance movements. I could be dangerous for them."

A few months later, Ganz was arrested a second time, and we never heard of him again. But we heard of other high-ranking Communists who were similarly arrested and executed, only to be "rehabilitated" years later; one was a surgeon whom we knew well from the Jewish General Hospital of Budapest and from the resistance movement.

More and more people were now escaping from Hungary across the border to Austria. But the border was increasingly more difficult to cross. One could not travel to places close to the border. Gendarmes swarmed, asking for identification on trains, buses, cars, and highways, and enquiring as to "reasons for being there." This procedure began fifty kilometres from the actual border. There was also the military border patrol, a tight, impenetrable force. After that came the barbed-wire fence, the minefield, more barbed wire, then the barking, sniffing, trained watchdogs with the police. There were turrets in the no-man's land with machine guns and sharpshooters. One had to be very careful. Hungarian and Austrian criminals helped people across the border for large sums of money, but sometimes there were false guides or dishonest criminals who robbed people and abandoned them. Sometimes they drove them around in a closed truck for half the night, took their money, and let the people out in the darkness near Budapest, saying, "There is Vienna."

A person could be shot dead at the border. These were lucky compared with the anguish of a series of wicked interrogations. A few years in jail was the minimum penalty, but it could also be much worse.

Although we knew we did not want to live in Hungary any longer, we wanted to finish our studies before we embarked on a dangerous border crossing.

Dreams and Tears: IX

Demons

All the things one has forgotten
scream for help in dream.

From Elias Canetti, *Die Provinz der Menschen*

In my lifetime, just like most people, I have had my share of peculiar and at times puzzling and frightening dreams or nightmares. Flying with flailing arms and legs, sometimes falling, finding oneself naked in public, or being chased are the occasional, everyday type of nuisance dreams that belong to the universal phenomenon of youth. But the nightmares that became my unwanted and diabolical companions for many years after the war were of an entirely different sort. I still find the description of them an unpleasant and difficult task.

The nightmares were inseparable from other symptoms, and each one of them must be described. They all started at approximately the same time, a few months after Liberation, and as time went on, all these manifestations increased rapidly in both frequency and intensity.

It is not so much the visual content of these nightmares that was agonizing or wicked. It was the accompanying emotional and bodily sensations that rendered them demonic and tormenting. On many occasions, the visual remnants of the nightmares were simple enough: images of war, killing, executions, and Nazis. I would not say, of course, that such content is not damnable or malignant by itself, but the real ordeal is the coupled mental and somatic sensations that created a dreary and sinister mood. The bodily feeling was not just anxiety but a sensation of choking, of being buried alive in soil or drowning in murky water. The result was an incredible loss of energy and a feeling of hopelessness that robbed all my strength for the rest of the day. Often, but not always, the nightmares woke me up and I would be covered in sweat.

I have already referred to my sleeping habit that the danger around me shaped during the siege. This consisted of folding the pillow into a ball under my neck and supporting my head with my arm, so that both of my ears would be free. After the war, and even today, this habit prevails. However, unlike the war years, once I am asleep, this precarious and less than comfortable position is no longer maintained unless I happen to have a nightmare. If that is the case, I struggle to retain this vigilant posture in my dream, and in doing so, I often scratch the left side of my forehead with my fingernail. Only the next morning when I am shaving do I discover the sharp scratch on my forehead, always in approximately the same location. At that moment, I will recall the content of my nightmare. I have many small scratch marks in that location. I used to cut my fingernails very short as a futile preventative measure.

There are other phenomena that have also become a source of torture, certainly not to a lesser degree than the nightmares. These are the frequent "daytime nightmares" that consist of unwanted, unsuspected, intrusive thoughts of "suddenly reliving" one or another actual dangerous situations of the past. On several occasions while writing these lines, I found myself groping to find the right word and repeatedly crossing out the word "memory." The concept of memory is misleading, since it sounds like the past and therefore does not carry the dynamism, the very nature of the experience. The "daytime nightmares" are not memories; they befuddle the senses and feel like they are taking place right now! It is actually reliving a past experience with the delusion that it is in the present—that it is just now happening.

How would you react if you suddenly realized that you are falling from the fourth-floor window and find yourself in midair, split seconds before you hit the ground? What if this occurs unexpectedly in the middle of your daily business? Or that you clearly hear the shot fired that is going to kill you now? Self-inflicted sensation of pain, like biting one's tongue or pushing one's fingernail into one's palm, is the psychological mechanism needed to bring oneself back to reality from the terrifying reverie, or to prevent oneself from shouting out loud in horror.

These phenomena did not last long—maybe a few seconds—but at the height of my suffering, they occurred several times a day. Such "attacks," when they occurred, disrupted my attention and interfered with my concentration. They also had their own autonomy. They were entirely unexpected and unpredictable and could not be voluntarily invoked. Like the panic attacks, they were imposed upon me by their own caprice. They continued for years.

A third symptom was the recurring sudden attacks of panic that happened during the day or night. At the peak of my difficulties, these took place several times a day. But this I have already described.

Yet I had a life to live, tasks to perform; I needed to study and progress, to make a living and still function despite all these symptoms.

Commonly shared by humanity is the delusion that we are in complete control of our lives. We relish this false belief because we like to be in control. It makes us forget our fallibility. The fact is that subtle amounts of chemicals influence our moods, not unlike the light filters that tinge the visual perception of our environment. Inappropriate absence or presence of these substances at critical sites in the body will misdirect our feelings and our conduct. But we cannot control the rate at which these chemicals wax and wane. Or can we?

At a later point in my life, I underwent five years of psychoanalysis. It was helpful in many ways and represented a cultural experience and a useful learning device in conducting psychotherapy on my own. But none of my symptoms were influenced in the least by the psychoanalysis. In time, some twenty years later, the symptoms began to fade. This coincided with other important events in my life.

CHAPTER 11

On the Road Again

Spring had come once again. It was March 1949, shortly after my twenty-fifth birthday. Three more months to graduation! We had written all but the very last examination and we had passed them with excellent marks. The one remaining test would be a cinch. It was so designed by the university authorities. Lici and I were so close to the fulfillment of our dreams that we could taste the sweetness of it. We were divorced by then, but a close friendship and my profound feeling of loyalty to her kept us together. But the world around us turned grim once again.

Driven by their career interests, most professors joined the Communist Party at least nominally. One exception was the highly respected Dr. Emerich Haynal, the gifted professor of internal medicine and *enfant terrible* of the university. He was openly and vocally anti-Communist, just as he had been an equally daring and outspoken anti-Nazi in times past. The only professor I knew who was an idealistic and dedicated Communist was Dr. Gegessi-Kiss of pediatrics, a brilliant physician and outstanding lecturer. But when the notorious purge of the Communist Party came, to our *Schadenfreude*, he was the only one to be kicked out from this elite club. Why? He liked abstract paintings. The Party liked "socialist realism," and Moscow did not tolerate abstractionism.

For the Communists, your taste in music, visual arts, and even the principles of biology were dogmatically prescribed by Moscow. The genetic doctrines of Trofim Lyssenko, the Communist commissioner of DNA, and I.V. Michurin, the mandarin of Soviet biology, eminently suited Stalinesque policies. They asserted that a genetic cross by grafting appropriate "mentors" on plants or animals would make them "trainable" to endure severe environmental conditions. This would bring the Soviet Paradise and the Five-Year Plan even more success, particularly when Siberian pineapples and bananas were harvested!

Although proven scientifically wrong, these semi-Lamarckian theories received the blessing from party-line enforcers in Moscow, much more so because Mendelian genetics was always at odds with Marx's scripture. This sounds almost humorous in retrospect, but it was not a laughing matter at the time. Several hundred dedicated scientists paid with their lives as "heretics" for having opposed the views of these two academic viceroys. The rest of them were coerced into a medieval and humiliating assent to palpable scientific nonsense. But Budapest, forever seeking a joke, found one: "Michurin and Lyssenko discovered a chimera between a giraffe and a cow; this way it can graze in Hungary and be milked in the U.S.S.R."

The true reason, however, why Dr. Gegessi-Kiss was expelled from the Communist Party was probably, as Sanyi Ganz, our Communist friend and former member of the Resistance Movement, said: the Party does not want "uncontrollable" idealists.

From the point of view of the Communists, my own record was very poor indeed. I never belonged to the Communist Party and I had the reputation, for good reason, of being an anti-Communist. I detested them and could not hold back my remarks, particularly after the provocation of Dr. Benedek and the Dunai affair.

The Iron Curtain was closing down rapidly. The number of students in our class was also dwindling, as many had already left for Vienna. "Dissidents," they were called. With the passing days, our apprehension rose steadily, as fewer and fewer students showed up at the lecture hall. We felt compelled to make a choice in haste, or else risk never being able to leave Communist Hungary. The choice was unfair and wicked. The decision was tearing us apart, but we could not live under a dictatorship again.

IRO (International Refugee Organization) identification booklet in Austria, 1949.

So we renewed our old connections with shady people—guess who? Yes, yes, Mr. Heisler was still around and still very active. He put me in touch with some "responsible Viennese businessmen" who just happened to be in Budapest. Mr. Heisler gave me their hotel room number but no names. I went to see them with my friend Imre Halasz.

The small hotel room was full of luggage. One of the "businessmen" was fussing and fretting over an enormous round of cheese that they had wrapped in a mink coat (after all, how else would you pack a thirty-kilogram round of cheese?), while the other was busy cleaning his revolver. This was not quite how I imagined responsible entrepreneurs from Vienna, even though the gun was elegant, small, and, one could say, for social occasions only. These business people did not give their names, let alone the name of the likely unregistered company for which they worked. In view of their anonymous status, we dubbed one of them "Cutface" and the other "Limper" for obvious reasons. However, they gave us their price and the date of departure: the day after tomorrow. Cutface and Limper would go in two separate cars. Lici would have a false Austrian passport. The price was such that I could afford the fee for only one person. Lici was on.

To wait in nerve-wracking insecurity gives rise to vivid and morbid visions. It is not a pleasant condition, but there was nothing else to do, except figure out what to pack in a single little suitcase. Poor Lici. She packed and unpacked that single valise again and again, hoping to cram into it a lifetime of supplies. Her university papers were most important, but alas, they took up a fair amount of space. Everything else Lici possessed was left behind. For a second time, we lost all our belongings. Finally, the time arrived, and Lici left. There was a question of whom she should go with. In the end, Lici went with Cutface while Limper went in the other car. I was left behind with my worst fears.

Two days later, the phone call came from Vienna. Lici had arrived. She was safe! She could not say much more on the phone, but later she gave a full account of her adventurous border crossing, and the fact that the other car, driven by Limper, never made it. Limper was arrested for smuggling at the border crossing.

Now it was my turn to go. But I did not have the money, only my own instincts, which I had to trust. The Austrian–Hungarian border could not be crossed illegally anymore, particularly without a guide. Even if one did cross the border, one would only be in the Russian-occupied zone of Austria. However, the Czechoslovakian–Hungarian border was guarded with less vigour because the other side of the border was just another Communist country.

From Czechoslovakia, one could still pass into Austria with less risk. I opted for this two-stage adventure.

The first thing I did was to write a letter to a border-town hospital. I chose the little Hungarian town of Balassagyarmat, a place that I had visited with a friend before with a similar venture in mind. I knew, of course, that my application for internship would be turned down, as only "politically reliable" people go to border towns. But at least I would obtain a letter written on hospital letterhead stating that they had received my application. That would be enough for me, but it meant waiting again.

Finally, the letter arrived. It was beautiful. Printed on hospital letterhead, bearing a round rubber stamp, it testified that it must be a document of importance. It said that they had received my application for an internship.

I had no time to waste. I decided not to say good-bye to my parents. Why should they be put through the agony of insecurity? I told them that I was going to a party and would sleep over at a friend's house. With that, I was on my way, all by myself. I did not take any suitcases with me but put all my university papers in my pocket and a pharmacology book in my other pocket (I still have it). So equipped, I took a bus, calculating exactly that my arrival in Balassagyarmat would be after dark. The bus rolled on, and I looked out at the familiar city scenery with bitterness in my heart. That was the last time I saw Budapest.

Soon the bus stopped, and the hated gendarme uniforms appeared and asked for papers. Their determination to support the Nazi regime in the recent past had now changed to a fierce support of the Communist government.

"What is the purpose of your trip?"

"Internship. I am going to do my internship in the hospital."

"Can you verify that?"

"Sure."

Unhurried, I found the letter and made as if I were yawning while I handed it over. The effect was perfect. It conveyed the unconcerned confidence of legitimate status. My past adventure with the Arrowcross death squad flashed across my mind. Closer to Balassagyarmat, the same scenario repeated itself with another group of gendarmes. Soon the bus arrived at the town and I immediately headed straight for the highway. I knew that the border was close, but in my excitement I lost my north-south bearing. Whatever it's worth, my remaining geographical sense was fine.

By then it was night. Suddenly I saw someone walking on the highway some distance away. The man, who did not spot me, marched towards me in the darkness. I thought that it was not a good time to make a new acquaintance, so I hid in the ditch. When he was just a short distance from me, a group of gendarmes suddenly materialized out of the darkness. They drove up quickly in an open patrol car, shouting at the poor fellow, who was probably in the same business as myself. He muttered something to the gendarmes but I did not hear it well. The full-throated sergeant shouted back at him like a foghorn: "Don't lie to me, you miserable worm! I saw you! You came from there, from Czechoslovakia!"

The sergeant major's firmly outstretched arm pointed in a particular direction, unmistakably revealing to me where the border was. I gratefully acknowledged the unintended help. Now I knew in which direction to go. (How lucky I was that they did not have a dog!) But I felt sorry for the little guy. It was also an intimidating reminder of what could happen to me at any moment. Life, at the expense of this pitiable unknown fellow, had brought an improbable chance for my benefit; something no sane, statistical calculation could have predicted.

The poor man was packed in the car and the gendarmes disappeared with him. Their vehicle left behind an evil smell. I waited for a while and then I approached the border. The Ipoly River was swollen, swift, and ice cold at that time of the year. Unfortunately, it came up well over my hips instead of just to my knees as I had been informed.

The other side of the river was swampy, and although I tried to walk very, very quietly, suddenly a startled and loud quacking sounded, like a frightful alarm, giving away my secret mission and scaring the hell out of me. A group of swamp birds rushed into the black night sky when I invaded their bedrooms.

By then, I was technically in Czechoslovakia. All of a sudden, in the distance I saw a Soviet soldier with his searchlight. For ten minutes I lay on my stomach in the mud, not daring to move. But in fact it was just a loose light bulb swinging on the side of the highway and interacting with my fertile imagination, with the help of the six cups of espresso coffee I had consumed earlier "to stay alert." No soldiers at all.

I was frozen. In the middle of the March night, the wet clothing clung to my shivering body, and my teeth chattered in the penetrating cold. My shoes, saturated with wet mud, made a loud, sloshy noise with each step. Finally, I found myself in a fallow field. A narrow trail wound up a hill to the outskirts of a small and somnolent village. I decided not to care what happened and asked for help at the first house. A man answered my knock, asking the obvious in Slovak, which I did not speak. But I bravely answered in Hungarian:

"My car broke down and I need some help."

"Your car, my ass! I have been a smuggler for thirty years. All I need is a glance. You came from over there." He pointed towards the border.

All I heard was the soothing, lovely word "smuggler." How rational. So it came down to a little bit of money. His corpulent wife got out of her bed to dry and press my only suit and shirt; after all, I was a customer, and business is business. Modestly, I hid my nakedness by lying down in her still-warm bed. Probably no one appreciated the lady's physical amplitude and the body warmth that goes with it as much as I did in my frosty state.

Soon another smuggler with a flatulent car was summoned, and, still in darkness, we left. The junior smuggler explained to me that he was going to take a longer back road rather than the highway that ran along the Slovak side of the Hungarian border. We stopped for a while near Krupina, a small town, and I got out of the car near a pine forest, inhaling the resinous cold air and gazing at the still-fallow valley through a milky, swirling morning haze. It brought back distant memories. I used the opportunity to relieve my distended bladder.

Before noon, we were in Bratislava, Slovakia's capital city, close to Vienna. To be sure, the border between the two cities was well guarded. But in Bratislava, I picked up some Zionist connections belonging to the *Bricha*[10] who said they would help me get to Vienna. By then, other refugees had joined us, and we exchanged information. We were to go to the Rothschild *Spital* in Vienna. "Wonderful," I thought naively. *Spital* means hospital in German, and hospitals can only be clean and well cared for. I desperately needed a bath. Maybe, as a medical student, I would get a private room with a bath. I certainly would ask the head nurse in her white, starched uniform.

But the Rothschild *Spital* was, of course, not a hospital at all. It was an incredibly overcrowded, filthy refugee camp located in the American zone of the city, on the Wehringer Gurtel, where a Polish Jew by the name of Mr. Teicholz ruled. People were lying in the corridors, and one could hardly move.

"Where is the bathroom?" I inquired.

"Where the shit is the deepest," came the answer, the truthfulness of which was immediately verifiable.

I phoned my parents long distance. By then they were worried sick in Budapest. Then I set out to find Lici. She had decided that Italy would be the best place to continue her studies. Soon she was on her way there, alone.

---

[10] An organization that promoted emigration to Israel.

* * *

More calamity! We could not get places in the Rothschild *Spital* and we were sent to another DP camp in the city, the Arzberg School. By comparison, the Rothschild *Spital* was a veritable Hilton Hotel. In despair, I slept on a bench in the nearby park for several nights.

I met a group of medical students in Vienna. Stephan Neiger had lived there for a few months and he was the dean of our group. He also spoke flawless German and had a rented room in the French zone of the city. I also met the ubiquitous Mr. Heisler, travelling freely with his diplomatic passport. He was pleased to see me. Heisler carefully listened to the account of Lici's border crossing and was pleased that she was safe. He regretted the fate of Limper, but consoled me. "He will escape," Heisler predicted with the certainty of an expert.

Word came that Lici had attempted to cross into Italy at the Brenner Pass. As none of us had a passport, much less a visa, all the travel and border crossings had to be done illegally. But having left the Soviet borders behind us, such ventures took on the quality of a game of fortune. They no longer represented a life-threatening situation. Indeed, as Lici tried to sneak across the Austrian–Italian border, she was spotted by Italian guards with their telescopes from far away. They made bets among themselves as to the estimated time of her expected and exhausted arrival. Then they arrested her with loud cheers and sent her back to Austria. She was placed in a DP camp in Salzburg. But she was morally defeated.

Meanwhile, in Vienna, Stephan Neiger negotiated by telephone with the dean of the medical school in Innsbruck. We were accepted at the university with three conditions: we had to be in Innsbruck by the end of April; we had to repeat the entire last year of the medical curriculum; and we had to rewrite (in German, of course) all of our examinations from the very first to the last.

As hard as these conditions were, we were delighted. But the first condition was the most difficult: how to get to Innsbruck. Usually the reliable *Bricha* organized safe transports through the Russian zone, but not until the middle of May. During Passover, these convenient border crossings were suspended. So to meet the conditions of the University of Innsbruck, we had immediately to make the precarious trip across the Soviet zone border at our own risk.

I reassured Neiger that Passover was renowned as a favourable time for Jews to get away from distressing situations and for making successful border crossings. We found a truck driver who would take us to the edge of the Russian zone, where we would leave the truck and cross the border alone in the forest. Meanwhile, the truck driver would cross the border legitimately and wait for us on the other side, in the British zone, near Graz. Other students, like Laci Revesz and Akos Talan, would be coming with us.

One evening, we were picked up by the rickety truck and travelled under a flopping, dirty canvas until the truck stopped. We were already slightly late. The darkness was fading. Warned to be very quiet, the driver pointed out the direction of the border and described the bend in the highway where he would wait for us. Then, once more we were in the dark forest, with the nerve-wracking snaps and crackles of dry twigs underfoot, our mouths parched and hearts palpitating. We glimpsed the unsuspecting Soviet border guard in the distance. Probably drunk, we hoped. Then we emerged cautiously from the forest.

The still leafless, bare tree branches, like black Brussels lace, sketched a capricious arabesque onto the apricot morning sky. We were on the highway, our beautiful truck waiting in front of us. *"Gruss Gott!"* But we remained very quiet until we got to Graz. The British zone! There, a sudden euphoria overtook us, an ecstasy, a blissful and exuberant mood. We were joking and frolicking. Finally, the lead-heavy Soviet dictatorship was behind us! We truly felt free!

From then on, whatever misfortune befell us, no longer would our very lives be in danger. If caught, the worst thing they could do was arrest us and put us in a DP camp until they cleared our status. This would mean that we would miss the deadline and lose yet another year of studies. Now we were in the British zone, and ahead of us lay the American and then the French occupied zones, and then Innsbruck, the westernmost city in Austria.

We had our share of excitement, too. We were nearly caught by the Americans, but in that zone we were able to fine a disheartened and hitherto hopeless Lici in the DP camp. We picked her up, and in less than an hour, we continued our venturesome enterprise. From Salzburg to Innsbruck we travelled in a coal wagon, a voyage that hardly improved our already less-than-debonair appearance!

Nocturnal Images: Return and Regret

"Ah! What is not a dream by day
To him whose eyes are cast
On things around him with a ray
Turned back upon the past?"

From Edgar Allen Poe, *A Dream*

I am travelling on a noisy, yellow streetcar in Budapest. As usual, the streetcar is packed full of people. The official selling tickets is collecting the fares from the passengers. With a sudden jolt, I realize that I have no Hungarian currency, only Canadian dollars. Dollars! How dangerous! Don't take them out of your pocket; they might see them. How did I get back to Budapest? Why did I come back? I am furious with myself. I have no Hungarian identification papers. The ticket collector will call the police, and they will ask for my documents. I have only Canadian papers. How will I get back to Canada? I must have been a damn fool to come back to Budapest. I may never get back to Canada now.

I wake up. Oh, it is that crazy dream again. Well, it passed.

CHAPTER 12

From Caterpillar to Butterfly

Innsbruck is wedged between the rugged peaks of Hafelekar in the north and the round-backed Patschelkofer covered with alpenrose in the south, both approximately 10,000 metres high and well above the tree line. Sitting on a plateau 1,800 feet above sea level, the town is bisected by the Inn River, a shallow current into which the waters of the smaller river, the Sill, are gathered. The old part of the city, with its narrow streets, seventeenth- and eighteenth-century arcaded buildings, and the sparkling *Goldene Dachel*, is a favoured tourist haunt. A Franciscan church in the park, built in the Renaissance style, contains the vast marble sarcophagus of Maximilian the First from the sixteenth century and a collection of old weapons and marble sculptures. Maria Teresa Street, the main boulevard in the downtown area, is lined with expensive hotels, restaurants, and boutiques and jammed with a maze of streetcar tracks. The prestigious university was built in 1677 and had always attracted students from all over Europe. Yet the population of Innsbruck was less than 100,000 in those days. We arrived in the early morning.

* * *

Professor Hitmayer, the dean of the medical school, listened to us with a glimmer of amusement in his eyes. We stood in front of him with soot only partly wiped off our faces and more than just traces of smudge on our bedraggled clothing from our rough border crossing.

Stephan Neiger and Lici spoke fluent German, but the rest of us were struggling with grammar, vocabulary, and accent.

"So, you made it!" the dean said.

"It was anything but easy."

"That I can well imagine."

So that was it. We were now students at the University of Innsbruck. The next step was to decide what to do. We were totally exhausted, having missed at least three full nights of sleep by then; we were famished; and we had no money. If we gave ourselves up to the French authorities as illegal and unregistered refugees, surely they would arrest us, feed us, and put us in a warm jail where we could sleep to our hearts' content.

Our gullible minds and empty stomachs made us dream up such nonsense. In front of the French Command Office stood a French soldier whose task it was to chase away everyone without exception. We approached him and wanted to see the commandant.

"*Sale Boche*," he said. "*Boche*" was reserved in the military tradition for "Germans." "Dirty Germans."

"No, no, you don't understand. We are not *Boche*, not Germans," we pleaded. "We are refugees." He shrugged his shoulders, a reasonable man with whom one could bargain.

"*Sale Étranger*," he said in a conciliatory tone. This left us momentarily stupefied.

"But we are Jews who came as refugees and have no papers," we dared him hopefully.

But he proved to be a man of firm democratic principles. He shrugged his shoulders again without hostility but with the attitude of a proud shopkeeper offering us a free choice of his fine wares.

"*Sale Juif*," he said, revealing his genuine impartiality in ethnic issues, and closed his shop.

But we did manage to get to see the commandant anyway. Very briefly. His secretary gave us a piece of paper saying that we could come back a week later. I have never been more disappointed in the disastrous inefficiency of the French military than at that moment. We found ourselves on the street before we could open our mouths. No jail, no food, no sleep! The height of bureaucratic bungling!

Fortunately, we found the secretary of the American Joint Distribution Committee. She did not help us but told us the office was closed. Perhaps we should go to the nearest DP camp.

"How far?"

"Oh, just north of Solbad Hall."

"Where is Solbad Hall?"

"Only fifteen kilometres from Innsbruck."

"But we have no streetcar tickets."

"Well, come back to see us next week or so."

So we marched for the rest of the day. The DP camp consisted of several barracks. The officer in charge told us that they had no place for us to stay. He had a tiny carpet in front of his desk. Like a vision, I imagined myself lying down on his carpet, wrapping myself in it and going to sleep before he finished the sentence. I found this mental picture irresistibly funny—or perhaps I was hysterical. I burst into loud laughter.

And that did it. All five of us broke out in a hurricane of uncontrolled laughter. I could not stop because I knew that they did not know what they were laughing at. This made the dam break, inducing a convulsion of more contagious laughter.

The officer was shocked to his bones. He had seen many kinds of reactions among refugees before—violence included—but never such a sweeping vortex of laughter. He became scared of the five crazy people. Places were found immediately. "No, the kitchen is no longer open, sorry. But breakfast will be available." Then my companions asked me why I had spread that contagious laughter. I explained, and we laughed some more.

The next morning, Laci Revesz moaned. His hat had disappeared. He had left Hungary with two suitcases, one large and one small. The large valise had been stolen at the Austrian–Hungarian border, and the small one at the Russian zone border. He still had the keys for the lost luggage and was guarding them with fierce determination, as if they were rare treasures. And now his hat was gone.

"For how long can they steal from me?" he rhapsodized at his misfortune. But he was to endure one more loss. In the interest of the well being of our small community, Laci's socks, for intense olfactory reasons, were confiscated, publicly fumigated, and formally buried the next morning in a solemn ceremony. We all delivered a brief and very poignant eulogy to the mourner.

We got some money from the American Joint Distribution Committee, a stipend of about US$8 per month. I also received £5 from Uncle Joseph in London almost every month for a year. Then we discovered that they paid cash for blood at the Surgical Institute. We were supposed to donate blood only once a month, but we managed to do it every two weeks, the only way to balance the finances.

And then we found the empty, bombed-out building at 14 Sill Gasse. This building originally belonged to the Jewish community of Innsbruck, so we felt entitled to move in. It still had some rooms that we could turn into a Jewish student home. We ate lunch at the YMCA. From the Quakers, we each got a suit. We discovered that there was a "Swedish breakfast" for those who were underweight. I qualified easily. The trouble was that it was served at six a.m. at the other end of town. The streetcar cost money. So I sold my Swedish breakfast ticket to one of our fellow students, Rabner, who just loved to eat (as evidenced by his waistline). And in those days, I loved to smoke.

But what we did not know was that at the Swedish breakfast, they took your weight weekly to document how the humanitarian donation turned into adipose substance. And Rabner was kicked out for he, according to the telltale records, had gained sixty-five pounds in a single week!

Laci Revesz was my roommate in the tiny cubicle made of cardboard in the student home. He was studying for his examination in internal medicine. Once in a while, he put aside his notes and walked around the room tapping the walls like a patient's chest. Laci, the internationally celebrated specialist. That is when he discovered a hollow sound just over my bed. His theory was perfectly clear, he said. Tomorrow, everyone was invited to a formal luxury dinner in the Maria Teresa Hotel. This building belonged to the Jewish community, he explained, and it was in that hollow that the persecuted Jews must have hidden their jewels! We were rich!

I did not have time to object before he made a hole in the wall with a hammer and found an empty space with a walled-in window. Of course there were no jewels, but from then on, the cold Alpine winds that lapped up the biting chills of the vast glaciers blew in through that hole just above my head. Laci said that this was very healthy for pulmonary tissues, and as a final authority on this question, he referred to *The Magic Mountain*.

Time was passing very quickly. We wrote one examination after another, and for most of us the German language was no longer a problem. Joseph came from London for a brief visit with his wife, Mary, the lovely aunt whom I met then for the first time. It was also the first time I had seen Joseph since before the war. We both shed bitter tears over our family members who had perished in the Holocaust. We confessed to one another the agony of our helplessness and the guilt about our very survival.

Yet we still found time to catch up on some wonderful writings that until then had not been available because of one or the other dictatorships. We eagerly sought out the works of Arthur Koestler, Franz Kafka, Albert Camus, and Sartre, all disillusioned former Communists; and George Orwell's books, which were naturally forbidden in Hungary at that time. Although I was familiar with the existentialist forerunners like Karl Jasper and Martin Kierkegaard, I felt that real existentialism was born in the air-raid shelters, on the battlefields, in the concentration camps, and in the resistance movements, rather than on the floor of academia. For us, George Orwell's work did not only spell a discourse about a hypothetical future, it also kindled painful memories from the past.

For us, Orwell's *1984* was already in the past.

One day, we had some visitors. Cutface and Limper dropped in. They were on a business trip in Innsbruck. Limper had learned a few words of Hungarian

Graduation at the University of Innsbruck with Lici, June 1950.

in jail before he escaped. We were very happy to see them and we embraced them. We decided to change the name of Limper to a more dignified one. He deserved it.

Tom Detre came to see us from Rome for a few days. It was a happy reunion.

Our humble student home in Innsbruck was definitely unsuited to receiving visitors. At times, guests wandered in and stayed for days or weeks. Nobody cared. Such were the two young men, one British, the other South African, who arrived. Probably college students. Mainly, Laci mentored them because he spoke some English. The British fellow, Tom Sharpe, was younger than us, and Laci used to hector him because of his boyish naivete in Middle European political matters. The two youngsters used to listen to our experiences in the war and our vehemently expressed political views. Then Tom Sharpe took off for South Africa, where his political incarceration eventually helped to launch his career as an author.

Some time earlier, my sister, Marta, and her husband, Jan Sebor, had left Europe and immigrated to Israel. That move gave my parents a chance to leave Hungary: people over fifty-five could leave Hungary if they had relatives in Israel. But they could not take anything with them and had to prepay their taxes for several years. This was exciting news. My parents arrived in Tel Aviv. True, they had nothing left from their previous possessions or wealth, but they were free.

We had no time for socializing outside the student home. We had little contact with the Austrian students. To avoid any anti-Semitic statements, we were always quick to announce that we were Jews. (I recall Otto Kahn's definition of a Kike: "The Kike is the Jewish gentleman who just left the room.") This pronouncement immediately unleashed a stereotypical answer. It was the same story we had heard dozens of times. How they loved the Jews. How they hated the Nazis. How they saved the lives of Jews. Encountering this so many times, we did our best to withdraw from them.

An exception was a fellow named Ziegler who said he used to be a Nazi. Then he explained that his parents were divorced. His father had been a journalist who did not support them, and Ziegler had lived with his mother in poverty. He was thirteen years old when the Nazis marched into Austria. From then on, he had military training, food, and clothing. Yes, he hated the Jews, although he had never met one. By the time he was thrown to the Soviet front, he knew the Nazis well. But it was useless to do anything against them. I liked Ziegler.

I had vague thoughts of specializing in tropical diseases and going to Africa, where physicians were well paid—US$400 per month, according to my information. But first, the graduation. Lici, Laci Revesz, and I obtained our diplomas exactly one year later than we would have received them in Budapest. It was June 1950. The three of us celebrated together. We had nobody else to cheer for us. It was also somewhat anticlimactic. How much work, how many long nights of studying, and how many abdicated pleasures that piece of paper had cost us!

With graduation, the monthly US$8 stipend from the American Joint Distribution Committee came to an end. We were no longer students.

Was I grateful to the University of Innsbruck for helping me to achieve my lifelong dream? For sure; mainly because I did not know then that the Anatomy Institute of that quiet alpine town still housed, "for teaching purposes," a large number of body parts of murdered Jews and anti-Nazis from various concentration camps.

I went to Germany to do my internship in Cologne, where I made the acquaintance of a German couple, the Rosens, who invited me to stay with them. But first, I travelled through Munich, where I found a small community of Hungarian Jewish medical students. Most of them lived with a lovely, crazy couple, Csilla and Mishi Grossman, in a big and sparsely furnished apartment where strangers came and went, eating and sleeping. I myself spent a few days in the convenient milieu of the Grossmans.

Once I asked Mishi, "Who are those two guys?"

"Which ones you mean?" Mishi asked.

I pointed them out to Mishi as they sat in shirtsleeves in his living room. "No idea," was his honest answer.

Cologne had been bombed with no mercy; miles and miles of housing lay in ruins. But the famous carnival spirit had returned, and the picturesque houses on the Old Market (*Alde Maa't*) still stood in their eccentric, disorderly fashion. There was even a carnival song about them in a vile *Kolsch* dialect (" . . . *Die Husche' bunt am Alde Maa't . . .*") and a sculpture was raised for the beloved fun characters Tunnes and Shale. The citizens of Cologne seemed to take pride in their laid-back nature that was so different from the German stereotype. Hamburg, the northern port city where the Tropical Institute is located, had been even more thoroughly bombed than Cologne. I registered for a six-month course in tropical diseases and lived in a Jewish old people's home on the once-elegant Rotenbaum Chasse, where I provided

A smiling Lici.

medical services in return for room and board. (That is where I diagnosed and treated my first case of lobar pneumonia.)

Hamburg was a fascinating city. The magnificent houses around the *Alster*, with their own port facilities and warehouses, reminded me of the sublime ambiance of the *Konigliche Kaufmann* from *The Buddenbrocks*, the refined, rich, and cultured families. In contrast was San Pauli, the same city but another world; the sailor town of Hamburg, the *Raperbahn* with its nightclubs, nude dancers, tattoo parlours, gambling houses, red-light district, and the "Little Erna" jokes.

I missed my family. When I finished the course, I decided to go to Israel. Lici stayed in Germany.

Nocturnal Images:

Random Thoughts of an Insomniac

We, the endlessly dared—how far we have come!
And only taciturn Death can know what we are
and how he must always profit when he lends us time

From Rainer Maria Rilke, *The Sonnets to Orpheus* II, 24
Translated by Stephen Mitchell

The background drone of the city has reached its lowest point and the streets are wrapped in darkness. This is the hour when almost everyone is sleeping. I lie on my back in my bed, lamps unlit in the room. For want of anything better, I watch the strange geometrics of the streaks of light on the ceiling, projected there by the complex laws of physics. They cruise on the white surface in one or the other direction, whenever a lonely car goes down the main road. But other "projectionists" are busy, too. Thoughts and memories scroll up, down, and sideways in my mind. This is the time for bizarre ideas and philosophies to uncurl.

Sometimes I wonder: what if I had been born into a Christian family—say, in Texas or Connecticut. Depending on the decade of my birth, I would probably have a crew cut, play football, and attend an Ivy League college. Likely I would have only insignificant contact with Jews, whom I would view mostly with indifference, perhaps with disdain, perchance with sympathy. Possibly I would have bad memories for other reasons.

True, I would have escaped the pain of persecution, but what about my identity? Where would my emotional immersion in the Jewish culture, Jewish history, Jewish destiny be? Yes, I could have turned many wasted years into useful training. Yes, I would have been saved from the horrors and deep wounds of the past, from the years of panic attacks and nightmares.

Surely I would have had other friends but not the friends I have now, whom I love and cherish. Who would remember my lost relatives and friends? Who would say Kaddish on Yom Ha'Shoah for Robert Markovitch or for Edith or for Zsuzsika? Would it be worthwhile to be free from these obligations and remembrances? What about solidarity and comradeship with other survivors? Would I give it up? I look sincerely into my soul and say, "No."

What if I had been born into a German Christian family, for example in post-war Hanover? Why does the world saddle me with guilt for what I have not done myself, for something I perhaps detest, for something that happened before I was born?

An insomniac has lots of time. So what about another scenario? What if I had been born into a Jewish family, let us say in Montreal? But then who, if anyone, would have saved Lici? I would not have been a survivor, a witness. I probably never would have met and married Edie. Nor would I have had to endure the years of torpor that my own government and circumstances compelled me to do, while half of my people were being murdered.

Ah! I take the scars, the nightmares, and the memories, pack them up in my rucksack and choose to be what I am—a survivor.

CHAPTER 13

Voyage to the Ancestral Shores

The French genius, Jean Francois Champollion "Le Jeune," read his papers to the Academy of Grenoble at the age of sixteen, was appointed professor of history at nineteen, solved the puzzle of the Rosetta Stone and the ancient Egyptian hieroglyphics, and died at forty-two. Surely he was more deserving than to have a rickety immigrant vessel named after him. But this scruffy little tub, proudly wearing the French tricolour, was cheerfully awaiting us in the sunny port of Naples, while Vesuvius retired for a smoke in the background. One look at its pitiable, worn-out hull convinced us that this floating disaster would never make it to Haifa. Surely it would sink.

And sink, it did. No, no, not just then, but two weary years later, halfway between Israeli and Lebanese waters. Some passengers were saved by Israel, some made it to Lebanon, and no one died. But back then, we still made our emetic crossing safely enough to Haifa. A former classmate, Stephen Lichtblau, the most recent M.D., also joined us hopefuls. We sang *Hatikvah* as we left Munich by train, where we had said good-bye to Lici before setting out for our ancestral homeland.

In Haifa, I had a joyful, tearful reunion with my parents and Marta and Jan. In just a short while, Father, against all odds, had established himself in business. He started to produce his electric gadgets after a sordid beginning when he washed cars for a pittance to put bread on the table. Marta worked as a freelance beautician; she had a kind of grocery cart loaded to the hilt with her paraphernalia that she pushed in the searing, subtropical heat to make house calls.

Times were gruelling in those years in Israel. After all, more than one million immigrants had arrived in those years in that tiny country, tripling the population. These immigrants included many survivors of the national tragedy that befell European Jewry, but in addition a large number of Jewish refugees came from the Arab countries, from Algeria, from Yemen. These Jews were sometimes forced to flee, barely getting away with their lives and leaving behind all their possessions. Israel was at war, food had to be rationed—*tzena*, they used to call it—but the basic principle of the government that no one should starve was maintained. Therefore, a few items, such as bread, which was very good, eggplant, and frozen fish fillets were free from rationing. Everything else, even oranges, was rationed.

Few of the newcomers, if any, had refrigerators. We had an old icebox, cooled by lumps of ice. Every day, we had to carry the heavy pieces of ice with big metal forceps, and the icebox was shared with many other tenants. This task was mostly Jan's job. At one time, Jan was an actor and had studied at the University of Prague. He still hoped to return to his profession, but all he could get were a few roles in a Hungarian theatre in Tel Aviv.

Photocopy of a drawing and signatures that was given to my father after the war by the illegal Slovak immigrants whom Father helped to escape deportation to Auschwitz and to survive the war in Hungary.

Life was difficult in that fledgling country. The recently arrived and destitute immigrant population outnumbered the original residents two to one. Most immigrants did not speak the language of the land. Immigrants kept pouring in from all regions of the world where Jews were persecuted, threatening a repetition of the biblical story of the Tower of Babel—this time in Israel.

We were often visited by Pipez, who now lived on a kibbutz. Sometimes he arrived with a pocketful of eggs, for such a treasure was readily available on an agricultural kibbutz. It was in Israel that we saw him for the first time after that heart-rending story in the Jewish orphanage in 1944. Later, he was almost killed by the Nazis, who murdered his grandmother and his two sisters, Eva and Zsuzsi, in Auschwitz, and his father, Henry, in the forced-labour camp. Pipez was the last scion of his family.

My parents rented one room in a *pension*, as did Marta and Jan, in Ramat Gan, near Tel Aviv. There, the facilities were shared and the climate was hard to endure. To my shock, I was informed that Mother had developed severe insulin-dependent diabetes and had to maintain a rigid diet. She therefore got a "special" rationing card, but when she cooked, using a small metal burner that Father had fashioned for her from discarded metal boxes, Mother regularly cheated. A large portion of her "sick ration" went into the family pot to improve the blandness of our meals. I invented a "cake" made of bread, molasses, and jam.

The first days in Israel. Mother, Marta, myself, Father, and "Pipez."

My parents did their best to show me around in the first days after my arrival. But in those days, the outskirts of Tel Aviv were covered with a vast expanse of red sand. At night, one could hear the whining and laughing of scavenging jackals. Scorpions were ubiquitous. Tropical illnesses like malaria, amoebiasis, and leishmaniosis, were still fairly common.

I soon paid a visit to the Sick Fund Institute, *Kupat Cholim*, where almost every physician began his or her professional activities. It was in downtown Tel Aviv on an old street named Samenhof that was lined with wild orange trees. The unimpressed administrators hardly looked at my diploma, which I proudly waved around whenever I had the chance. Instead, they told me to go for a few days to an outpatient clinic in the small town of Petach Tiqva, where another physician would show me the local routines.

Next morning, I was on my way, taking a bus to the dusty little town. I soon found the clinic and the specified colleague, an old physician with white hair, short pants, rosy cheeks, and a sunny nature. He asked me many questions, some professional, some not. Then he insisted that I sit in with him while he saw his patients. Sometimes he casually asked me how they treated such cases nowadays in Germany, or what else the diagnosis might be for the patient we had just seen.

What a linguist he was! He communicated with ease in German, English, French, and Russian. He was also fluent in modern Hebrew and Arabic. Incidentally, the latter was his hobby. He collected Arabic folklore. His friendliness had no limits. He invited me to his house for lunch. He was a widower and prepared the food himself while I looked around his den. Books were piled from floor to ceiling, as well as in the middle of the room. A diploma hung on the wall. No, it was not a diploma. A closer look revealed that it was a beautifully scripted letter of gratitude on his retirement from many decades of teaching internal medicine in Genf. Then we chatted about medical literature.

Later, I came to the conclusion that this "showing me the routine" was actually a sort of informal examination. There were too many people with too many phony diplomas after the war. In the *Kupat Cholim*, some friendly officials showed me a Tel Aviv hospital, the *Tel Ha'Shomer*. One of the administrators drove me there in his car, the height of elegance. I still remember that his car was a DeSoto. How could he afford this? It must have cost a fortune! Back in the main office, I met some more officials. All were well dressed and looked well-to-do. We spoke German.

"Do you have any special interest in medicine?" one of them inquired.

"I certainly do," I answered.

Bitterly, the horrendous times I had suffered through came to my mind. The friends and relatives I had lost in the *Shoah*, the student years, the hunger, my livelihood from blood donations, Mother's illness, the panic attacks that had made my life so difficult, Lici's TB, and my divorce, all flashed through my mind one by one . . . and the DeSoto.

"What might it be?" came the question. My bitterness turned to anger.

"To make money!" They all laughed. I did not.

"In that case, we have just the right post for you. It pays double the official salary, and you pay no income tax."

"Where is it?"

"In Eilat."

"Where is Eilat?" I asked.

"Well, it is difficult to explain now, as you do not seem to know the country well yet. Come to the airport tomorrow morning and we'll take you there."

My very first post as a legitimate physician! I was excited. I asked others, where was Eilat?

"A few miles west of Hell. But don't worry, it is just as hot," was the answer.

My ignorance at not connecting Eilat at that moment with its vast history was unforgivable. Immortalized in the Old Testament is King Solomon's Canticle of Canticles (Solomon 1:7, ". . . *umbilicus sicut crater eburneus . . .*"—"a navel like an ivory crater"), which was inspired by the enchanting Shulamite Queen of Sheba from Al'Yaman and Ethiopia (*The lily of the valley, the flower of Sharon*), while Solomon's gold-laden fleet waited in the port of Etzion Geber, the modern Eilat—Aqaba. Many subsequent Jewish rulers, such as Hiram, Jehoshafat, and Uzzia, benefited from the wealth of Eilat's once-rich mines. But this was twenty-seven centuries ago. Since then, only devastation has followed, as if an angry nature had turned her back on this desolate land.

Vast mountains of indifferent sand had choked this once-famous place into a dry oblivion. Rocks cracked from the rapidly alternating oven-like midday heat and cold desert nights. Tough plants survived here and there by having waxy, leather-like leaves that parsimoniously retain every trace of moisture. Fauna and flora had evolved a frugal, fluid-conserving metabolism. Enchanting layers of beige and brown contrasted with the striking blueness of the sky that stretched far away without a trace of white cloud above us. The dominance of these colours made the deep green leaves of the odd desert tree stand out like emeralds.

Peculiar little bundles wrapped in cloth were hung by unseen hands on the branches of these solitary trees. It was said that the Bedouins had placed them there and that they contained an emergency supply of water. Swinging in the constant wind, the water became quite cold. Removing them might cost the life of the owner as he crossed the desert because he counted on their being there.

The right arm of such a thief was a small price to pay according to the harsh laws of the desert.

Is the desert a *"soulless place where the sky is the king . . . where ugliness is ubiquitous,"* as Albert Camus portrayed it? No, on that point I disagree with him. The desert has its own magic!

We met in the early morning at a military airport near Tel Aviv, and guess who flew the plane? Zolo, my own cousin. He frequently flew to Eilat in his military plane, a Dakota. These Dakotas were old warhorses, with an oval cut out on the side for parachute jumping (open during the flight!), and simple handholds, like on buses, for "comfort."

It took nearly an hour to get to Eilat. The arrival was overwhelming. It was early summer. The heat was tremendous. We had to be careful not to touch any metallic objects that lay exposed to the sun, lest we burn our fingers. Somehow, the fine sand got into everything. It squished between my teeth, rolled into tiny hard balls in the corners of my eyes, covered the fine membranes of my nose and throat, and got stuck in my ear canals.

Walking in the desert is exhausting. Your body bends forward to meet the never-ending hot wind, while your feet sink into the burning sand with each step. Where there is no sand, the scattered rocks are an equally harsh impediment. The Negev; it seems that the landscape has defied the passage of time; the terrain remains unaltered since Biblical times. I imagined meeting a group of ancient Hebrews, led by Aaron, crossing the desert and scouting the canyons and ominous cliffs on their way to the Promised Land. We were lulled into the misapprehension that we did not sweat. In fact, we did, but we could not notice it as it dried instantly. When we licked our lips or hand, it tasted very salty. This was the way to get rapidly dehydrated!

In 1951, Eilat was a pioneer town with a population of 400 people, mostly construction workers from the "Solel Bone" Company, building the first housing project for a nonexistent but hopefully future population. No electricity was available, but in the evening, tractors were used to generate some power, along with the by-product of a disproportionately large output of decibels.

People slept outside in the sand under the stars. A single, crumbling ancient Arab building, Um-Rash-Rash, which looked like a barn, was the "downtown." It was owned at that time by a Dutch couple, the Piementhals. Daringly it was called a hotel, the *malon*—what chutzpa! The drinking water was rationed. Some water was brought in from Ber Ora quite a distance away, but it contained perilously high levels of magnesia.

Besides construction workers, there were also some criminals (I still have the newspaper clipping) who were given a choice between jail or being free and working in Eilat. Wisely, most of them chose jail, despite the high hopes of Ben Gurion, who held a childish belief that Eilat would become a booming community someday. Sand, heat, and flies were the only things in abundance in Eilat.

On the positive side were the incredibly blue and surprisingly cool waters of the Red Sea, with high mountains on both sides of the bay and a span of transparent azure firmament. The Red Sea was not red at all. What was red, however, was the mountain range that embraced this magnificent bay. In the bright daylight, it was an almost indelicate orange colour, which turned to a glowing copper, as though the nearby copper mines of King Solomon had found their molten content on the surface of the reef. As evening approached, the rocky cliffs turned from red to mauve, then to navy blue, until finally they became one with the night sky. Soon the desert was silvered by moonlight.

All around, the silence of the desert ruled (once the electricity-generating tractors were turned off, thank Heaven!). Silence without any background noise, a silence that a city dweller has never heard, a silence that makes the ears buzz from hearing one's own circulation.

And the spectacle of the desert sky! On the very first night, lying on the sand that still radiated the daytime heat, I gazed at the starlit sky and thought that it was not a coincidence that science, philosophy, and religion all began in this region. Did I hear perhaps a strain of faint Pythagorean astral music? I found myself hypnotized into the arithmetical compulsion of counting the stars above me. Beyond the planets and the known constellations like the Big Dipper, Canus Major, and others, I playfully connected these heavenly bodies to form mystical, geometric figures, as if it were a Rorschach test, to contemplate the endlessness of the Universe, its ultimate Purpose, and the unremitting passage of Time.

One never got enough sleep in Eliat in those days. When the tormenting heat of the day finally eased, everyone felt relieved, somewhat revived, and therefore neither wishing nor able to sleep. The boisterous youngsters were shouting, their vivaciousness bursting forth. The management showed old and silly movies, using the electric current provided by the noisy generators, but they might as well have been silent movies in the midst of that hellish noise. (Maybe they were.) A sheet was hung in the sand as a movie screen. This was sometimes used for target practice by pistol-toting youngsters who were impatient to end the conflict portrayed by the actors; so they shot the villains on the screen prematurely.

So no one slept. But the trouble was worse in the morning. With first light came the invasion of flies—flies that quite sensibly slept miles away from the noise created by our less-wise species. And now, well rested and lively, swarms of them were ready to start their daily fly business. You covered your face with a sheet, but it was too hot to endure. Between the heat and the flies, one could only console oneself with breakfast, inevitably accompanied by both plagues, the flies and the heat.

I had a male nurse, an experienced army medic, a *hovesh* who took care of much of the business. I found out (also a saved newspaper snippet) that Eilat had not been able to get a doctor until now. I was the first civilian physician in Eilat. But what in the world could have prepared me in Budapest, in Innsbruck, or even in the Tropical Institute in Hamburg, for all this? For the scorpions that crawled into your shoes at night . . . for the sea urchins like hedgehogs in the water near the shore, just waiting to penetrate the skins of unsuspecting bathers and cause painful inflammations . . .

My inexperience earned me some embarrassment, particularly from my *hovesh*. When I asked him to take the temperature of a patient, he laughed, the bastard, like a barking dog, bending over and slapping his thighs with his palms, until I, pink in the face, understood that we had only a single thermometer—and it was strictly for decorative purposes. The usefulness of this precious instrument was limited by the simple fact that the outside temperature in the shade was 120°F.

But slowly I learned. Once in a while, Zolo arrived in his Dakota and brought me cool, fresh water from the plane, where it was always available. Rarely, tourist planes came and stayed for a few hours, bringing pretty American girls who were withering from desiccation and overwhelmed by us, testosterone-driven macho men with one-track minds.

Since I was the only physician in Eilat, I was also the government physician. One day, I received notification from the Ministry of Health, written in a highly diplomatic tone, instructing me to do a Wasserman, a blood test for syphilis, "on the female population." This was the two prostitutes. I told my *hovesh* to bring both women early the next morning so that we could send the blood samples on the departing plane. But they disappeared, and for a while the town had no female population. For that I earned more contempt.

On one of those first days, I got an emergency call from one of the border *kibbutzim*. The message came via an old-fashioned camp telephone that had to be cranked to bring it to life. The message was that one of the boys had suffered a heart attack on that distant border *kibbutz*. A Moroccan driver with a jeep was available.

Then I made my first mistake: "Drive as fast as you can," I instructed him. The reckless daredevil! How his evil eyes sparkled as he bared his tobacco-stained teeth in a grin! What he failed to tell me was that we would have to travel a serpentine mountain road at night, near the Egyptian border, with no headlights. "But the moonlight," he said, "is good enough."

The mountain road was only half finished. When I arrived, my legs were shaking. I asked the two kibbutzniks at the gate what had happened. They were busy eating a meat conserve from the can with their bayonets. One pointed his bayonet toward the only barrack. There I found a muscular young fellow holding his side while he turned and twisted on his bunk from agonizing back pain. The pain went down both of his thighs. He was sweating (who was not?). I looked at his urine. A faint tinge of blood? Maybe. Heart attack, like hell! He had kidney stones that were stuck in the ureter.

Now what to do? I had to give him something for his pain. I drew some morphine and some atropine into a syringe, turning, this battle-scarred tough guy into a whining little boy. "*Zrika, zrika*," (needles) he moaned over and over again. He got his injection, and I decided to transport him to the nearest "big city," which was, of course, Eilat. He was put in the jeep, and the harrowing return trip on the rough serpentine road commenced.

The credit really must go to my Moroccan driver. The morphine soothed the patient's pain, the atropine relaxed his smooth muscles, and halfway to Eilat, the jeep shook out the kidney stones. But I earned respect and recognition for my vast medical knowledge, even from my *hovesh*. I harvested the sweetness of my triumph, keeping any self-doubts to myself.

My attempt to build a filtering device on the water tap to remove the magnesia was a naïve engineering effort that failed. The high magnesia content was a real problem. If people drank as much water as they needed, they got terrible diarrhea and consequently lost even more fluid until they became dehydrated. Ben Gurion is crazy. There will never be a city here.

Many adventures, medical and otherwise, had passed in Eilat before I fell sick and weak and began to have diarrhea myself. But as I did not drink that water, it must have been caused by something else. Then nausea and vomiting joined my misery, and I barely knew how I arrived at Tel Aviv. It was an amoeba that plagued me—*Entamoeba histolytica*. It took quite a while for me to recover, but when I went back to Eilat, I still did not feel well. It was worse when I had to walk against the wind, in the ankle-deep hot sand.

Somebody planted a few tiny trees near the shore. We used to give a few drops of our precious drinking water to these unfortunate kidnapped saplings that deserved better. Some died, but some lived, and they are now the oldest trees in Eilat, at Um-Rash-Rash, near the Red Rock Discotheque.

A boy was shot by the Egyptians near the border. He had an abdominal wound, and there was no way of knowing what the bullet, which had penetrated him from the side, had damaged. There was also the chance of hemorrhage. He had to be opened up. I was by myself, without any professional help, and had to do the surgery on a stretcher. I thought of Dr. Bela Molnar while I dealt with the emergency. I sweated so much that I felt close to dehydration by the time I finished. One construction guy with a sense of humour, which I could appreciate only in retrospect, called out to the patient, "Move over, pal. Let the Doc lie on the stretcher." But the patient was all right, tolerated the air trip to Tel Aviv well, and did not sue me for malpractice. (By now, he does not have a case.)

An unexpected visitor arrived. She was a cheerful grey donkey, shaking her big head up and down and blowing air through her nostrils, clearly flirting with me. She ate some of the filling of my mattress and seemed to declare her friendship; but when I tried to sit on her back, she looked at me with reproachful eyes and immediately lay down. I understood her disapproval of my rude behaviour towards a lady friend. Communication was difficult; she vocalized only rarely and then with some awkwardness. I sympathized with her language difficulties and understood that she preferred to chat with body language.

She followed me around for a while, flicking her long ears back and forth, sometimes in different directions, carefully listening to our discussions. Now and then, she tried to chase away the flies by skillfully vibrating parts of her hide. She clearly came from Aqaba, to the despair of her Arab owner, who got her back eventually after a complicated international deal via the United Nations. She was not just any kind of donkey!

Soon, however, I became ill again and had no choice but to return to Tel Aviv. There, I slowly recovered and began to work in the neighbourhoods of Petach Tiqva, Ramat Chaim, Givat Rambam, and other little settlements. I made a lot of house calls. The difficulty with house calls was that many of the streets were so new that they had no names. "The second green house, left from the railway crossing." You got there, and all the houses were yellow. And so on.

The nearby refugee settlement was full of Moroccan Jews. They spoke a language that was, amazingly, supposed to be French but sounded more like Arabic. I had my adventures there, too. I was called to a barrack "urgently."

There, an elderly man, unconscious, had obviously had a stroke. His six sons towered around his bed.

"Make him bleed! You must cut his vein and bleed him!" they advised me, kindly and forcefully, about the latest advancement in medical science.

"No . . ."

"What? This is our father! Make him bleed . . . or somebody will bleed anyway!"

I had a large fifty-mL syringe in my bag, and started to draw blood from him. Nowadays not many physicians can say that they treated a patient by bleeding in modern Israel, where outstanding specialists were performing delicate neurosurgery, and medical research had made huge steps forward. But the land was always a spectrum of extremes from the ancient to the avant-garde, all under one roof.

In those tumultuous years, severe epidemics of poliomyelitis ravaged many parts of the world, including Israel, where I have seen my share of tragedies, particularly in the immigrant camps. In 1951, no vaccination existed.

It saddened me, but it was clear that I could not make much money in the emerging new state. At least that was the way I felt then, mainly because I was full of impatient aspirations. In my stateless passport I still had a "return visa" to Germany, where I could apply for overseas emigration. The winter arrived, but it was not cold. An almost incessant rain fell in those last few days, mostly just a drizzle, but from time to time, a sudden cloudburst brought plump and lusty water drops that plopped against the window. The Ayalon, usually a dry river bed most of the year, swelled into a tidal current until it overflowed its shores, creating a veritable lake between Tel Aviv and Ramat Gan.

* * *

The miniature Italian liner *Philippo Grimani*, with her lazy crew and choleric master, was peevishly waiting in Haifa just before dawn. My parents were with me at the port, Mother waving good-bye with a deep sadness in her eyes that singed my soul. Soon the journey began. A mélange of feelings— sadness, guilt, defiance, and fear of an unknown future—took hold of me. Leaning against the railing, deep in thought, I watched the ship riding the row of slow, heaving peaks and rapidly plunging valleys moulded by vast masses of foamy salt water and listened to the monotonous creaking of the worn-out keel. I was so alone! By morning, we would be in Piraeus, Greece.

* * *

New Year's Eve in Rome. The train arrived from Venice, where the *Philippo Grimani* had docked. The master of the ship quarreled with his staff, threw his cap on the floor, and danced and trampled it in his fury. He was so funny that everyone laughed except the crew—they had seen better performances from the master.

On the train from Venice to Rome, I was seated beside a mild-mannered young Italian priest whom I mercilessly tortured throughout the trip while I tried to refresh my Italian at his expense. He probably earned quite a few brownie points to enter Heaven. Close to midnight, I settled into my cheap hotel room and looked out the window. This was when the war broke out.

* * *

At the stroke of midnight, the windows of the neighbourhood flew open, and old chairs, damaged porcelain pieces, and broken picture frames flew out onto the street, which was now completely empty. Italians knew better than to walk on the streets on New Year's Eve at midnight. Peacefully wandering cats ran for their lives, howling. Then, "Happy, happy New Year! *Il capo di anno. Buona fortuna!*" Everyone kissing and toasting. Except myself. I had no one to celebrate with. The chipped cups, bringing bad luck, and other similarly cursed items flew out the window as they did year after year, to bribe the incoming year of 1952! What will it bring? Again, I felt alone. I decided to call Tom tomorrow.

Dreams and Tears: X

A Sentimental Journey: Past or Future?

The sea was sapphire coloured, and the sky
Burned like heated opal through the air

From Oscar Wilde, *Impression de Voyage*

Ever since my original adventures, I have returned from time to time to the renascent city of Eilat, the site of my first job as a physician. But this time, I had stayed away for many years. Therefore, the last trip brought a surprise. We could barely get a reservation in one of the many luxury hotels that fringe the azure bay, even though it was out of season. We arrived in the evening hours, just when the mountain range turned into an unlikely lavender blue. But the streetlights already sparkled and the forest of multicoloured neon lights twinkled, illuminating the modern city that spread far beyond what we had ever dared to imagine. Everything was air-conditioned—the department stores, movie houses, malls, and hospitals. The Club Mediterranee was a marvel. The restaurants offered a choice of French, American, Russian, and Oriental cuisines, and fabulous seafood ranged in abundance from the stylish establishments to the small eateries. Discotheques and nightclubs opened their doors long after we went to sleep. Masses of eager-to-speed taxis waited impatiently at traffic lights, carrying holidaymakers back and forth.

Next morning, I could not wait to walk in the direction of Um-Rash-Rash, to see whatever remained of the *malon*, our "hotel" at that time, the single building around which we used to sleep under the stars. I passed yacht clubs with splendid sailboats and motorboats and walked along the sandy beaches shared by all the hotels. It was December, but the beaches were packed with people, many of the beautiful European girls enjoying the warmth of the sun in topless bikinis. It was still early morning, but the cobalt sea was full of swimmers and people snorkelling, speaking many languages—a veritable Babel. A city of youth. The tourist boats gathered their passengers for aquatic adventures, while the buses competed with them, offering tours to Jordan or Egypt, King Solomon's mines and the desert. There were no flies to be seen.

The tiny building remains from Um-Rash-Rash have become a national monument. A sculpture commemorating the Negev Brigade stands in front of it. The trees that we planted some fifty years ago are still there at the side of the Red Rock Hotel and are now the oldest trees in Eilat. Some young people were playing in the park that surrounded the historic building of Um-Rash-Rash, and I could hardly restrain myself from collecting them around me to narrate the story of the Old Eilat.

It also occurred to me that even from my one-time salary as a starting physician, I could have bought half of Eilat's real estate then, and it would have made me the richest man in Israel. If only I had listened to that dreamer Ben Gurion!

CHAPTER 14

Die Wanderjahre

Tom and his jealous cat Cili lived a life of leisure in the bourgeois neighbourhood of Rome's Via Ruggiero Fauro. Tom rented a furnished, four-room apartment. He was still a final-year medical student, but he had to provide himself with the particular lifestyle to which he had become accustomed. Considering his circle of friends, especially his girlfriends, and his bachelor parties, this demanded quite a sum of money. He earned this by working under Professor Binessoni at the Ministry of Health, as well as in several other agencies. He was also a "consultant in mental health issues" at the International Hospital Monte Verde in Rome and at various other places. By then, his command of Italian was impeccable. For transportation, he used a motorcycle.

When I called him to say that I was in Rome, he was delighted, and in his gracious and persuasive manner he insisted that I become his houseguest. Immediately. It did not take any particular urging on his part for me to move in.

Tom was in his morning mood when I arrived, trying to wake up and making espresso coffee—many cups of it. We listened to each other's news of our adventures. Cili found a comfortable niche for herself on the couch, curled up, and ignored me as she went to sleep, her "motor" going. I chatted with Tom about my experiences until suddenly Cili was up, hissing, her back curved, her fur standing on end. A moment later, the reason for Cili's hostile stance walked into the room.

She was a young, vivacious, leggy, shapely British woman named Edna, dressed in a white nurse's uniform and spreading breezy charm and beauty. As was frequently the case, Edna was slightly late for her hospital duty at Monte Verde. She was surely worth a second glance. She smelled of soap, had thick reddish-blonde hair combed up under her white cap except for a short, capricious lock that unbeknownst to her mischievously hung down on her sleek brow. She wore almost no make-up, only a touch of pale, natural-coloured lipstick.

She spoke English to Tom. My English was nonexistent in those days, so we switched to Italian, which Edna spoke poorly. I immediately felt a great attraction to her. Tom (in Hungarian) denied that they were lovers, but Cili, in her unforgiving attitude to Edna, informed me otherwise in cat language. Yes, at one time, yes—but it was long ago, conceded Tom. Now he had "others." And "others," to Cili's hysteria, he indeed had in great numbers.

Tom gave Edna a lift to the hospital on his motorcycle. She smiled, and a sudden saucy breeze pressed her white nurse's uniform against her lithe, young body. Wrapped in this fashion, for a fraction of an unchaste second she looked more nude than if she were naked. I saw Edna's long, graceful legs as she swung them over the back seat of the motorcycle and sat on the pillion, her skirt riding up to reveal, for a split second, the tops of her white stockings, tight garters, and a stretch of pale skin under the billowing material. Tom revved up the motor, and Edna did the same with my furtive erotic fantasies. Then they were gone.

That was the magical epoch following the war when the Americans discovered Rome. That was the pre-Fellini era, when the Via Veneto near the Villa Borghese was more Hollywood real estate than Italian. In the tepid January sunshine, in one square kilometre, the movie moguls, stars, and international courtesans of both sexes easily outnumbered the overworked gossip columnists and paparazzi. The Via Veneto was the place where things happened. The city was in a frenzy to accommodate the world. And Tom was part of this whirling social white water.

Tom introduced me to some of his friends and colleagues, an array of students, professors, and just bright people who shared a common proclivity for humour, the entry ticket into Tom's circle. They were the upper-class Roman intellectuals, very urbane, with charming manners and natural elegance. We met either in Tom's house or in espresso bars. As I once did in Budapest, I again enjoyed animated discussions and heated arguments, although I was severely handicapped by my limited command of Italian. And there was never a shortage of well-dressed, long-limbed Italian beauties with outstanding minds and satiny olive skin. *Le beau monde*. And the *demi-monde* as well.

I had plenty of opportunities to see in Rome, as I walked around the remains of the ancient city, the crumbling walls that in my imagination still echoed with the famous lamentations of the past, the drama of Cato (". . . *ceterum censeo . . .*"—"other than that I suggest [that Carthage should be destroyed]"), and Cicero (". . . *quo usque tandem abutere patientia nostra . . .*"—"just how long you wish to abuse our patience"), and so many others. Unhurriedly, I saw many museums, galleries, and churches. I savoured the spirit of modern Rome, admired the peacock-like *carabinieri* with their white gloves and shiny swords. But most of all, I loved to watch the street scenes of people milling about and so easily excited, theatrically protesting to the Creator with eyes turned to heaven, hands gesturing, confiding their indignation to the All-Merciful.

I marvelled at the well-known tourist sights: the Colosseum, the Forum, the Old Appian Way, and the Pantheon. I stared at the beauty of Bernini's fountains, the Piazza Navone, the boutiques on the Via Condotti. I strolled in the Trastevere. Slowly ambling up the Ponte Fabricio, I surveyed some of the less popular sights—the old hospital in the Isola Tiberina, the ancient Thermae, the subterranean Basilica at the Porta Maggiore, with its neo-Pythagorean past. With the melody of Respighi's *Feste Romane* in my heart, I walked around the ancient streets and saw the busy marketplace at the Piazza Campo dei Fiori where the "heretic" Giordano Bruno, the itinerant Renaissance philosopher-writer, was burned at the stake.

Edna lived in the same building as Tom, and for one reason or another I found excuses to visit her. These were the years of my erotic peregrinations. One evening, I found her just as she came out of the shower, covered with a gossamer sheet of something. The limpid folds of the fabric suggested her graceful lines. We both felt ready. I embraced her and felt her hair gently brushing against my face, her divine curls now falling below her shoulder. I kissed her, and she breezed against my lips without pulling away her willowy, lithe body: "No use, I am frigid." She said it in a matter-of-fact way that made it believable. It sounded like an aphrodisiac. My body pressed hard against her curves. Very slowly and gently, we became lovers.

She had some set habits. When home from hospital duty, she loved to take long, leisurely showers and to use perfumed body lotions. She had a drawer full of rainbow-coloured panties, some plain, some suggestive in satin trimmed with lace, some made of silk with scalloped edges. She called them "knickers," and changed them several times a day. This habit had nothing to do with hygiene but seemed to give her pleasure.

Her favourite colours were chartreuse, lavender, and turquoise. Once I teased her in broken Italian that perhaps she should wear all three, one on top of the other. She did not appreciate the remark. In the hospital, she always used a pale lipstick that matched her lips. But when off duty, she wore stunning lipsticks chosen from her remarkable repertoire to fit her mood: shimmery coral, velvety pink, berry red. I loved to watch her putting on lipstick. She made the act into an ultra-feminine, sensuous performance that required her total devotion, forming an open, curled "O" with the rim of her tightened mouth, as if she were making love to her lips. Through her make-up mirror, I watched her slowly apply the satiny pigment of her whim to her lips. Then she blotted off the excess creamy coating, signifying the end of the ritual.

She used to lie on top of me naked, the tips of her soft fingers playfully stroking my cheeks, lips, or eyebrows, while mine were gently raking the fine arch of her spine or caressing the nape of her neck under the weight of her tumbling reddish-blonde tresses. She often gazed deeply into my eyes as if trying to read my thoughts and whispered to me in English, first a rapid, silky banter, then a non-stop, more serious chatter, soliloquizing in a hushed tone, all the while aware, but choosing not to care, that I failed to grasp her meaning. I realized that these loquacious narratives must have been important for her and perhaps allowed her to drop her inhibitions, for she knew that our relationship was shamelessly physical.

As she twittered away, she sometimes blushed girlishly for reasons I could not grasp. At other times, her eyes suddenly filled with tears, the saltiness of which I kissed away. I often wondered what she was telling me. Perhaps she was saying that this was an exception, she was usually not like this at all. Perhaps she was explaining that what made her so devilishly daring was the very fact that I did not speak or understand her language.

Soon enough, I had to move on. I was to go to Cologne, but Edna persuaded me to take the longer route so that she could accompany me to Paris, where we could spend a few days together. I happily accepted this suggestion. Tom wished us a good trip, and we took the train from Rome.

The locomotive emitted a series of short, rapid puffs of steam, and almost imperceptibly, the train began to move with the familiar, repetitious, metallic rhythm and tedious tugs and throws, forcing upon us the monotonous choreography of train travel. Edna and I were alone in the second-class compartment. Soon we left behind the Etruscan plain and the carefully cultivated fields.

The trip was tedious. One can kiss for only so long, and we tired of our cumbersome conversation. Then the famous old Simplon Tunnel, which takes quite a while to pass through by train, challenged us. So we switched off the lights and in the darkness indulged ourselves in the carnal rites of the satyr Silenius and Dionysus. Towards the evening hours, we arrived at the busy, whirling, rain-splattered station in Paris, where the colourful neon lights were reflected in the dark mirror of the rain-slicked pavement.

We stayed in a very small and cheap hotel on the Boulevard Haussmann. But small as the hotel was, it surprised us with its amazingly vigorous nighttime traffic that carried on with unceasing vitality. We fell on the bed exhausted, but we were kept awake for a little while longer by our fatigued senses, which continued to mimic the long-endured noises and motions of the train ride.

Edna's self-declared frigidity was long in the past. Paris and Edna! Oh, how I loved to discover her body, her slender waist—the charm of the Tuileries and the Boulevard Saint Michel; the hollowness of her ticklish neck—the Place de la Concorde and the Louvre; the two gentle dimples on each side of her lower spine, just above her buttocks—the Arc de Triomphe and the Sacre Coeur cathedral; the roundness of her breasts—Montmartre and the Opera. How I remember the Eiffel Tower that Robert Delaunay revered as the feminine symbol of Paris! How I recall the semicircle of a slight purplish furrow, revealing the ghost of the elastic in her panties that drew an arc onto her tender skin. Money we did not have, but we still saw everything in Paris, including the Louvre, "from the outside" only (except the Eiffel Tower), and we were hungry most of the time. We ate junk food. So much for French cuisine.

The last day arrived. Edna went south, to the Gare de Lyon. I was destined to go to the northeast to the Gare de L'Est. I took her to the Gare de Lyon. I wrapped her in my arms, and she melted into my embrace. Then she clung to me tightly, as if in despair. I inhaled her intoxicating femininity. But our kiss tasted sad. It conveyed an unspoken good-bye. I wanted to turn around and watch her depart, but she insisted that I not follow her departure with my eyes. She picked up her luggage and—clink, clunk, clink, clunk—her high heels echoed evanescently on the stones of the Gare de Lyon behind me; clink, clunk, clink, clunk—the diminishing sound of her rhythmic walk faded out of my sphere and from my life forever.

* * *

Lici was working at the Max Planck Institute in Cologne. She looked awful. Dark circles framed her eyes and she had obviously lost weight. I was shocked. The shadow of death had taken over her face. Tired? All the time. Night sweats? Fever? Yes, maybe. Cough? Incessant. I barely needed to do the physical examination to hear the amphoric breathing in the right upper lobe caused by the cavity in her lung.

In nearby Merheim, I knew Dr. Jentgen, the head of the Hospital for Chest Diseases, from my earlier internship. Lici was admitted immediately, for her condition was grave. I found work as a *locum tenens* for a busy German family physician, Dr. Hans Horn, and this provided me with a modest income. I visited Lici almost every day, bringing her delicacies that she did not even care for. Her condition steadily declined, and I grew desperate.

One day, Lici told me that she had dreamed about Cecil, her mother, who had died in Auschwitz. In the dream, Cecil told her that she must eat sprouting wheat to get well. I got hold of some wheat and put it on my windowsill to sprout. I was unsuccessful with the first trial because the neighbourhood sparrows discovered the cache and had a feast. Eventually I succeeded in growing a supply for her (it is rich in Vitamin E). I was amazed at the primitive recesses of my own mind. But faith is a powerful, though uncharted, remedy. ("Use every new method while it works," William Osler used to teach.) Lici also needed a pneumothorax. Chemotherapy, which was just around the corner, was not yet available.

Lici was engaged to Laci Revesz but he was in Sweden trying to pave their way for emigration. It was impossible for him to return to Germany. Ever so slowly, Lici got better, and her immigration visa to Sweden arrived. Where was Edna, the charmer, now, I wondered. I applied for an immigration visa to Canada.

* * *

Immigration ships seem to share some hidden property, some inherent secret disposition. The Dutch *Groote Baer*, which used to deliver troops to Korea until wear and tear rendered it unsuitable for this noble task, was waiting for us in the Rotterdam harbour. For some time now, it had been an immigration ship. However, it had already been sold for scrap metal, and this last trip to Halifax was her valedictory performance. A seemingly inoffensive and harmless smell of diesel oil, tar, and fish dominated its hull. Only much later, when the October waves of the North Atlantic caught the ship broadside and created a whirling motion that our stomachs faithfully replicated, did we realize that a logarithmic increase of the penetrating smell had been reached. This established a circular, irritating connection with the brain's disgorgement centre. Interestingly, a few passengers must have anticipated all this because they were profusely seasick while the *Groote Baer* was still tied up in Rotterdam.

The ship was at sea for a very long time. A wild rumour began to circulate that the captain was seasick. In our "stateroom," where fifty or sixty men slept with but a single sheet of metal between us and the raging salt water, everyone was sick. One poor fellow, whose name I do not know because he failed to introduce himself properly, was vomiting so hard that he dislocated his jaw. Fortunately for him, I had had ample experience in correcting this problem due to my previous exposure to electroshock treatments, where such dislocation was, in those days, a frequent occurrence.

In the midst of all this, I thought nostalgically of the Canadian Pacific shop window in Budapest, where the model of that magnificent ship, *The Empress of Britain*, with a tennis court on the top, had tempted me throughout my childhood.

My fare was paid up to Halifax, where I entered Canadian immigration, an experience that I do not now recall at all. It was early October 1952. Where should I go now? I knew nothing of North America and less about Canada. But I knew that I must move to a big city. From high school (remember how poor a student I was?) I recalled that there were two large cities in Canada: Montreal and Toronto. It really did not matter where I went, since I did not know a soul in North America.

I had a few other problems as well, such as my diploma. It was not valid in Canada. Money was no problem—I had $40. The language was a critical issue; for some reason, Hungarian, German, and Italian were not good enough here. With the other immigrants, I went (or was pushed?) to the railway station. The elderly clerk, whose German was very poor indeed, helped to decide my fate: Montreal was cheaper than Toronto by two dollars, so that was how I came to live in Monteal.

When I arrived, it was already dark, although it was only six o'clock. On the train, a young man with a Jewish look and matching accent told me that he had already rented a room in Montreal. Why not go with him? I had to go somewhere, and it did not matter where I went. My immigrant friend indeed had a room on Esplanade Street, which I recognized as a Jewish area. My soul mate's landlady spoke fluent Yiddish, something that I had picked up in various DP camps; liberally mixed with German, I could communicate with her. She had a lady friend, Mrs. Segal, who lived nearby on Fairmount Avenue and had a room to rent. Eight dollars a week.

I was exhausted when I arrived, but first I wanted to see the city! So I went to the corner of St. Urbain Street, and with a sinking heart I compared the sight with Rome's Via Veneto. I felt defeated. The good thing about this location was that I could always find my way home. I learned that when I smelled fish for the second time, I had to turn left.

Next morning, I was on my way to the local university. What is it called? McGill? Okay. Where is the library? Like a bouncing billiard ball, I eventually found everything I wanted. I sat in the library with the *Canadian Medical Association Journal* and a dictionary in front of me and I began to read the latest publication. From the back, where the advertisements were. At first, I was confused. I did not know the difference between an intern and an internist. There were plenty of hospitals looking for interns. I made note of two of them: St. Luc Hospital and the Montreal General Hospital.

"Where are they?" I asked my landlady in a language that I considered to be Yiddish.

"First you go to the St. Catherine Street," she explained, St. Catherine Street being the most popular location in Montreal. But I interrupted her.

"Where is St. Catherine Street?" I inquired.

"Oy," she said.

The way Mrs. Segal explained it, the two hospitals were in the "same block," one side French, the other English. This was almost true, but not quite. First I went to the French hospital, the St. Luc. (It did not matter because my French was no better than my English.) At the St. Luc Hospital, I confidently asked for the medical superintendent. I explained my predicament to Dr. Tetrault. We spoke "international," mingled with whatever, and in turn, he conveyed to me something that I clearly grasped: "Don't call us, we'll call you."

So much for the French hospital. I set off for the English job. As I followed Mrs. Segal's instructions faithfully, I went down the street and entered a different hospital in the same block. Again, I asked for the medical superintendent. They pushed me through a labyrinth of corridors, opened a door, and I found myself in front of Dr. Tetrault again!

On the way home, I bought some aspirin and took three tablets. I was tempted to take them all, consoling myself that I would begin to pack immediately. I had had enough of Canada.

No, I did not go back to Europe. I became depressed instead. I spoke all the wrong languages. I consoled myself by buying a Parker fountain pen, like an important person would own, for $8. How irresponsible! That represented a week's rent and half of my remaining finances. But I needed a boost.

Consider fate. If Tetrault had hired me for that measly job, I would now be writing these lines in French . . .

A few days later, I was at the Royal Victoria Hospital. They sent me to the Allan Memorial Institute because "Dr. Cameron speaks German." He did not, but he knew someone who did. Who? Dr. Heinz Lehmann in Verdun, the medical director of a large, English-speaking mental hospital.

It was a long bus ride to Verdun. Mental hospitals in those days were financially deprived. Because of that, they had special permission to maintain an as yet "unqualified" medical staff of immigrant physicians. I was hired as a "general physician" for the institute. I was to live in, get three meals a day, uniforms, and a salary of $150 per month!

I was delighted. In my overflowing joy, I hardly listened to the job description. I was to look after Northwest House, a building with 400 chronic patients, including taking their histories, doing physical examinations, giving electroshock treatments, medications, etc. I was also to do some physical examinations and necessary treatments for the "TB ward patients." I had to do urine analyses for the entire 2,000-bed hospital (about thirty tests per day).

In the evening, I was the "hospital pharmacist" and had to dispense the drug orders to the head nurses. I also had to concoct different preparations, such as a diarrhea mixture, cough syrup, etc. A handwritten, dog-eared recipe book was my helper. We, the book and I, did not trust each other from the first moment. "Take a pound of opium," the book instructed. Indeed. A pound of opium. The hospital never had weaker mixtures than in those days. It was like preparing minestrone for 2,000 people, but more dangerous. And I also had to share night duty with the psychiatric residents, my turn coming twice a week and every second weekend. Dr. Lehmann told me this would be the last time he would speak to me in German—henceforth, it would be English only.

By then, it was early November. On the first of December, I received $150. They deducted a few dollars for tax. By telegram I sent $120 to my parents in Tel Aviv for a refrigerator. I felt somewhat better.

* * *

There was a joyful celebration in the border kibbutz. The crop looked promising and the hard work seemed to pay off well. Pipez was particularly happy. This was 1954, his sixteenth birthday, and his friends were all cheering along with him. Soon, he would be in the army, a moment he was so fervently waiting for. They danced and sang and drank orange juice. When the time came, the *Kumzitz* ended. They took the truck to return home. But the truck sped away prematurely. Pipez fell off. He did not move. Soon it was clear that he had died instantly of head injuries. In his wallet, they found a picture of Lici.

Tibor Lenz, "Pipez," in his last days of his brief life.

* * *

The nightmares? Of course. They kept recurring with no let-up. The panic attacks also continued. I often wondered if I would ever be free of them. It cost me so much energy and left me exhausted, over and above the minimum workday of fourteen hours.

Nocturnal Images:

The Question

Was it a vision, or a waking dream?
Fled is the music: do I wake or sleep?

From John Keats, *Ode to a Nightingale*

At one time or other, every survivor raises the question: why me? Why did I survive? How many, who were cleverer, faster, or richer than myself have died?

The easy answer is that survival was entirely a chance occurrence. It is a question of good luck. While this seems to be true, it is somehow difficult to believe. If so, the will of a Supreme Being must be presumed. This compounds the puzzle. Why was I the one who was spared? How many perished who were better, more religious, more devoted than I? Was I saved so that I could tell my story? But everyone has a story to tell—how many were killed who could have accomplished such a task far better than I? Why was I chosen?

How much of what I call "myself" arose simply by the unfolding of my genes? How much was sired by events I chose, or was kindled by the ill-fated misadventures I was forced to endure? How much of "myself" do I like? How much do I begrudge or grousingly acknowledge? How many things have I bettered within myself?

How can I cure myself?

CHAPTER 15

Struggles and Losses

The years spent in Verdun's mental hospital were now behind me. Those were historic times when psychiatry suddenly and unexpectedly began to advance, bringing incredible changes to this field of medicine. Finally, broken loose from the world of superstition, psychiatry entered its most exciting phase and grew into a biologically grounded fledgling science. These changes were particularly evident under the leadership of Dr. Heinz Lehmann. But this is the subject for a different book.

I was in the midst of redoing my examinations. All of them. For the third time. In Hungarian first, then in German, and now in English. It is more disgusting to pass the same examinations three times than it is to fail them. But that was not enough. One year of "rotating" internship was also required. I completed that at the Montreal General Hospital; that is, in the old Montreal General Hospital that is still on Dorchester Street, strategically located between Chinatown, the port, and the red-light district. This teaching hospital of bygone days was still permeated by the spirit of Sir William Osler, who had worked there fifty years earlier. The venerable institution ran on a shoestring budget, on ossified principles, on the slave labour of the candy-striped student nurses, some unpaid nuns, and the cheap labour of the interns. Unpaid supervisory senior staff worked solely for admitting privileges. I still recall nearly verbatim the twenty-seconds-long "welcome speech" given by Dr. Thomson, the chief resident:

"We are a very generous hospital," he said. "It is true that we pay a salary of only $25 a month for interns, but out of the goodness of our heart, we will see to it that you won't be able to spend it!"

How true it was! This was that bittersweet time when with a total annual income of $300, I did not have to pay any income tax. And something more. We got three meals a day, if our stomachs could tolerate it (Old Montreal General Hospital! I still remember your wicked "Spanish rice" dish), and as many clean uniforms as we happened to need—sometimes three a day. In the interns' quarters, the rooms were shared by two interns. So even if you were not on call, you were awakened by the phone ringing for your partner, who happened to be on night duty. Every second night, you were on night call, followed by a full, ordinary working day. Every second weekend, you were on call from Saturday morning to Monday evening.

On a table near the window in the Emergency Room was a small cup filled with change. Above it was a red button. Amateurishly laid wires led out from the window frame and ran across the street to a sleazy Chinese laundry. When a Chinese patient came in who could not speak any other language, and this was a frequent occurrence, you rang the laundry and a worker came over to interpret. Sometimes he spoke less English than the patient. Sometimes the patient and the worker began to talk at length to one another in Chinese. Who knows about what? Families or politics, you were frustrated and completely left out. Then you gave some change to the worker and used your imagination to end the stalemate.

Work in the Emergency Room was a tedious, dog-wearying task that continued around the clock. Young women were brought in bleeding from incomplete abortions; we also had people injured in car accidents; victims of pub brawls requiring stitches that would put a *couturière* to shame; suicide attempts. One gruelling night, when my roommate, Dr. Pollack, was on call, the phone rang shrilly at 3:30 a.m., waking both of us. The Emergency Room nurse told him that a patient had walked in "hearing voices talking to him in his head."

"Call Ear, Nose, and Throat," mumbled Dr. Pollack, attempting to go back to sleep. Another untiring buddy was Wallace Troup, later a cardiologist in Ottawa.

The student nurses were fuelled by enthusiasm for their profession. If not, they just could not make it. A crooked seam on a white stocking, a loose button, a forgotten pair of scissors hanging on a gauze string tied to a starched apron—these were enough to lose one or even both free afternoons in a month. The pride of the Emergency Room was the row of 100-year-old basins for washing hands. They had a million tiny cracks latticing their surfaces but were sparkling clean and shone radiantly from the vigorous scrubbing by the student nurses. This job started their day at five o'clock in the morning.

The student nurses lived across the street in a separate building and had strict curfews. Elderly, narrow-lipped, suspicious Hesperides, who all looked alike, sat at the entrance door, ready to bark at any male who dared to enter the building.

Some of the student nurses wore intriguing pieces of underclothing. No, no, don't get any risqué ideas, now! I observed this delicate garter belt but once, in the Emergency Room. A candy-striper happened to develop acute appendicitis. While she was being examined, I saw her two-way stretch garter belt that held up her stockings while at the same time keeping her blouse tucked in without a wrinkle. Perfection had to be maintained.

Everything was regimented. Dr. Thomson's instructions to the residents were that they were supposed to be on the ward by six o'clock in the morning, not a minute later, "freshly shaven, in clean uniform, with sharpened pencils and notebook" to follow him on rounds. The giant surgical wards "L" and "M" each contained fifty beds. The head nurse saw to it that the bed linen was straightened, the patients were looked after, and all the staff were present for the "military inspection." Then Dr. Thomson led the parade. He made his rounds and rattled off different orders and laboratory tests that he wanted done "immediately." The interns feverishly made notes. He also expected the interns and residents to be in the operating room by eight a.m., "all scrubbed and dressed for surgery."

The task of assisting for the operations was finished by two o'clock in the afternoon, and if you were lucky, some cold leftover food was waiting for you in the kitchen (cold, lardy Spanish rice. Yuck.). But you had to hurry, because by then the new admissions were lining up on the ward, waiting to have their histories taken and their physical examinations, while anxious patients and relatives waited eagerly for discharge with accompanying instructions. At the same time, the indignant head nurse made sarcastic remarks "about the good old days, when interns really worked instead of crawling around leisurely." Oh, yes. You had to do your own urine analyses, white blood counts, red blood counts, haemoglobins, and hematocrits on your new patients, from blood taking to complete end results, without any laboratory assistance. You had to have your own equipment for it (pipettes, cell-counting chambers, etc.). That was just for morale. The lab redid it more accurately anyway.

Life was no easier in the Emergency Room. You had to go on ambulance rides—of course with screeching sirens—and carry the heavy emergency bag. You never knew what to expect. DOA—dead on arrival—was the simplest. But it could be a heart attack, a delivery, a street fight, a stroke—you name it. Lots of drunks. If no ambulance calls came, whatever was going on in the Emergency Room queued up and awaited your attention. Small surgery. Removal of a nail. Opening an abscess. Bleeding stomach. Chest cold. Fracture clinic. Vascular clinic. Set up intravenous drips. Syphilis clinic, where Dr. Robert Jackson taught me to do spinal taps. "Place a Miller–Abbot tube." ("What's that?") Hypochondriacs. Panic attacks, like my own, were received mostly without any sympathy.

Women in those days did not have many rights. A married mother could not sign an ordinary "consent for treatment" form in the hospital for her children, not even in an emergency. The husband had to be summoned. This was a complicated task, particularly when the husband, say a travelling salesman, was out of town. One exception to this rule was if the woman had been widowed. In that case, her signature was accepted. Since every unpleasant task was given to the student nurses, I overheard one of them asking in her weary voice, "And where is your husband?" (Meanwhile, the child's scalp was bleeding.) "My husband is dead. I am a widow." The eyes of the candy-striper lit up and the cheery words slipped out: "Very good!"

As you can see from my portrayal of this bygone world, there have been enormous changes not only in medicine, hospitals, nurses' training, and internships but also in the way society regards women.

At last I finished all of my requirements. I completed the all-important L.M.C.C. examination, but I still could not enter into medical practice. In those days in Quebec, you had to be a Canadian citizen to practise medicine. By then, I had been in Canada two-and-a-half years; to acquire citizenship, one needed five years of continuous residence in Canada. But I had to make a living for the remainder of the time, much more so because my parents were arriving from Tel Aviv.

The only way to make a living was by specialization, by becoming a resident physician. While my primary interests were either neurology or endocrinology, I was always fascinated by psychiatry as well, if for no other reason than because of the gnawing wish to understand why human beings are capable of descending to the cataclysmic beastliness and sinister depravity that I had observed during the war.

Two other factors were pushing me towards a specialization in psychiatry. One was that a year from my previous experiences in Verdun would be accepted in the four-year specialization program. The other, quite frankly and less poetic, was that a psychiatric residency paid a slightly higher salary than any other specialty—up to $300 per month.

An additional motive in favour of psychiatry was the fact that in the early fifties, Montreal was a veritable Mecca for the neurosciences. There was a conglomeration of outstanding experts, researchers, teachers, and fabulous clinicians, like Dr. Heinz Lehmann, a pioneer of modern psychopharmacology; Dr. Charles Chagass, the EEG wizard; Dr. Ewen Cameron, the catalyst of research; Dr. Theodore Sourkes, Dr. J.H. Quastel, and Dr. David Quastel, all neurochemists; Dr. Hebb at McGill, the mover and shaker of the psychology department; Dr. Wilder Penfield, neurosurgeon and a dean of functional neuroanatomy; Dr. Hans Selye, the explorer of the stress concept; Dr. Erik Wittkower, psychoanalyst and the guru of psychosomatics; Dr. Alistair McLeod, teaching analyst; Dr. James Olds, researcher of the brain's reward system; and Patrick Wall and Ronald Melzak, the experimenters of the gate theory of pain, to mention but a few.

Just as I finished my internship and began my residency in psychiatry, a joyous event took place: my parents arrived from Tel Aviv. Now it was my turn to show them around Montreal. I brought them into the midst of the sizable Jewish-Hungarian society that gathered in the four or five espresso bars on Stanley Street, where the dominant language in those days was Hungarian. This was 1956, the year of the Hungarian uprising against the Communists and the large Hungarian immigration to Canada that followed. My parents had no shortage of social contacts and new friends. One might justly ask what the reason was for our cautious avoidance of so many Magyar gentiles. Some of the first graffiti on the walls of Budapest during the 1956 uprising boasted: "Itzig, this time we won't take you all the way to Auschwitz." ("*Itzig, most nem viszunk Auschwitzig*," rhymes the affirmation in Hungarian.)

If the resident's salary was not designed for maintaining one family, not even if supplemented with moonlighting (the forbidden practice of seeing patients at a cut rate at night), it certainly was less than sufficient to maintain two. Money was always short.

Lici had had her chemotherapy and her TB was now in the past. She settled in Sweden, married Laci Revesz, and at the beginning held a prominent position in internal medicine. Then she divorced both—internal medicine and Laci. Now she is a well-recognized, senior psychoanalyst in Stockholm with an international reputation. We correspond to this day, and on rare occasions we meet at various conferences.

My sister, Marta, and her husband, Jan, obtained U.S. immigration visas and on their way to the States spent a few months in Montreal. Mother insisted on learning English. She enrolled herself in an English language course and became an ardent visitor of the galleries and antique shops ("just to look"). Father could not be held back. Although he was then sixty-seven years old, he found himself a job in a metal factory, Rubenstein's, and planned to patent his inventions and open a small factory all over again. He did speak four languages, but no English or French.

When I arrived in Canada, I had no idea about the existence of a French population in Quebec. I discovered French Canada all by myself. Now I regretted my high school Italian. I wished that French had remained in the curriculum because I would have been better off. But Quebec was not at all unfamiliar to me. In fact, there were many similarities between pre-war Hungary and Quebec. Both were Catholic countries, both were ruled by a small inner circle of inbred elite and by conservative policies, and both were firmly influenced by a powerful church—the Roman Catholic Church. Yes, I would not hesitate to ascribe a distinctly feudalistic flavour to both Horthy's Hungary and Duplessis's Quebec. Both were palpably anti-Semitic. In Montreal, as elsewhere in North America, many places, such as hotels and clubs, declared themselves "restricted," meaning that Jews were not allowed to enter. What else was common to the two countries? Both shared a social, political, and religious system that produced uneducated, cheap labour. This, of course, was readily exploited by others.

There was, however, one significant difference between Hungary and Quebec. Even though Hungary was a Catholic country, the Church could never enforce the creation of large families. The dream of the Hungarian peasantry was firmly set on the possession of a piece of land. This is why so many of them migrated to Canada. Large families carried the danger that the family farm would eventually splinter into nothing. They chose to live by the principle of "one family, one child" (*egyke* in Hungarian). In Quebec, however, the French Canadians had very large families, and in their early teens, the children dropped out of school to help the family earn a living.

The French Canadians spoke a patois, a "bad" French, but most of them also spoke good or poor English; while the English Canadians spoke only their own language. True, the French language was obligatory in high school, but unlike in my youth, it was regarded as "a subject to be passed, not a language to be learned." It was only much later that I learned to appreciate the unique culture of French Canada. Since then, enormous changes have taken place in Quebec. Now the language is "pure French," and their newly gained pride reminds me of the early Zionists who also rejected Yiddish, the language of their forefathers, the ghetto language, as they turned away from the "soul food," Jewish kitchen, and the culture of the Diaspora.

* * *

The grievous task now facing me is to describe the agony of Mother's last few months of life. This renders my writing once more a stinging, distressing undertaking. With Mother's passing, a great chunk of myself died, too. Many painful images surrounding Mother's illness remain shrouded in dim obliteration in my mind, too hurtful to focus on.

My parents' sunny arrival in Montreal was soon followed by Mother's illness. First, she had only an abdominal discomfort that she attributed to her usual and frequent gastric afflictions, a weakness on the maternal side of the family shared by many of us. But the discomfort soon grew to become a grim malady, and Mother's diabetes tended to get out of control. The pain increased, as did a rapidly advancing abdominal swelling. An ascites developed. Test after test failed to reveal the cause of her trouble. Scores of outstanding specialists examined Mother, became frustrated, and made repeated, cautious references to "the stress of the recent immigration, to psychosomatic factors."

I did not believe any of these feeble explanations, and in my agony, I anticipated a calamitous illness. I was, unfortunately, right. The fluid in the abdominal cavity was an indication of that, and by then I recognized Mother's malignant disease. As time went on, the growth advanced and her suffering worsened. The vicious tumour had diabolically metastasized into the very hearts of each one of us, where we felt the reverberation of Mother's pain.

Melancholy memories, aching images, nostalgic recollections tortured us. Our miraculous survival a dozen years ago kept coming back in my memory. So we "won't live forever," contrary to my belief, a notion born in the daze of the happiness of liberation.

Doctor, psychiatrist, whatever . . . I was just a hurting child wanting to cry for his mother. But I was not allowed to show her my hurt—not to her, not to Father, not to Marta. Marta, too, did her very best and she, too, kept her suffering to herself. I recalled my special "mental photograph" of Mother's youth and beauty. I remembered seeing the frightful past images, how Mother was hunted by the barbaric Nazis on a distant, rain-splattered day. I recaptured Mother's dreams and her painful losses. The swell of the tears I held back choked my throat.

My parents' fortieth wedding anniversary was approaching in mid-August. My heartbroken father brought forty long-stemmed red roses to the hospital, and their fragrance filled the sad room, roses that harkened back to Buda, to Father's rose garden and to happier times. Tears were rolling down my mother's cheeks. "White roses would be more appropriate," she said, giving away her awareness that she knew the end was near. Father quietly exchanged the red roses for white ones.

Two weeks later, I was in the hospital with Mother. It was two o'clock in the morning. Mother's suffering still went on, although she was no longer entirely conscious. Her body parts were giving up; her liver and kidneys barely functioned. The night nurse appeared with a syringe of morphine. I knew that in Mother's condition this amount of morphine was too much for her. The nurse knew it, too. She stopped, looked into my eyes, and I nodded my head. Nothing was said. And my beautiful, loving mother was dead twenty minutes later.

I also knew that from then on, for the rest of my days, I would have to shoulder the torment of guilt for that nod and carry the dark memory of that tragic night. But I would do it again.

Dreams and Tears: XI

A Seraphic Diary

A tear surges up,
surges up to be shed,
for life is complex precisely because
it is cut short

From Yevgeny Yevtushenko, *A tear*
Translated by A. Boyars and S. Franklin

Jewish survivors of the Nazi carnage in Budapest often wondered about the fate of Raoul Wallenberg. The recurring question always had been accompanied by the typical survivor's guilt: "I am here; where is Wallenberg?"

The same emotional undertow generated a widespread dissatisfaction with the search efforts. Overall opinion held that not enough was done to find and liberate this revered hero. Probably this is true. The cumbersome machinery of the USSR did not permit a reliable flow of information to reach the Western world, although many unconfirmed rumours were floating around.

Sweden, despite her cautious attitude towards her dangerous neighbour, repeatedly brought up the question with Soviet visitors. Because of a mass demonstration with the main theme, "Where Is Wallenberg?" that was organized by the editorial staff of the Swedish newspaper *Expressen*, Krushchev's Stockholm visit was ruined and almost cancelled. Similarly, Kosygin, Gromyko, and others had their painful moments in Stockholm and at home on account of the Wallenberg issue. One important hint as to why the Soviets "had to" kill Wallenberg is the confession of an ex-colonel of the KGB, Oleg Gordievsky, who wrote in his memoir that he had tried, apparently unsuccessfully, to recruit Wallenberg as an agent.

Many private and official delegations made inquiries in the USSR, including the then secretary of state, Kissinger, Senator Moynahan, President Carter, U.S. Congressman Tom Lantos and his wife, Anette, and others. Many witnesses had seen or heard of Wallenberg in various different Soviet prisons and *gulags*, but these witnesses or their relatives were secretly threatened by the KGB. Some disappeared or died mysteriously. Some influential members of Wallenberg's family could and should have done more to free him.

But Nina Lagergren and Guy von Dardel, Wallenberg's half-sister and half-brother, repeatedly negotiated with Soviet officials—Nina in particular. The last time was in 1989, when they met with Gorbachev. In the spirit of *Perestrojka*, they were given sympathetic promises by Gorbachev, who ordered an immediate search in the Lubianka prison. This was effective to a point. Among other personal belongings of Wallenberg, his passport and his Budapest diary from 1944 were found by Vadim Petrovitch Pirozhkov, deputy chief of the KGB, and Valentin Mikhailovich Nikoforov, deputy foreign minister. Nina Lagergren brought back the diary to Sweden, where the newspaper *Expressen* published it page by page on January 13, 1990.

Lici sent me the photocopies of the appropriate pages. On the fateful day, in Wallenberg's handwriting, the note shows on *Lordag* (Saturday) 5th August 1944 at 16:00, five names, including "Mrs. Koranyi." On *Mandag* (Monday) 7th August 1944, another notation appears: "10:00 a.m.—5 *fanger* (prisoners)." That was when I was reunited with Lici. My eyes filled with tears as I remembered Wallenberg by this silent reminder from his grave. He really showed the world that a single man could make a difference in fighting evil.

CHAPTER 16

New Challenges

I had no idea how to start a private practice. Open an office and just wait? None of the multitude of university courses I had taken on three continents and in half a dozen countries had dealt with this basic subject, even though in those pre-medicare days, private practice was almost the only choice for a young physician. I finished my residency and continued to work as a researcher in the Queen Mary Veterans' Hospital, where I enjoyed the last shelter of an epoch of salaried jobs, despite the meagre livelihood it provided. The pinch was felt mostly in the last third of each month. In exchange for total independence and self-mastery, I soon had to quit this convenient refuge.

I liked my position at the hospital, which was full of new and old friends. Guess who else worked there? For one, Katherine (the one-time "streetcar conductor" at the time of the Nazis in Budapest); she was doing her residency in internal medicine. Csilla Grossmann (the owner of that crazy, open-to-everybody home in Munich) was completing her training in pathology. Though we were all very busy, the coffee breaks got longer and longer. We had so much to gossip about.

Another attraction and new friend was Blossom Wigdor, the psychologist who was not only extremely knowledgeable and endowed with a sharp mind, but was also very attractive. She was well aware of both her keen intellect and her physical assets. With a pair of lovely, long legs tightly hugged by the flawless film of nylon stockings, we suspected she was the secret inventor of the miniskirt, soon to become the fashion.

My superior was the young Gerry Sarwer-Foner, an extremely energetic and ebullient man, an enthusiast with a considerable waistline. Blessed with an insatiable appetite for work, publications, research, money, politics, smoked meat sandwiches, cherry pie, and refined French cuisine, Gerry possessed an ego with two whirring wings.

When Gerry moved, I took the sublet of his office on Sherbrooke Street. I summoned all of my courage and bought a set of tasteful office furniture at the distinguished store of Valiquette. Good grief! I felt I would be an old fogey by the time all this was paid off. At the same time, I purchased a secondhand two-toned Buick. I was thirty-four years old and this was my very first car. I also had a largely empty, one-room, rented apartment.

I met Gerry regularly for research discussions that he set up in different restaurants (probably because at home, Gerry was kept on a strict diet by his hopeful wife, Ethel). This is where I came to recognize Gerry's fine talent concerning gourmet food. Eventually I became better acquainted with French cuisine, something that I had missed in Paris. Happily, these were research meetings, and I, as a humble research fellow, was exempted from paying for them.

Psychiatry was a fascinating arena, its scope unfolding rapidly in front of our eyes. To be sure, the old-time mental hospitals were still around. These were severely under-financed institutions, and in the absence of effective treatments, they mainly warehoused mental patients under poor conditions. The desperate treatments available for severe mental illnesses still involved hydrotherapy, a leftover from ancient times, although the hydrotherapy room was no longer in use in Verdun. But the dubious insulin coma treatment was still a daily practice. Electroshock treatment was then a mere fifteen years old. It was helpful for some depressions but was largely a failure in the treatment of most cases of schizophrenia. The worthlessness of the early lobotomies, a crude surgical solution to a subtle neuropsychiatric problem, had also been the product of the same despair, and its sad outcome soon became glaringly evident. Of course, we had sedatives, mainly the awful-smelling paraldehyde, discovered by Cervello at the end of the nineteenth century, and the barbiturate found by Baeyer in 1864, but these drugs had no lasting influence on the course of the illness.

In the 1950s, there was a double damnation for the taxpayer: tuberculosis and mental illness. Tuberculosis was a veritable killer, particularly for young people; and under poor social conditions the cruel disease spread through entire families and whole communities. By law, the acutely infected people were quarantined in TB sanatoria, sometimes for years, at the cost of many personal tragedies. Fresh air, nourishment, and bed rest were thought to be the best cure, although pneumothorax (filling the chest cavity with air and collapsing the lung while the cavity healed) was also widely used. But there was always a shortage of beds in the TB sanatoria. In these close-knit communities, with their peculiar subculture and altered time concept, unspoken house rules prevailed. More and more new institutions had to be built.

If crowding in TB sanatoria had been a problem, the situation in mental hospitals was much worse. Mental illness was totally incapacitating for its victims, but it was not a killer like TB. Individual philanthropy was palpably less generous for supporting mental hospitals, and the frugal government support was much less for the mentally ill than for the care of any other condition. Not long before, mental hospitals were still referred to as "insane asylums." When a new mental hospital opened, it was full that very same week and had a waiting list.

Depressed and manic patients were discharged from time to time; people with organic brain syndrome and senile dementia died, and their places were filled from the hard-pressed waiting list. Gradually, the hospital population became entirely schizophrenic. Schizophrenia is an illness of adolescence and the young. People were admitted to mental hospitals at age eighteen or twenty and remained there for the rest of their lives. When the hospital population was almost entirely schizophrenic, there were no more discharges, and a new hospital had to be built.

Mental hospitals were built on the outskirts of the cities, where farmland was the cheapest. To save more money, all were constructed on the same architectural plan. If you knew your way around a mental hospital in Halifax, you would be familiar with the one in Vancouver.

But then came the beginning of psychiatric wards in the general hospitals.

Our knowledge of biochemistry and pharmacology, even to this day, does not permit us to achieve exact "molecular targeting," the production of the ideal drug without any side effects, the distant hope of progressive minds. Most medical inventions occur by serendipity (a term coined by Horace Walpole in 1754 after the fable, *The Three Princes of Serendip*), through a fortuitous chance discovery (although Claude Bernard used to say that "chance prefers the prepared ones"). Such chance eventuality yielded penicillin for Fleming and changed the practice of medicine. This is also how modern psychiatric drug treatment was born.

How old is pharmacology? Did it begin with the human race? Hominoid, perhaps? Or Lucy? Still earlier? It cannot be! Yet animals are known to seek out specific plants for certain conditions, a phenomenon that did not escape the attention of the modern pharmaceutical industry. They still maintain observation posts in the few areas of rainforest that are still left. Serving man's vain interest in immortality, an enduring curiosity around primitive religion, magic, demonology, and psychomimetic drugs is forever kept alive.

All these go far back in human cultures and all meet at Delphi, in Homeric Greece, at the Temple of Apollo, above the entrance of which is carved, "Know Thyself." There, the Pythian maiden, the adulated Sybil, chewed her sacred roots that put her in a trance, and in this altered state of mind, her famous oracles were conceived and recorded.

By then, the North African sand, with its contemptuous indifference for time, had buried the Kahun and Ebers papyri that had been written a millennium earlier and listed some 700 prescriptions. The *Solanaceae* family of plants contains mandragora ("mandrake"), atropine, scopolamine, hyoscine, and datura roots, with its peculiar, distorted mannequin-like shape that readily became the source of witches' brews, voodoo, potions of charm and longevity, and that imbue the consumer with strange mental distortions. This temporary distortion of perception, feelings, and thoughts underscore the occult power of these "secret" formulas. Grouped around the transient mental effects of some drugs, different religions arose. One such drug was based on the South American plant ololiuqui, and a ceremony surrounding it had been described by Hernandez, the conquistador Cortes's physician. Another such religion was the peyotle church that was portrayed so well in Reco's book of *Magische Gifte*.

The Middle Ages also did not escape repeated mass poisonings by the wheat fungus *Secale cornutum*, which invaded the wheat fields from time to time and caused temporary madness in the entire community. In retrospect, these epidemics, called ergotism, turned out to be a sort of mass LSD trip.

The late nineteenth-century and early twentieth-century literature began with DeQuincey (*Confessions of an Opium Eater*, 1822), who first used the term "tranquillizer," followed by Sigmund Freud's short lived addiction to the "harmless" cocaine, a "theoretical shortcut to happiness" (listed as such but ruled out in his *Future of an Illusion*), and by the enthusiasm of Havelock Ellis (*Mescal: a New Artificial Paradise*, 1897) and Aldous Huxley (*The Doors of Perception*, 1954) for mescaline.

But nothing fuels the human imagination more than War, perhaps because innumerable problems demand instant, life-or-death solutions, and money is no object. This leads us to the often ill-fated yet vital convoys of the Second World War. These ships were not manned by professional sailors. The crews were simple, ordinary folk—civilians. And the poor souls puked all the way to Soviet Russia and sometimes, when they happened to survive the German submarine attacks, all the way back. So did the early clipper flight crews. The demand went out to the pharmaceutical industry: anti-emetics were needed, good ones, and right away.

And indeed, one after another, some excellent anti-emetics that are still in use came along. Among many others was the intestinal and bladder antiseptic methylene blue, which had been used against intestinal parasites since the last century. Because of its anti-emetic and antihistaminic properties, it was tried for seasickness, but it had unpleasant side effects. It was manipulated chemically to become chlorpromazine, and Laborit tried it for the treatment of surgical shock in 1951. He did this because of its remarkable ability to render the patient "indifferent" to his or her surroundings while remaining conscious. It also had a good sedative effect and was harmless. However, nobody knew anything about it. The Rhone-Poulenc Company approached two groups of scientists: Pierre Deniker and Jean Daly in Paris and Heinz Lehmann in Montreal.

Lehmann was reluctant to try it at first. He asked the staff for six volunteers before he would give it to the patients. At that time, I had been in Canada for one year and was working under Lehmann. I felt that as a new immigrant I had to prove myself worthy of the job; I volunteered along with five nurses. I was given fifty milligrams of chlorpromazine intramuscularly. Dr. Lehmann wished that "no placebo reaction" should mislead us. After the injection, we were told to continue our usual activities.

My day began by giving several electroshock treatments. After the second one, I was out. I still remember someone taking my blood pressure, and Lehmann saying, "Oh it is just a placebo reaction." I remember nothing after that. A deep sleep enveloped me, for which both the chlorpromazine and many months of overwork had so well prepared me. I slept and slept. I was the first person in North America to get chlorpromazine.

Deniker and Daly preceded Lehmann's publication of the results by about two months. The clinical trials on patients were most interesting. Not only were patients well sedated, they also stopped hallucinating. Why? Lehmann thought that the chlorpromazine did more than just sedate. Even the quality of the sedation was different. The patients were no longer irritable or combatant, yet they were fairly alert and they were able to get around and live their lives.

Chlorpromazine was not the only new drug. Another was reserpine or rauwolfia, so named by the German botanist Leonard Rauwolf. This drug, used in ancient times in India, was called "snake root" or "insanity herb." Muller synthesized it in 1952. Nathan Klein and later Sarwer-Foner were among the first to describe its effect on the mentally ill.

That same year, two new drugs were developed that benefited schizophrenic patients. True, reserpine had little clinical usefulness because of its side effects. However, it was also used for treating high blood pressure, although it caused severe depression in patients so predisposed. But reserpine, more than others, spurred more research. How do these drugs work? Reserpine radically reduced serotonin levels in the brain.

Hofmann in Switzerland worked on synthesized ergotamine. In the process, he accidentally poisoned himself with LSD-25. Turning mistake to benefit, he recorded the drug's effects, the hallucinations, the mental dislocation that he experienced—the first of the "bad trips." What was amazing was that such a tiny amount of material could cause such a huge effect—a quarter of a milligram! And this prompted the question: can it be that in schizophrenia, the brain produces its own hallucinogens? A metabolic dislocation? This resulted in more research, and by 1954, several chemical theories were proposed for schizophrenia. We felt the excitement of believing that the "final answer" was just around the corner. Days away, maybe weeks. Today we are more cautious. The enthusiasm has waned and we are many years older.

In 1949, botched research in Australia by Cade resulted in the discovery of the usefulness of lithium in manic-depressive disorders. It took a long time, however, before this preventative medication became popular. Meanwhile, an anti-TB drug, isoniazid, was discovered. It was observed that isoniazid made the often-depressed TB patients bloom and beam. In 1951, Daley tried it on depressed patients in Paris, and it worked very well. Thus, the first family of antidepressant drugs was launched. In the same year, Hafliger and Schindler were working on antihistaminics and found the first of the tricyclic compounds. In 1957, Kuhn found imipramine, another antidepressant medication that is still in use today. All these drugs and the halo effect of research work that surrounded them fed into a common pool of accumulated knowledge on mental illness.

Within a blessed decade, from 1947 to 1957, the profile of psychiatry had changed. The real difference, of course, was made by the drugs. Their use rendered most patients much more amenable to psychotherapy and rehabilitation. This meant that additional mental hospitals did not need to be built, and many of the old ones were closed. First, we cheered these events, then we stopped rejoicing. The premature closing of mental hospitals and the insufficient resources for rehabilitation resulted in a dramatic increase in street people in big cities.

With all these changes, psychiatry still retained the humanistic and cultural profile that had slowly emerged since the birth of Romanticism.

* * *

But what about my own, personal misery? The nightmares? The panic attacks that still tortured me regularly? There was nothing available in terms of treatment that I knew about at that time. Imipramine would have been most helpful, but back then, this was not yet known. So I had to put up with the misery of my symptoms for a few more years.

Tom Detre came for a visit. He was working at Yale University and his career had progressed by leaps and bounds. On this short visit, I brought Tom together with Katherine Drechsler. They actually knew each other from Budapest but had not been particularly close. With the help of Csilla Grossmann, we brewed a complex strategy and kept fanning the flames of Aphrodite until Tom began to make many more trips to Montreal. Katherine and Tom were soon married.

My private office on Sherbrooke Street opened with a fanfare. It is a pity that no one else heard the trumpets. I had three patients who were sent to me by Dr. Saul Albert, my former chief at the Jewish General Hospital in Montreal. But then disaster struck. Two of my patients left for a summer vacation. What was I doing with a single patient? It was not even an urgent case. The last time I was on holiday was in 1942, sixteen years earlier. In my trepidation, a car pulled up near to me and I heard a friendly voice:

"Hi, you, what are you doing? You gonna be hit by a car if you are not careful!"

I turned around and it was Mishi Grossmann.

"Hi, Mishi. What am I doing? I just decided to go on vacation for one week."

"Very good. And where are you going?"

"To your place."

Mishi Grossmann was not at all surprised. He was never surprised. He worked in a TB sanatorium at Prefontaine in the Laurentian Mountains. He had an apartment in the sanatorium because he was on call twenty-four hours a day, every day. But this did not wear him down at all. He carried out his duty with casual ease. When he disappeared for a few hours, he phoned in every hour to the hospital.

"Fine," said Mishi. "We will find some consultation work for you. When are you coming?"

I bent further down and only then noticed the two ladies who were sitting in the car. My eye got stuck on the young woman sitting beside Mishi. She impressed me so much that I could not speak.

"This is Erwin, the shrink," I heard Mishi saying, then her name, but I did not hear it well; Edith . . . no, Edie . . . something like that. Then Mishi ran out of patience and was on the move.

"When are you coming?"

"Tonight!" I shouted towards the moving car.

That was a quick decision. But that woman's face kept coming back to me. Yes, of course she was beautiful but in a racy, esoteric way. Her slender womanhood was unsuccessfully hidden under her casual slacks and blouse. What splendid, thick hair she had! In my reverie, I could almost feel the soft caress of those shiny, luxurious locks on my fingers as I ploughed into the body of tempting, twisting, bronze riches. And those playful, luminous grey eyes radiated humour and intelligence. Maybe she won't be there tonight at all? Maybe she is married? What was her name? Edith? Edie? Maybe she is one of Mishi's endless procession of lovers, a cursed compulsion or nervous habit that was ruining his marriage to Csilla? Ah, no.

Later in the afternoon, I was on my way, driving to Prefontaine. The drive took about two hours, through picturesque little Quebec towns and rural regions, dogs chasing muddy tires, passing village eateries and gas stations, churches and idyllic country taverns, sometimes slowed down by ancient, moribund jalopies crawling in front of me. Dubious, souped-up vehicles passed me with hair-raising speed, splashing mud all over,

I knew the TB sanatorium well. I made consultations there frequently; they paid $10 for an afternoon's work, usually three patients. I was disappointed when I arrived. Where were the girls? Oh, the girls. They were in the hotel, of course.

"Why? Should I invite them?" asked Mishi. The devil, he was teasing me, but he had already picked up my attraction to Edie, and now he knew it very well. "After supper, we will have a card game." Mishi was a gambler and played cards every single night. "Meanwhile, we have problems with some of our patients. When are you going to see them?"

Joseph Rothbart, the newly appointed and very young executive director of the sanatorium, joined us just as Edie showed up with Bozse, her woman friend who had originally come from Hungary and settled in New York long before the war. Edie, I learned, also came from Budapest, so the language of the evening was Hungarian.

We ambled languidly up towards Mishi's home in the slowly waning, rose-coloured light of the dusk, so typical of the summer sky of the North. The weak rays of twilight had gilded Edie's hair a surrealistic red as it fell below her shoulders. She had smooth and impeccable porcelain skin that seriously tempted me to touch and caress her. The shape of her face, the structure of her nose, her broad forehead, all spoke of a strong character. Her lips were made up with a matte carmine lipstick, and she wore a light, smokey-blue eye shadow that emphasized the grey of her eyes. Her bronze hair was piled up and twisted into a chignon. A breeze fluttered her light dress that hugged her hips tightly as she directed her grey eyes, like flashlights, on me with curiosity. So far, we had kept silent, but my message was clear to her. I could not help noticing how her magnificently shaped breasts tented the airy material of her dress, sculpting slight horizontal folds in the stretched fabric and accentuating her imposing womanly figure.

We spoke of many things, while uncharacteristically Mishi grew impatient. "What's the matter? I thought you guys and dolls wanted to play cards. Let's get at it. Time is money!" First, the three of them played cards while I talked with Edie. Then Joseph joined us, but my body language clearly indicated that he was not welcome just now. Conforming to the laws of male solidarity, Joseph soon withdrew with a knowing smile on his face. I spent that evening and late into the night talking to Edie. When the two of us were left alone, we switched to English. We did not even notice it.

I was surprised by the strong, unexpected emotion that suddenly ambushed me. It was a feeling I had not experienced for a long, long time and it made me feel alive, bewitched, and exuberant. Will I be hurt again as before? Is it the inescapable love again? Am I being fair to Edie?

We spent the next few days in a dreamy, summery mood. Neither of us was naïve. We both knew life well, were familiar with love and pain, had been acquainted with divorces and losses. We searched for common roots, fragments of the past to share. Perhaps we met in Budapest? Who knows . . . No, we had not met. Yet we had been in the same places so many times that I could not believe that our eyes, even as children, had never before locked on each other. In school, in the synagogue, at sports events? Edie had the same "map" as a child—the same important places: Hauer's pastry shop, the city park, the amusement park. She knew the same best benches, half-tented by overgrown greenery on Margaret Island where generations of teenagers had smooched. She was Jewish, she was a survivor of the Shoah. Like myself, she had lived through the Nazi times in Budapest. No two people could understand each other better. The bitterness of her youth remained untold for a long time; her very own tears and dreams remained covered for a while longer.

When finally we kissed, our lips touched softly and lingered for a long time. Before we assented to our passion, her lovely eyes were moist.

Edie, my love, my wife, and my devoted partner for life.

* * *

And so, my travelogue through my younger years draws to an end. I will try to close the old, worn-out volume and may open a new one.

Three months later, I arrived in New York and Edie was waiting for me at the airport. In the taxi driving toward the city, I placed a small diamond ring, my mother's, on Edies' finger. She was overwhelmed by her emotions.

"When do you want the wedding?" she asked.

"Now."

The wedding was a simple one. Edie's sisters, Eva and Ila, and my sister, Marta, were at the wedding with their husbands. Then we were packing Edie's belongings in Mishi's car, and I returned to Montreal, a married man.

A new future lay ahead of us.

Nocturnal Images

The Answer

What matters our creative endless toil
When, at a snatch, oblivion ends the coil

From Johann Wolfgang von Goethe, *Faust*
Translated by Peter Salm

Edie and I had been married for a couple of years and were living in our rather empty apartment on Montreal's Plantagenet Street. We enthusiastically admired its beauty. It was ours. It surrounded us with a tender, cosy warmth. True, we had hardly any furniture, no carpets, and no curtains. But we had a gorgeous antique Sevres vase that stood in the middle of the large, barren living room floor and two cushions in the corner. All we needed to do if we wanted to move was call a taxicab.

In contrast, my office where I saw patients was lavishly furnished on credit. Once a week, I worked in the clinic at the Jewish general Hospital where I treated public patients and supervised residents. Once a week, I lectured at McGill University. These I did, of course, for no remuneration—just for the sake of belonging to these prestigious institutions. The lower steps of the ladder. My daily routine started at seven a.m., and my wife picked me up in the office at nine or ten in the evening. I worked six days a week and on the weekends I attended to my house calls, did my paperwork, and tackled my research.

I was halfway into my psychoanalysis. I saw a senior teaching analyst, Dr. Alistair MacLeod, five times a week. Although there were many Jewish and Gentile analysts in Montreal, most from continental Europe, I chose someone who was an outsider in Jewish matters because of my roots and life experiences. As time went on, I learned many things about myself and others. But the panic, the nightmares, and the other symptoms of depression and anxiety remained unchanged. They defied all possible explanations and interpretations. All in all, the analysis was also a valuable immersion in cultural, anthropological, and philosophical matters. But the therapeutic value of it was disappointing. This situation has been described repeatedly by psychoanalysts concerning Holocaust survivors.

After a particularly tiring day, I fell into an unusually deep sleep. I got up in the middle of the night and, drunk with somnolence, eyes still closed, I headed towards the bathroom. I cautiously avoided a chair in the darkness, not wanting to bump into it and wake Edie. The bathroom door was open and a sliver of moonlight had thrown a feeble shaft of pale yellow through the window. Suddenly I was face to face with Him: an immaculately dressed SS major. His uniform covered his muscular body, the armband with the swastika was on his left arm, and the iron cross decoration sat in the middle of his chest. His face was somehow familiar and was replete with sarcasm. I could wait no longer. My right fist shot out with all the power I could muster. There was no way to hold back the punch when in a fraction of a second I recognized the face: it was mine.

Yes, it was I in the SS uniform. Within the next split second, the large bathroom mirror fragmented into a myriad of pieces with a thundering shrill of glass. Edie, now up, sleep torn from her beautiful eyes, scared speechless, heart palpitating, looked at my right fist, bright red and profusely dripping blood. What happened?

What happened? If only I knew. I have never stopped seeking The Answer, not since my liberation. What makes people so rotten? Animals kill for food only. Anger and hatred have nothing to do with it. But where does the evil ghoulishness of man come from? Of the many clever theories that have been proposed, particularly by Konrad Lorenz (*On Aggression*), none has been able to offer a sufficient explanation.

I remained without sleep for the rest of the night and for many nights thereafter, pondering. What is The Answer? Neuroanatomy? What is the common denominator of the beast and human brain? The answer is the limbic system, the site in the brain where basic, crude emotions are generated, the site of the Freudian Id, the human animal, the brain part I liked to call "the organ of adaptation," or, for that matter, the organ of maladaptation. But the limbic system in animals remains uncorrupted provided they stay in their natural milieu. Domestication, a form of corruption, is the abrogation of hatred. Or is it? Is hatred therefore hard-wired in the human brain? But what happens to the social-moral filter? Can personality be changed? I recall a Roman proverb from my childhood that Uncle Baer taught me, a single sentence that opposes the views of the psychoanalysts: "*Expellas naturam furca tamen usque recurret*" ("You may expel nature with a fork but it will return just the same").

The Nazis must be expelled. But the Nazi is crafty and knows how to hide and how to come back. Where do Nazis hide? I learned that comprehension and insight surface only slowly and indirectly in psychoanalysis. Yes, of course. The Nazi hides in the safest and most unsuspected place: within every one of us, within all of us. Until you trap him, expose him, and subjugate him within yourself, he can "get away" and nobody can control him. The Nazi can be confronted only by yourself. It takes courage to face him. We cannot eradicate prejudice permanently and then lean back, content. We must be on the alert and find him again and yet again, always in his new disguises, in his newly repainted camouflage. That's how the Nazi seeks to return. The task is to continually weed out and prune the evil.

So a lifetime of searching, thinking, and suffering finally led me to The Answer, a worn-out commonplace. But is not civilization built on clichés? In my heart, I am like the very best and no different from the very worst, but never in my actual deeds. This is the watershed.

My chronicle is now exhausted. A happy ending? Perhaps. I survived. Lici is alive. I achieved the dream of my vocation. I married Edie. But everything has a price, and the survivor must pay. He must redeem his existence with the pain of the remembrance, with the sorrowful memories of lost ones, with the obtrusive, abhorrent, and uninvited moments when he is assailed by the past and with his doubts. Survivors themselves created the notion that "the best one of us has perished." To what degree is this true? How does it reflect on me? It seems that I am finishing my memoir with more uncertainty than elucidation.

Well, this is the story of my youth. But life did not end there. Differently tainted dreams and tears burgeoned, and more peaceful smiles, happiness, and healing followed. New adventures, fresh quests, and untrodden paths of learning beckoned. The recording of these, however, is for another time.

Edie in 1958.

My beautiful mate, Edie.

Once more, Edie, my beloved spouse.

References

I wrote this memoir employing my own resources, notes, and remembrances. But I needed to confirm past events, historical conjectures, names, places, and dates. For these purposes, the following sources were utilized:

Abley, Mark, "Sweden's abandoned hero." *The Ottawa Citizen* (Aug. 16, 1997), p. B-2.

Andrew, Christopher and Oleg Gordievsky. 1990. *KGB—The Inside Story*. HarperCollins Pub. Co.

Bierman, John. 1981. *Righteous Gentile*. New York: Viking Press.

Choko, Marc H. and David Jones. 1990. *Canadian Pacific Posters 1883–1963*. Meridian Press.

Gonda, Laszlo. 1992. *A Zsidosag Magyarorszagon 1526–1945* (*The Jewry in Hungary 1526-1945*). Budapest: Szazadveg Publ.

Levai, Jeno. 1948. *Raoul Wallenberg*, 2nd ed. Budapest: Magyar Teka Publ.

Marx, Karl. 1959. *A World without Jews*. Translated from the German original and edited by Dagobert D. Runes. New York: The Withdom Library (a division of The Philosophical Library Inc.).

Morse, D. Arthur. 1967. *While Six Million Died*. New York: Hart Pub. Co.

Shirer, L. William. 1960. *Rise and Fall of the Third Reich*. New York: Simon and Schuster.

About the Author

Dr. Erwin K. Koranyi, a practicing psychiatrist in Ottawa, is the author of three technical books and has contributed eleven chapters in different textbooks and over fifty scientific papers in refereed journals. Dr. Koranyi is professor emeritus (psychiatry) at the University of Ottawa.

As a Jewish boy in the dark world of growing Nazism in Hungary, he vainly dreamt to become a physician. Instead, his life became a precarious daily struggle and continuous mortal risk as he endured Nazi persecution and helped his beloved ones to survive. They lived through the Holocaust in part with the help of the heroic Swedish diplomat, *Raul Wallenberg*. Koranyi and his family endured untold losses during the persecution until they were liberated from the Nazis by yet another Evil Empire.

More adventures and adversities coloured his medical studies in Hungary, and after dangerous border crossings, he finally reached freedom and obtained his much-desired MD degree in Austria. He practised medicine in the then-fledgling country of Israel, and subsequently settled in Canada. Here, he specialized in psychiatry at Montreal's McGill University, where he later taught.

Dr. Koranyi married Edie Rosenbaum, also a Holocaust survivor, and a lifelong dear partner. In 1970, the University of Ottawa invited him to join its staff, and he has been repeatedly honoured as a distinguished teacher.